Front Line and Fortitude

To Sandie

I owe you so much for your selfless and untiring help and encouragement to complete this story. When I was about to give up you stepped in. With your fresh mind and enthusiasm, I was able to pick up from where I had stalled and continue the challenge to bring this story to the outside world.

The hours you spent with me deciphering bad writing, tweaking and refining, searching through historical records, such as they were, were invaluable, as was your persistence when we hit brick walls, until we both felt there was no more out there which we could access.

Without your support the manuscript would have remained somewhere in the depths of my computer tormenting me every time I logged in, never to be completed, let alone published. I feel sure that although you never met 'Ria, as the family called her, you have probably ended up knowing her almost as well as we did.

Thank you so very much.

Author's Note

For countries and cities whose names have changed or been modernised since the mid-twentieth century, I have retained the names as Maria wrote them, which were those in use at the time: principally Abyssinia (Ethiopia), Burma (Myanmar), Bombay (Mumbai), Madras (Chennai), Calcutta (Kolkata) Rangoon (Yangon), Mongmit (Momeik) and Maymyo (Pyin Oo Lwin). Similarly, Quetta is referred to throughout as being in Northern India, as the events described in the book predate the creation of Pakistan.

Contents

Glossary of Terms and Abbreviations

ALFSEA	Allied Land Forces South East Asia
Basha	A dwelling or shelter, a tent
BESA	Bengal Entertainment Services Association
BOR	British Other Ranks
CAS(B)	Canteen Army Stores (Burma)
Char	Tea
CCS	Casualty Clearing Station
CBID	Canteen Bulk Issue Depot
Chinthe	Mythical lion found guarding the entrance to pagodas and temples in Burma. WAS(B) emblem: a black Chinthe on a red square background which was worn on the uniform beret. Bronze Chinthe pins were worn on each collar
Dekho!	The magazine of the Burma Star Association, from a Hindi word meaning 'Look!'
DUKW	An amphibious vehicle: the letters are not an acronym but a manufacturer's production code.
ENSA	Entertainment National Services Association
FANY	First Aid Nursing Yeomanry
GOC	General Officer Commanding
GPT	General Purposes Transport
IO	Intelligence Officer
IOR	Indian Other Ranks
KOSB	Kings Own Scottish Borderers

Kukri	Distinctively curved Nepalese knife associated with the Gurkhas
L of C	Line of Communication
MDS	Main Dressing Station
MTO	Motor Transport Office
Mufti	Military slang for civilian attire
NCO	Non-commissioned officer
POW	Prisoner of War
POL	Petrol, Oil and Lubricants
PTI	Physical Training Instructor
RAPWI	Recovery of Allied Prisoners of War and Internees. Established in February 1945 at the HQ of Lord Louis Mountbatten to help free the prisoners of the SEAC zone.
SEAC	South East Asia Command
Toc H	International Christian charity organisation formed in 1915 during WW1 in Belgium by The Reverend Philip 'Tubby' Clayton, Bubbles Clayton's uncle. Named after Talbot House, the original soldiers' rest and recreation building at Poperinge during the First World War, 'Toc Aitch' being TH in the phonetic alphabet used by radio operators at the time. An organisation which still operates to this day.
VAD	Voluntary Aid Detachment
Wads	Cakes/buns
WAS(B)	Women's Auxiliary Services (Burma)
WRNS	Women's Royal Naval Service (Wrens)
WVS	Women's Voluntary Service

Foreword

by Dame Vera Lynn

I remember seeing the lovely Wasbies (Women's Auxiliary Service: Burma) when I was out in Burma all those decades ago. There were not many of them but they performed sterling work; not only at staging points but also when the front-line troops came back to base camp, a team of Wasbies were there working in excessive heat in mosquito-infested jungle clearings.

The Wasbies ran the mobile canteens to keep our boys fed and watered and as the saying goes 'an army marches on its stomach'. They always worked with a smile on their faces and were in great demand wherever they went. It's good to know their story is now being told.

'Maria': Jeanne Elspeth Pilbrow, MBE, later Holroyd (née Holford-Walker)

Introduction

This story is based upon the life and diaries of my maternal aunt, who was born Jeanne Elspeth Holford-Walker, in 1917 in the village of Wool, Dorset, but was known as Maria throughout her life to both family and friends, most likely after her paternal grandmother.

In 1924 she emigrated with her family to Kenya where she spent an idyllic childhood, growing up on a cattle farm in the drylands of Nanyuki, north of Nairobi. Maria met and married her husband, Peter Pilbrow, in Kenya in 1939 but left in 1942 in order to follow him to India where he had been posted with the King's African Rifles, whom he had joined upon the outbreak of the Second World War.

I first met my aunt in 1953, after she had settled in London following the end of the war and in 1979, after I too moved from Kenya to England, we became very close. When she died in 1988 she left behind a conundrum – a decrepit cardboard box containing a cache of scrappy notes, both handwritten and typed, a scruffy little diary, and numerous battered photograph albums. At the time of her death I was grief-stricken and in no frame of mind to explore the contents of the carton in any great depth, although a brief inspection suggested they were worth keeping. I cleared Maria's house and the box was put away in a cupboard, where it remained for fifteen years.

It wasn't until I had sold my business and had more time on my hands that I started to think about the contents of the box. Initially I couldn't bring myself to pry: I still felt it unsettling and a little uncomfortable to ferret around in Maria's private life. However, the itch eventually became a scratch and curiosity got the better of me. One cold winter morning I peeled off the disintegrating brown tape and opened the battered container. The contents – notes, diary and photos – were in no sequential order but appeared to be a record of Maria's extraordinary history and they set me off on an eight-year journey to piece together the details of her astonishing exploits. This was to prove a daunting task as she had rarely spoken of her past and there were many gaps and questions which required research and investigation.

Initially I typed up, in chronological order, everything I had and knew, starting with her early years as the feisty middle daughter of a settler family who emigrated to Kenya following the First World War. This was relatively easy to record, as I was already aware of the family history, but when it came to Maria's war journal, this was a different matter. Maria wrote of being with the Women's Auxiliary Service (Burma), abbreviated to the WAS(B) and known affectionately as the 'Wasbies'. I knew next to nothing about this period of Maria's life. All I remembered was that she had left Kenya at some point during the course of the Second World War in order to meet up with her husband, who was serving with the Army in India. Apparently, once there, she opted not to return to Kenya but rather to join the war effort in South East Asia.

As I read through the combination of typed and handwritten pages, newspaper cuttings and telegrams pasted into the albums, the context of her war experiences began to fall into place. I learned that Peter's battalion took part initially in the East African Campaign against Italian forces in Abyssinia – now Ethiopia – and Somaliland. Doubtless she felt his absence keenly, so soon after their marriage, but during the first years of the war at least he was close enough to come home when he had leave. She had married him in spite of her parents' disapproval, displaying for the first time the determined and independent streak which was to figure so prominently throughout her story. When he was posted to Northern India in 1942, he managed to secure permission for her to join him for the period of his training at the staff college at Quetta, and she had no hesitation in leaving behind everything she knew and crossing the ocean alone in order to be with him.

Not long after she reached him, however, it was apparent their relationship had begun to falter, at least on his part. We don't know what it was that first drove a wedge between them – and nor did Maria herself, as her initial hurt and puzzlement at his increasing distance makes plain. Crucially, however, and against his express wishes, she chose to remain in India under her own steam, which led to her joining the Wasbies, which led in turn to the war diary which forms the main body of this book.

*

The Wasbies were formed during the Second World War and initially operated in India and Burma, but who exactly were they, and what was their role? When I began my research few people had heard of them and in the beginning I could find no relevant historical reference or information. Fortunately, I was able to contact a couple of Maria's close friends who I knew had worked with her during the war and they were able to enlighten me.

The campaign in the Far East started when Japan declared war against Britain and the United States in December 1941, bombing the US naval base of Pearl Harbor and attacking British forces in Malaya, Singapore and Hong Kong. The WAS(B) was formed shortly afterwards in January 1942 to work mainly on cypher duties with the British Armed Forces in Burma. The WAS(B) organisation had been in existence only a few weeks when the Japanese invaded Burma from the south, and the Wasbies had to evacuate back to India, where they were disbanded. A short time later, Ninian Taylor, an indomitable woman who was to become the WAS(B) commander, suggested to the military hierarchy that a canteen service could be established which would provide a taste of home in the form of tea and cakes (known amongst the troops as char and wads) and a friendly smile to the serving men. The service, which was to operate under the umbrella of the British Army, would offer both static and mobile facilities, the latter operating from the rear of converted Chevrolet vans. The idea was accepted and Mrs Taylor set about the task of enlisting and training her team of women. The majority of her recruits were young, some the daughters of civil servants and colonial expats from Britain and Australia, others the wives of military personnel and missionaries, most of whom had been living in South East Asia when war broke out.

Once the Wasbies were in full operation this put canteens, staffed by British and Commonwealth women, within the sound of Japanese guns. Mobile units were sent to establish canteen shops and tea counters at all the major staging points within the Burma and India theatre of war. The Wasbies came to be eagerly accepted by Divisional Commanders of the Fourteenth, and later Twelfth Armies for offering not only tasty fare but also a little bit of warmth and cheer during a time of darkness and drudgery. They provided a valuable morale boost all along the route from base camps to forward fighting zones throughout the duration of the war in the Far East. It was the highlight of a soldier's weary and trying day to find that there was a Wasbie canteen in the vicinity and the beastliness of their existence could be forgotten for a brief moment over a cup of tea and a treat along with a welcoming face. Hence it was not a surprise to the girls to find trees deep in the forests or jungle bearing little hand-scribbled notices saying 'Wasbies welcome'.

In 1943 South East Asia Command (SEAC) was set up to be in overall charge of Allied operations in the South East Asian Theatre of WW2. Lord Louis Mountbatten was appointed Supreme Allied Commander and General William Slim was appointed Commander of the Fourteenth Army, later known to many as the 'Forgotten Army'. It numbered over one million men under arms, one of the largest Commonwealth armies ever assembled, and this is to whom the Wasbies were assigned.

Maria joined the Wasbies in 1944 and her work with the troops of this campaign began in March of that year.

She remained with them until the Wasbies were eventually disbanded in 1946. Throughout this time, whenever she was able to write it up, she kept a personal record of events and her response to them – this was the small, battered leather-bound diary I later found amongst her effects.

Reading her vivid first-hand account of these intrepid women and the difficulties that they faced made it even more surprising to me that nothing had been written about them at that time, and certainly nothing which gave them the acknowledgement that they deserved. I later found there had been a limited edition government booklet published in 1947 of which a copy was given to each of the Wasbies. Maria's copy was not with her effects, but was subsequently given to me by her nephew, my cousin.

After the war was over, Maria was awarded an MBE in recognition of her service. This last discovery came as a complete surprise. Such was Maria's modesty that she never mentioned receiving her award, which I found along with its citation in the same drawer in which she kept her precious letters. It appears from correspondence accompanying the medal and citation that she did not attend any ceremony to receive her MBE, opting for it to be sent to her by post. She had previously been mentioned in despatches and was also the holder of campaign medals: the Burma Star Medal for her service in India and Burma, the 1939–45 Star which was awarded to all members of the armed forces for operational service overseas, along with the War Medal 1939–45 which was also awarded to all members of the armed forces involved in the Second World War. She was one of six Wasbies awarded the MBE and four of them were founder members including Ninian Taylor and Lois St John, her assistant commandant, so the fact that Maria was honoured in this way was a clear indication of the regard in which her contribution to the war effort was held. It was this fact, together with a desire to see the Wasbies given their due, that first made me think that her story deserved to be not just a private family memoir but a full-length book.

*

The process of unravelling and writing Maria's story was a rollercoaster of highs and lows: fascinating insights followed by frustrating brick walls and then eureka moments. Deciphering the diary itself was no easy task. It was pocket-sized, the handwriting cramped and difficult to read; service personnel were not supposed to keep personal diaries, lest the information in them should fall into enemy hands, so she had to keep it hidden. Maria kept hers stuffed inside her bedroll, which goes some way towards explaining its distressed condition. Moreover, as is clear from its contents, often she was writing it in the most trying of circumstances – within earshot of artillery fire, in inhospitable terrain or monsoon weather, in jungle clearings or burnt-out villages or in towns devastated by recent battles. Sometimes she wrote in ink, which in places has bled through the thin paper and obscured the writing on the other side; sometimes in pencil, which after all these years has become very faint. Apparently on occasion, when neither of these was available, the troops had to use sharpened charcoal twigs to write their letters home. Thankfully, Maria did not have to resort to this expedient.

Keeping the diary evidently inspired her to write further. In the first few months following the end of the war, when she was back in Rangoon and the Wasbies were involved in the Repatriation of Prisoners of War (RAPWI), her team had been allocated a static canteen at Mingaladon airfield, where the POWs were first met. It was here, of an evening, that she started to elaborate on her notes in a partly typed journal, and this gives a clearer, expanded account of some of the more condensed and cryptic passages in her diary. In instances such as these where the journal gives a more detailed version, I have incorporated the relevant passages with the diary entry.

Maria also collected and kept every letter (both personal and official), movement order, flight pass, telegram, photograph, newspaper clipping, invitation, menu or interesting scrap of paper which came her way. These, in family tradition, were all faithfully pasted, scrapbook-style, into the photograph albums I found, and enabled me to piece together and add colour to her life in the army with the Wasbies. When dated, and they weren't always, these also helped me enormously in confirming the timeline of events.

In addition, there were many publications and organisations which provided invaluable information about the Second World War and placed Maria's exploits in accurate historical context and, as the years went by, the internet became an increasingly useful tool. However, it was individual people who offered the most valuable and unexpected material, adding background, filling in gaps or corroborating details. In one such example, Maria had kept a record of a flight to Calcutta on an aeroplane intriguingly nicknamed 'Chinthe' – the Chinthe being the mythical creature which was the Wasbie emblem, as well as that of the Twelfth Army. Wanting to find out more about it, on impulse I decided to phone the RAF Museum and spoke to their curator, Gordon Leith. He was able to confirm not only that there was indeed an aircraft named Chinthe but, that it was the personal Dakota of General Stopford, Commander of the Twelfth Army, and that the pilot was Flight Lieutenant Dennis A. Woolfe, all of which accorded with the details Maria had kept. He asked if I would like a copy of the pilot's log for the relevant week, together with – thrill of thrills – a photograph of the aircraft and the pilot.

And so the tale slowly came together ...

*

The book is structured so that the central three parts are Maria's own first-hand account, beginning with her departure from Kenya in 1942 and ending with her repatriation in 1946. These are bracketed with two biographical sections, one detailing her early life in Kenya and the other her return to civilian life after the war.

The reader may wonder why, if the wartime diary is the crux of the book, the first part is given over to Maria's upbringing in Kenya. The tough life of the pioneers, miles from anywhere, with the railway not reaching them until ten years or so after they moved there, having to be self-sufficient not only in food production but also in supplies and medicine – there were no doctors, nor vets for the livestock – made for resourceful people. All of this played a major part in the person Maria became, enabling her to do what she did, to go to India, stay on, and cope with everything her war service threw at her.

I grew up in Kenya myself, and Maria's older sister Grizel is my mother. I knew the family home very well and had taken all the journeys described in the first section of the book including the wonderful train journey between Nairobi and Mombasa, although of course when I did the journey it was not so primitive and in fact became quite luxurious. Thus, for the first fifteen years of our lives, her experiences and mine were not dissimilar. However, those whose interest lies exclusively in the war chapters should feel free to skip this section if they prefer and start at Part Two.

*

At the end of the long journey that brought this book into being, some mysteries remain. One thing that no part of Maria's notes or diary makes clear is what happened to break up her marriage. Nor do we know exactly why she chose to stay on in India rather than return home. A desire to prove herself? The hope that perhaps, by staying where Peter was, they might still be reconciled? There are certainly elements of that within the diary. We know that she kept newspaper cuttings of war reports which enabled her to keep track of his whereabouts in Burma, but they only met again the once, and that more or less by accident, when his battalion and her canteen crossed paths in a jungle clearing.

Sadly, their relationship could not be rebuilt. Realising that there was nothing for her in Kenya, she opted instead to be repatriated to England and start her life afresh. But had she not felt compelled to strike out on her own and join the Wasbies, this book of course would not exist. Her resilience and her determination are what drove her, and I hope that this account does justice to the memory of those forgotten women of the Forgotten Army.

Maria's diary: the start of a long journey.

PART ONE

Early Life in Kenya

1924–1942

Maria's father, Allen Holford-Walker, came from a military background. His father, Brigadier General Edgar Holford-Walker, had served in India and Egypt and was decorated after the Battle of Tel-el-Kabir in 1882. Allen went to the Royal Military College at Sandhurst, from which he joined the 1st Battalion The Argyll and Sutherland Highlanders in 1909, serving with them initially in Malta and India. Following the outbreak of the First World War his battalion was posted to France in 1915, where he spent time in the trenches. Wounded in action, the nature of his injuries prevented him from returning to front line duties as an infantry officer. Instead he applied to join the Machine Gun Corps and was assigned to the Heavy Section, which operated the early tanks.

In August 1916 he returned to France as commander of twenty-five tanks for 'C' Company, with his younger brother Archie amongst those under his command. Both brothers took part in the battle of Flers-Courcelette on the Somme on 15 September, where tanks were used for the first time against the enemy, and again in November 1916 at the battle of Ancre, after which Allen was awarded the

Military Cross in the New Year Honours list in January 1917. He remained with the newly renamed Tank Corps for the rest of the war, although his previous injuries led him to spend several periods in hospital during this time.

Following the end of the war, employment in the civilian sector in England was scarce, with a great number of ex-armed forces personnel seeking work. This situation affected not only enlisted men but also returning officers, for whom there were not enough professional jobs to go round. To this end the government set up the Soldier Settlement Scheme to Kenya in 1919. Unlike the wider settlement schemes which saw thousands of ex-servicemen emigrate to Australia, New Zealand, Canada and South Africa, the Kenya scheme was aimed almost exclusively at the officer class. Applicants had not only to have served during 1914–18 but to have substantial financial resources, sufficient to fund them during the initial stages of the venture, to purchase land and equip a farm. Allen met the required criteria of ex-officer status and, with his wife Joan's private means, was eligible for the scheme, so he applied for passage to Kenya, under the terms of this programme.

Allen had married Joan Barrington Moody in Farnham, Surrey in December 1914. She too came from a military family, and one which moreover had set its stamp on British colonial history. Amongst her antecedents were Major General Richard Clement Moody of the Royal Engineers, who would go on to be the first Lieutenant Governor of British Columbia and the first British Governor of the Falkland Islands; his brother Hampden Clement, commander of the Royal Engineers in China; and their father, Colonel Thomas Moody, commander of the Royal

4

Engineers in the West Indies. Another great-uncle had served as a British army chaplain in China, the Falklands, Gibraltar, Malta and the Crimea. Her father, Thomas Barrington Moody, was a navigator with the Royal Navy whose career took him to Brazil, Australia, Hawaii, Canada, Japan and China before returning home to teach navigation at the Royal Naval College, Greenwich.

With such a tradition of travel and settlement overseas on both sides of the family, it is perhaps not surprising that Allen and Joan should have grasped the opportunity. Added to this they were close to Joan's maternal cousins, Raymond and Logan Hook, who had emigrated to what was then British East Africa in 1912. Raymond was well known in the colony and had established a worldwide reputation as an excellent hunter, trapper and expert in Kenya's wildlife. This often involved him arranging and escorting shooting safaris for the rich and famous from America and Europe. He had now lived in Kenya for some years and was in a position to offer the family a great deal of assistance and advice regarding their move to a challenging new life. With young children and little knowledge of what such a migration might entail, this information was priceless.

At the time Allen and Joan made their decision to emigrate, Maria was seven years old. The family, consisting of Maria, her older sister Grizel aged eight, and young brother Fionn aged two, left Whitmead, their home in the village of Tilford, near Farnham in Surrey, to start a new life a long way from England. On 27 November 1924 they departed from London's Tilbury Dock bound for Mombasa on board the SS *Mulbera*, the flagship of the British India Line. Built by Alexander Stephen and Sons of Glasgow to carry 158 passengers – 78 first class and 80 second class – she was launched on 14 February 1922 and remained in service on the East African route until 1954.

The voyage took three weeks, via Gibraltar and Marseilles, across the Mediterranean and through the Suez Canal into the Red Sea, calling at Port Said in Egypt, Port Sudan and then Aden, before finally entering the Indian Ocean to head south along the East African coast, arriving in Mombasa just before Christmas on 21 December.

No doubt the journey for the children was enormous fun: a continual series of parties and games from morning until evening. Every day there was something going on and they were kept entertained and busy most of the time, leaving the adults to enjoy the trip without having to keep the children occupied and out of mischief. The adults too enjoyed on-board entertainment, and found time to play deck quoits, attend fancy dress parties and partake in games with the two girls.

SS *Mulbera* at sea. Courtesy Kevin Patience

According to the family album, which was faithfully kept by Joan and contained a great number of photographs and newspaper clippings relating to their boat trip and early lives in Kenya, one of the highlights of the journey was when the Duke and Duchess of York, later King George VI and Queen Elizabeth, joined the ship in Marseilles. This was their Royal Highnesses' first visit to the African continent, where they were to enjoy a private holiday and safari touring Kenya and Uganda, without too many of the trappings of an official visit.

The Duke and Duchess travelled in a normal first-class cabin on board the ship. They were sociable and joined in most evening entertainment, mixing freely with the passengers. One cutting describes how they took part in Father Neptune's ceremony on crossing the Equator. The hoary old sea god and his henchmen decreed that tradition be observed. His court let the Duchess off lightly: even he could not withstand her charms! However, he did demand that she swallow a potion of mysterious preparation, and when she had complied she was supplied with a free passport to his tropical domain. The Duke, however, was duly sentenced and, with good humour, wearing only a vest and a pair of shorts, permitted himself to be soaped, shaved and then ducked as was the custom when 'crossing the line'. But he had his revenge. Calling for volunteers he led his storming party, with a rush, to the bridge. They swarmed up the ladder and seized the captain, hauled him to the deck and ducked him.

The Duke and Duchess were known to be passionately fond of dancing and they exacted full enjoyment from a fancy dress ball held on board. The Duke was dressed as a

Venetian boatman and the Duchess as a Spanish dancer. Both costumes were improvised. The Duchess danced with both passengers and members of the crew, with the Duke also selecting his partners from amongst the passengers and when it came to the Eightsome Reel their Royal Highnesses had everyone beaten hollow: the Duke was not allowed to forget that he had married a Scottish lassie.

All too soon the sea voyage was over and the ship turned toward the port of Mombasa. The family's first distant sighting of the East African coast was Mombasa old port, dominated by the imposing façade of Fort Jesus, a solid and forbidding structure built into the coral rock face overlooking the Indian Ocean. Mombasa is one of a number of picturesque ancient Arab towns on the coast of East Africa, steeped in history, having been subjected to many invasions and sackings over the centuries. It is a port from which, over millennia, the Swahili and Omani Arab people have sailed their dhows between Dar es Salaam, Zanzibar, the Persian Gulf and India during the monsoon season, carrying all manner of lucrative cargo ranging from exotic spices to slaves.

Probably the first most notable European connection with East Africa was the discovery of Mombasa by the explorer Vasco da Gama in 1498. He had been appointed by the Portuguese King, Manuel I, to lead an expedition to find a maritime route to the East, and it was during his voyage that he ventured into this port whilst en route to India. Nearly a hundred years later, in 1593, King Philip I of Portugal ordered the construction of Fort Jesus to help protect the entrance to Mombasa from other would-be marauders. Portugal was one in a long line of countries that invaded this strategic coastal town, and this magnificent fortification bears the architecture of many occupations, standing proud to this day.

As the SS *Mulbera* neared the coral reef which runs down most of the East African coastline, the vessel slowed down to be boarded by a special pilot who was required to navigate the ship through the tricky *malango* (entrance in this natural barrier), leading into the old Kilindini Harbour which nestles between Mombasa Island and the mainland: *Kilindini* very appropriately being the Swahili word for 'deep water'. The hazardous nature of the approach was evidenced by the skeleton of the steam ship *Ahmadi,* which went aground in 1909 and whose engine protruded above the water for many years and was known locally as 'The Elephant Wreck'.

With the Indian Ocean now receding behind her, the *Mulbera* slowly and carefully manoeuvred her way past the two headlands of Ras Serani on Mombasa Island and Nyali on the mainland, where giant ancient baobab trees stood sentinel on the cliff overlooking the mouth of the harbour. It was here the ship would drop anchor.

Once anchored securely, the steam-driven derricks swung into action as preparations were made to unload the cargo and baggage, there being no purpose-built quay offering berthing facilities at this time.

Soon after the *Mulbera* moored, the Governor of Kenya, Sir Robert Coryndon, came on board via the ship's ladder, which was attached to the side of a vessel enabling the movement of passengers on and off ships when no quay facility was available. Sir Robert met the royal couple to organise their speedy disembarkation and transfer to the governor's residence, before they all boarded a newly painted, private train which would carry them up to Nairobi.

Fascinated, the girls watched the fanfare surrounding the Royal arrival in Kenya. The Duke and Duchess left the *Mulbera* on board a special launch which bore the Royal Standard in the stern. The Duke wore the white uniform (with blue sash) of a naval captain and the Duchess looked dainty and refreshing in a cream frock and white pith helmet. On the shore every building sported decorations, bunting and greenery of some description. From the flagstaff hung a stream of coloured flags which signalled 'Welcome to Kenya'. Passengers watched at a distance as the Duke and Duchess landed and heard the massed crowd of many races burst into hoarse cheering. The impression the Duchess made in the centre of that multitude of dark faces and exotic colouring was memorable – a little cream figure in the midst of flamboyant Africa.

After the thrill of the royal spectacle it was the family's turn to leave the ship. They joined the queue of passengers waiting to disembark via the same precipitous boarding ladder, and on looking at the waiting launches bobbing on the water below it would have seemed a long way down. The descent in the clothes of the day was rather alarming. Allen, wearing a smart tropical suit and hat, managed reasonably well, although poor Joan struggled, dressed as she was in a long-sleeved ankle-length dress and a wide-brimmed hat to protect her face from the sun. She descended in a rather gingerly fashion, followed by the children's governess, carrying Fionn and, encouraged by Allen, Maria and Grizel brought up the rear.

At the foot of the steps were motor boats ready to ferry passengers to the jetty leading to the customs sheds where they awaited the arrival of their luggage. A clamour of dock hands and porters assisted with the movement of everyone's goods and chattels, which had to be hoisted up from the holds and transferred to the shore on lighters for inspection and clearance.

The heat and humidity of Mombasa was crushing. An attempt had been made to disguise the unlovely surroundings of the harbour and wharf with sun-shading palm fronds. Despite this the sun beat down, there was no cooling sea breeze to ease the cloying hot atmosphere and everyone just wilted. Their clothes stuck to them uncomfortably, and soon there was a general air of ill temper, uncertainty and frustration. This, along with the slightly chaotic and lengthy arrival procedure made it seem like an eternity before Allen managed to locate, process and sort out the family's possessions, enabling them to leave the dock. Once their belongings had been cleared, Allen arranged with the necessary authority for them to be stacked onto *hamali* (hand) carts for transportation to the railway goods shed ready to be loaded aboard the train which would leave for Nairobi the following morning.

A few motor cars were parked in the square outside the port along with an abundance of rickshaws, more hand carts, animal-drawn wagons and masses of porters jostling noisily outside the customs area ready to take passengers and their belongings to hotels and other local destinations. Allen, Joan and the family took rickshaws to spend the remainder of the day and that night at a nearby hotel prior to their departure the next morning for the 24-hour journey to Nairobi. During the rickshaw ride they noticed that all the government offices had been closed and it appeared that no one in Mombasa intended to do any work that day. Every effort was to be made to ensure the Duke and Duchess enjoyed a resounding welcome to Kenya.

The following day, with the next leg of their journey due to commence, the excited girls and the rest of the family had risen early, soon to make their way, again by rickshaw, to the station ready to board the train, which was due to leave at eleven o'clock. On arrival at Mombasa station Allen checked that all their belongings had been stowed in the baggage van, after which they all clambered up the steps into their allotted compartment in a smartly painted cream and brown Uganda Railways first-class carriage. It was not long before the robust American-built Baldwin B Class steam locomotive pulled slowly out of Mombasa at the start of its long haul north-west. The carriages had no corridors, there was no dining car and the loo facility, which for some reason children always seem to be in need of, and usually at the most inopportune moment, was located at the end of each compartment. When the lid was lifted, you could see straight through to the ground, so the children were given strict instructions not to use it when in a station.

The locomotive crawled slowly off Mombasa Island across Salisbury Bridge and onto the mainland. The single line track snaked its way inland, with the engine chomping its way through enormous quantities of coal, imported from England and India. With the engine belching a trail of smoke and steam skyward, it climbed slowly up from sea level on its journey to the capital situated at an altitude of 5,500 feet, some 300 miles away. It wasn't long before the palm trees of the coast slowly gave way to the bush as the train crossed the thorn-tree landscape known as the Taru Desert. The carriage was hot and dusty and although it did have blinds, it was too warm to pull them down during the day, and the family wanted to view the countryside as the train carried them on the first leg of the journey. So, they had to contend with the soot and dust blown in through the windows, and it was not long before they were all covered with a fine coating of grime.

The views stretched endlessly for miles either side of the train. After leaving the coastal region, there were no towns or villages as such and the land was uncultivated – this certainly was wild country, so different to where the family had come from, and Maria later wondered how her parents felt about their decision to venture into the unknown. Apart from a few high rocky outcrops, scrubby bush and tall intricately constructed terracotta coloured anthills, the scorched land was pretty flat. It stretched endlessly towards the distant misty blue ridge of the Yatta Plateau, the world's longest lava flow. The high Taita Hills stood prominent to the west and in the far distance, on a clear day, Mount Kilimanjaro, Africa's highest mountain with its distinct snow-covered apex, could sometimes be seen towering above the grasslands of Amboseli on the border between Kenya and Tanganyika (now Tanzania) in the south-west.

For the first leg of the journey, Joan had organised a picnic lunch and drinks to be supplied by the hotel. The train stopped frequently to take on water, enabling the

Baldwin B Class Locomotive and passenger train outside Mombasa.
Courtesy Kevin Patience.

passengers to alight and stretch their legs. Dinner and breakfast breaks had been planned en route for passengers to avail themselves of a meal in the railway refreshment room, which was in a Dak bungalow situated beside the track. Meals were pre-ordered by the guard, who sent a telegram up the line advising of the number of passengers and meals required for each journey. Dinner was at Voi, a hundred miles inland from Mombasa. The breakfast stop next morning, prior to arrival in Nairobi, would be at Makindu, in a dusty little railway hut about a hundred miles south of the capital.

Late in the evening the train pulled into Voi, where throughout the stopover the giant engine continued to grumble and groan like some huge live fairy-tale monster, with steam hissing out loudly from somewhere underneath. The night was very black as the two girls strained their eyes into the unfamiliar darkness, which they now knew harboured many mysterious wild beasts.

The refreshment establishment at Voi, which had first been licenced to sell liquor in 1910, along with serving meals, also offered much-needed washing facilities to the hot, dirty, dusty and soot-covered travellers. The building was rather scruffy and sparsely furnished with basic government-issue, locally made wooden tables and chairs. There was little adornment and the rooms were lit by paraffin lanterns, there being no electricity in those early days. As far as Maria remembered, the meal itself was no culinary delight, but then would one really expect this in the wilds of a newly emerging country?

At Voi, it was the family's first experience of the sights and sounds of an African night. Buzzing mosquitoes bit any exposed arms and legs, moths and other insects fluttered around the lamps and lizards and geckos crept across the floors and up the walls in pursuit of an appetising bug. In the distance what sounded like a lion grunting, jackal yipping and the spine-chilling sound of hyena fighting over a far-off kill were all a little unnerving.

The children were already rather nervous, as during the journey up to Voi their parents had recounted the true tale about a pair of man-eating lions which roamed the Tsavo area in 1898 when the railway line from Mombasa to Uganda was under construction. Apparently, they resorted to attacking humans due to the lack of antelope and other small game animals in the area, following an outbreak of rinderpest disease and a severe drought. Their hunger and desperation for food had driven the starving cats to become man-eaters, taking some of the Indian and African workers who were building the railway bridge across the Tsavo River. Unsurprisingly, the labourers immediately downed tools and refused to continue working until the unfortunate creatures were tracked down and shot. Being so young, the children had listened wide-eyed, and of course found the story very frightening, although at the same time rather exciting. They made sure the window of the carriage was kept tightly closed throughout the hours of darkness, just in case.

When they re-boarded the train after dinner, bedding had been laid on the seats in passenger compartments and travellers hunkered down for the night with the sway of the carriage and the rhythmic clickety-clack of the wheels on the track soon lulling most of them to sleep, only to be woken at regular intervals throughout the journey when the train stopped at a number of scruffy little halts along the line for the locomotive to take on water. No matter what the hour, the passengers were met by a noisy throng of local folk with naked small children, scantily clad bare-breasted women and men wearing nothing more than a loincloth, all offering locally grown fruits and foodstuffs to some of the third-class passengers who made the long voyage sitting on wooden slatted benches. Not a comfortable journey. Their belongings, including live chickens, legs tied together to stop them escaping, and probably the odd goat, were squashed in alongside them. Judging by the noise and excitement at each brief stop it was obvious that the train was a highlight, not to mention a lucrative few minutes, in the local purveyors' otherwise quiet, pastoral lives.

After leaving Voi the railway line continued through the hot, dry wilderness of what is now the 8,000-square-mile Tsavo National Park, home to an abundance of wild animals, large and small, beautiful and ugly. Black rhino and huge herds of elephant and buffalo roamed Tsavo. Alongside these large animals, zebra, giraffe and gerenuk, a long-necked, delicate browsing antelope, together with a myriad of other gazelles either grazed the dry grass or browsed on stunted trees and bushes which might offer a little morsel of nourishment. Also living in this area were the predators: lion, leopard and cheetah, hyena, wild-dog and jackal – all struggling to exist in these sun-baked, red sandy scrublands through which the railway track had been laid.

Breaking up the bush-entangled landscape through which the train was travelling there was a scattering of the extraordinary-looking but magnificent baobab trees, similar to those standing sentry at the harbour entrance in Mombasa. They were quite striking with enormous bulbous trunks and the most strange, thick and leafless, arm-like branches from which hung huge pendulous seed pods. These trees, which appear to thrive in this harsh bush land, are semi-succulent and are believed to be amongst the oldest living species in the world, with some of them aged up to 2,000 years or more. They are home to a host of beasts and birds, and are nicknamed 'upside down' trees. Local tribal folklore believes that when God made the world he became frustrated and angry, ripping the trees out of the ground and stuffing them back into the earth upside down. It's true to say their branches do look more like roots, particularly when the trees shed their leaves in the dry season to conserve moisture.

Travelling through the night, the train stopped for breakfast at Makindu, with the family looking forward to reaching Nairobi and meeting up with Raymond. On arrival, however, their first impression of the capital was one of noise and utter chaos, with the jostling locals clamouring to help disembarking passengers unload their goods and yelling at each other either in their tribal languages or Swahili, none of which at that time could be understood by any of the family. The station was dusty, grimy and smelly, with an abundance of flies, but thankfully, although blisteringly hot, the air was not as sultry as Mombasa had been.

Waiting at the station was Raymond, and it wasn't long before he and Allen managed to deal with the storage of the family's possessions and they were soon on their way to the Norfolk Hotel at the edge of town. Raymond had decided to break the journey before continuing the last difficult and arduous leg by oxcart, via Thika, the end of the railway line, to their final destination – Nanyuki – where Raymond and his brother Logan lived and where the Holford-Walker family were to settle. It was not until 1931 that the railway line finally reached Nanyuki.

Raymond was a tall, imposing, authoritative man, with a tanned weather-beaten face. He was partially blind in one eye, sported a goatee beard, had a great beak of a nose and the children found him very scary looking. He certainly had a presence, was organised and efficient and obviously well respected by those with whom he came into contact. He was extremely well educated and well informed and Maria remembered her mother saying he would often read Egyptian hieroglyphics just to amuse himself of an evening.

Once out of the station, the family headed the short distance to the Norfolk Hotel via rough, dusty roadways on which an assortment of handcarts, horse-drawn buggies and ox-wagons, rickshaws and bicycles plus a few motor cars all shared the same thoroughfare. Along the roadside there were busy little stores, with corrugated iron roofs overhanging the street, offering a little shade to shoppers and pedestrians. Most of the shops were run by Indian immigrants selling all manner of goods from pots and pans and basic household necessities to farming essentials. There were butchers and grocers, drapers and tailors selling textiles and making clothing suited to the hot tropical climate. Government offices and banks occupied larger stone-built premises, but on the whole Nairobi was still a small but growing capital.

It didn't take too long to reach the hotel where Allen and Joan could take stock of their surroundings, having agreed to a few days' break before undertaking the somewhat intimidating final leg of their journey. The few days spent in Nairobi, including Christmas, gave Raymond the opportunity to purchase some items which he needed, in addition to a number of things he recommended Allen and Joan should stock up with whilst they were there. This involved, amongst other things, a visit to Wardles, the only chemist, to obtain an adequate supply of tropical medicines suitable for both animal and human use.

A few days later the little family party boarded the train to travel the short distance of approximately thirty miles to Thika, where Raymond's staff and ox-carts were waiting at the station. After their arrival Raymond first took them to the Blue Posts Hotel, giving them opportunity to refresh themselves as this would be the last glimpse of civilisation for several days. True to form, Raymond wasted no time in supervising the loading of goods onto the ox-carts for the last stage of the journey and they were soon on their way.

Thika is located in an area where the stunning African flame trees grow in abundance and Joan marvelled at their vivid orangey-red blowsy flowers, which were an unexpected and wonderful splash of colour against the rolling landscape. She had never before seen trees with such flamboyant and luscious blooms; in fact, they were the first of many stunning flowering trees they were to encounter in this extraordinary country with its enormous variation of vegetation, terrain and altitude.

Raymond, who always wore tropical attire – a battered and none-too-clean old felt bush hat, well-travelled scruffy khaki bush shirt and shorts with sturdy leather boots – now carried over his shoulder a heavy-calibre hunting rifle. He carried his gun not only for protection but also to shoot for the pot. He was a very fine shot, in spite of the poor sight in one eye, and was well accustomed to shooting either birds (guinea fowl, sand grouse and partridge being particularly plentiful in the area) or, alternatively, antelope, which would of course feed his staff as well as the rest of the party during the trip. It was normal for farmers to live off the land, which included game meat and wild fowl in addition to farm-reared cattle and sheep along with home-grown fruit and vegetables.

So there they were: a little caravan of new settlers trekking slowly and laboriously up the dusty road to Nyeri, where they would break their journey at the White Rhino

Hotel before continuing onward to Nanyuki. Initially the plan was to stay with Raymond's brother, Logan, who owned a small hotel in Nanyuki: the Silverbeck, named after their family home in England. The journey from Thika to Nanyuki spanned a distance of approximately eighty miles and the ox-carts had to travel over un-made-up rutted and corrugated *murram* (laterite) roads. Progress was slow, hot and dusty. December was the hot dry season, consequently the road was in a very rough state and it took a number of days for them to reach Nanyuki.

Initially they travelled through fertile land which later became coffee plantations, then onward through forests where the soil was a deep rich red in contrast to that at their destination, which was more dry and sandy with only a scattering of thorn bushes on sweeping grasslands stretching for miles into the distance.

During the journey nights were spent under canvas: they were cold, as the altitude was over 6,000 feet above sea level, so the family had to huddle around a camp fire to keep warm in the evenings when the equatorial sun went down promptly at six o'clock. Camp fires were lit at dusk and kept stoked throughout the night, not only against the cold, but to deter predators. The oxen were uncoupled from the wagons, watered and overseen by a herdsman, then left to graze until it was dark, after which they too settled down at the camp perimeter. Most animals lay down, chewing the cud and slumbering peacefully, ready for the next leg of the journey, which started before dawn the following day.

Early evening was the time when Raymond, Allen and Joan would pull up their canvas chairs around the camp-fire for a drink whilst supper was being prepared by the servants.

Allen and Joan would talk to Raymond about what the future held, or just listen to his stories of encounters with rhino, elephant and buffalo, lion and best of all, beautiful leopard and cheetah. Raymond was well known for organising safaris for wealthy hunters, mainly on the slopes of Mount Kenya or the Aberdare Mountains, in addition to which he had a team of staff trapping a variety of wild animals, which he kept on his farm prior to shipping them to zoos around the world, and they soon learnt that this awe-inspiring and interesting man had a special passion for cheetah.

During these evenings the girls sat with their governess and she either read to them, which was difficult with only a hurricane lamp for illumination, or, alternatively, they looked up at the ebony skies as she pointed out some of the stars and planets in the universe above. There had been a new moon on Christmas day, so the skies were dark with only a sliver of silver indicating its presence, allowing the swathe of the Milky Way to twinkle like fairy dust alongside the bright diamond of Venus, the 'evening star', always the first to shine when the sun went down. Soon Venus would be joined by more stars including the red planet Mars, only it wasn't really 'red', more of a golden copper colour. Lower in the sky was the distinctive Southern Cross, a constellation none of them would have seen before. Their governess would tell them about some of the other planets which could be identified such as Jupiter and Saturn. On one occasion she sketched the outline of one of the more recognisable constellations – the Greek mythological hunter Orion drawing his bow and arrow.

At 5 a.m., just before dawn, hot tea was brewed for everyone and the children were given a warm milky drink before an early breakfast and departure at sunrise. The African team driver would issue a piercing whistle, which instantly had the oxen on their feet, stretching and ready to be harnessed to the wagons – a primitive arrangement of rawhide thongs and ropes attached to the yokes which were placed over the necks of each pair of beasts before they were leashed to the wagon's *disselboom* (shaft). The lead animals had ropes placed round their horns and these were used by one of the staff, who walked beside them, to guide the team along the rough track.

After breakfast, Joan, the children and their governess all climbed on board a wagon whilst the men mounted their sure-footed local Somali ponies, and at the crack of the driver's long *kiboko* (hippo-hide whip) the beasts moved off and the day's trek began. The oxen were docile creatures and were never struck with the whip, responding without question to the driver's command, accepting without complaint the arduous lives they led. They ambled along at their own slow pace, in harmony with the rhythmic whistle or song of the African staff. Although the going was rough and slow, and at times the wagons rocked and swayed precariously over the uneven ground, it was nevertheless a tranquil, unhurried mode of transport, allowing the family to soak up the atmosphere of their new environment.

At midday, when the sun was at its hottest, the caravan would stop at a suitable spot, often by a stream, for everyone to stretch their legs and have something to eat – most likely a tin of 'bully' (bully beef) and biscuits, and perhaps some fruit. The cattle grazed for a couple of hours before the trudge began once more until late evening when camp was set up again, having travelled maybe twenty miles in the day.

The African staff provided by Raymond consisted mainly of Masai, Samburu and Kikuyu. They were intriguing to Maria and Grizel at first as the tribesmen were pretty scantily clad, the Kikuyu in skins whilst the Masai and Samburu wore either skins or a terracotta cloth called a *shuka,* which was knotted at the shoulder and draped over the body, leaving little to the imagination. Some of them had fancy braided hairstyles and the Samburu decorated their bodies with a coating of fat mixed with red soil, probably to repel flies and mosquitoes, resulting in them looking even more curious: the girls had, after all, never seen dark-skinned people before their journey began. A number of these wild-looking men also wore beaded jewellery round their necks and in their ear lobes, which had been cut and stretched to form big loops from which their adornment dangled, and also round their ankles or wrists.

For personal protection most of the Samburu and Masai tribesmen carried a *mkuki* (spear), and the Kikuyu a *rungu* (wooden club). Spears were usually carried by the younger Masai *morans,* their name for a young warrior. Raymond explained that it was Masai custom to believe that a *moran* was not considered a man until he had killed his first lion with a spear, but he assured them that they would be unlikely to meet one of these felines during their travels, or at least he hoped they wouldn't. Raymond's rifle was the only protection against any unwanted encounters.

For the children this was just the beginning of a huge thrilling adventure, but it must have been a daunting and challenging period in Joan and Allen's lives. They would very quickly have to become self-sufficient, not only having to grow their own vegetables and cereals, but breed and tend animals for milk and meat, something they had never done before. Shop supplies were few and the only store quite distant from the farm. They would also have to take care of animal and human ailments, tending to a number of strange tropical illnesses, along with snake or insect bites etcetera, without the help of vets, doctors or hospitals. They relied upon the small quantity of medicines purchased whilst in Nairobi. The alternative was to mix up herbal potions from basics obtained from the one and only provision store in Nanyuki, which brought supplies up from Nairobi, by ox-cart, when the road conditions permitted.

On arrival in Nanyuki the family quickly settled at the Silverbeck. The hotel was located in the most beautiful spot, with wonderful gardens and a splendid view of the not too distant snow-capped Mount Kenya, with sparkling icy glaciers nestled between its three craggy peaks. Batian was the highest at 17,057 feet, Nelion and Point Lenana were lower, although still snow-covered. The mountain was a spectacular sight which could be enjoyed from the veranda of their little *banda* (cottage), one of half a dozen or so built in the grounds of the main building.

The cottage was a relatively small timber affair with a shingle roof, and it was certainly on the primitive side. There was no electricity, so paraffin hurricane lamps were used for illumination at night. Furnishings were home-constructed and sparse and there was little in the way of plumbing or sanitation as we know it today. The bathroom contained only a round enamel basin with jug. This was placed on a wooden washstand with a small mirror above. To the side was a galvanised tin bathtub which was gravity-filled from a converted forty-gallon oil drum containing water pumped from the Nanyuki River. The drum, which was located outside each *banda*, lay over a stone construction under which a fire was lit each afternoon to heat the water in time for an evening bath. The loo was a 'long drop', situated in an outhouse behind the living accommodation in the back garden, and the family were all advised to give the wooden 'sit upon' above the pit a jolly sound kicking before use, in order to dislodge any snakes, scorpions or other creepy crawlies that might be lurking within. Maria found this a little disconcerting at first but it wasn't long before it just became a way of life, and actually it was quite exciting if anyone did find something untoward in residence.

A special feature of the Silverbeck was the location of the bar. When building his hotel, Logan had paid particular attention to where his bar was to be positioned. It actually straddled the Equator and was, and still is, always a talking point for visitors who liked to debate on which side of the hemisphere they would prefer to take the weight off their feet, imbibe and enjoy their alcoholic, or otherwise, refreshment whilst discussing their day's activities and adventures in this remarkable wild country.

*

The family remained at the Silverbeck until March 1925, when Joan and Allen purchased a farm of 1,800 acres from a Dutchman, one of the early Voortrekkers from the Cape in South Africa who had made the journey north to East Africa some years before, also by ox cart. The farm was situated about eight miles out of the tiny town of Nanyuki, a short distance from Raymond's ranch. They decided to name the farm Killean after an estate in Argyll, Scotland, not far from where one of the family ancestors originated, and it was here they started their new lives as settlers.

The farmhouse was a small stone building containing very few mod cons and, much to Joan's dismay, little in the way of a garden, apart from the odd flowering shrub and scruffy tree. It really had no redeeming features at all, other than a beautiful view of Mount Kenya. Spartan but functional was what one expected to find on farms in those early days. Farmers worked hard and didn't spend time on beautiful gardens. Creature comforts were few and far between as there was no electricity or plumbing to speak of, and kitchen facilities were basic to an extreme with only an old wood-burning, cast-iron Dover stove which had to be coaxed into life every morning and kept fed with a supply of wood throughout the day. A large kettle seemed permanently on the boil and two small flat-irons remained on the back of the stove ready to press the daily hand-washed and sun-dried laundry. All in all, this was certainly no cosy family abode.

One of Maria's vivid recollections a few months after they moved onto the farm was the sound of the rain falling onto the rusty corrugated iron roof of the house. It was quite deafening, particularly during a hailstorm, although after a while, especially when tucked up snug in bed, it was a strangely comforting sound. March was the start of the long rains and it was soon discovered the roof was prone to the odd leak, requiring buckets and bowls to be placed strategically around the floor to catch the dripping water. If one had to get up during the night to find the loo, or in the children's case a pot, these were not easy to navigate round when half asleep with only a candle for illumination.

The rains were soon followed by the cold dry season from June to the end of August, so initially things must have looked pretty bleak to Allen and Joan, who were finding it difficult enough to acclimatise to their new, somewhat uncivilised and challenging environment, not to mention farm issues with staff and animals both domestic and wild. In particular, Maria remembered being terrified by the blood-curdling call of hyena, which used to attack and take calves during the night. Some nights the low rasping sound of leopard on the prowl could be heard and they too were prone to killing calves or sheep, with the victim either missing or found mauled with the onset of daylight. Other wild animals would get into the maize crops, pulling up and eating the precious harvest.

For these and many other reasons, farming proved more of a challenge than Allen envisaged and it was no wonder that some of the earlier settlers had been forced to give up the struggle to exist in this harsh country. It was blighted with animal diseases, drought and subsequent bush fires, and in some years the invasion of huge locust swarms. These would appear overnight, darken the skies well into the following day and decimate everything in their wake, leaving total devastation and the need to buy in feed for the livestock until the grass grew back.

In spite of the initial lack of comfort Killean was a captivating and idyllic place in which to grow up, and Grizel and Maria settled in very quickly, exploring and having great fun. Raymond soon provided horses for Joan and Allen and ponies for the girls, who quickly learnt to ride, and it was not long before they also acquired a number of pets including dogs, cats and rabbits.

As children they loved to visit Raymond's farm – it was a total menagerie with a mass of animals of all descriptions, domestic and wild, wandering freely around the farmyard. Even his house was like a zoo. He had buffalo, eland, zebra and other wild beasts mixing with the domestic animals that populated his garden, often straying into the house if they had half a chance. Everywhere you turned there was some sort of animal underfoot – it used to drive his long-suffering wife, also named Joan, to distraction.

Allen bought a Model T Ford motorcar along with a tractor and necessary agricultural machinery. With help from Raymond he engaged staff and purchased a team of oxen enabling them to plough and plant crops. Of course the family had to learn the local language of Swahili as none of the farm workers understood a word of English. Motor vehicles were somewhat unreliable and by today's standard very underpowered, travelling at speeds of around thirty miles per hour at best, when the unmade-up roads permitted. It was many decades before the roads would be surfaced with tarmac. In the wet weather they turned into deep, glutinous almost impassable mud, with vehicles often helplessly slithering off into the ditch, having to be pushed out by local farm workers, dragged out by oxen, or a tractor if there was one on a farm nearby.

In addition to crops, mostly maize, Allen slowly started to build up a herd of pedigree Ayrshire cattle from imported stock, which he kept along with a herd of local beasts. The Ayrshires, which acclimatised well to the harsh conditions, provided milk and cream not only for the home but also to send to the local creamery, where it was churned into butter and sold countrywide. In those days, butter was mostly tinned in order to preserve it, as there was no such thing as refrigeration. The local *Boran* cattle were bred and sold for beef.

Allen had always taken a keen interest in horses, particularly thoroughbreds, and became involved in pioneering the breeding of racing stock in Kenya. He bred and trained his own string of thoroughbreds from imported English stallions and mares. In later years he was ably assisted by Grizel, who remained a successful trainer and breeder throughout her long life in Kenya, winning the 1975 Kenya Derby with a horse named Highlight, whose dam's lineage dated back to a mare bred by Allen in those early years.

Shortly after they moved onto the farm, Allen and Joan decided to build a permanent and more comfortable home. The new house was designed by them, built from locally cut stone and completed in 1926.

In later years, I myself came to know this house well, and a greater contrast to the primitive conditions under which they lived for the first few months can hardly be imagined.

Great care was taken with the plans of the new home, which was positioned in order to observe the best possible view of Mount Kenya; outside, jacaranda and flame trees were planted while herbaceous borders and a central fishpond all drew the eye toward the distant mountain. Room proportions, layout and interiors were carefully designed, especially for the drawing and dining rooms which led onto a covered veranda, on which the family would usually take breakfast in the warmth of the early morning sunshine.

The finished drawing room was elegant, furnished with family antiques. Fine leather-bound volumes stood on the bookshelves and watercolours of the old family home at Whitmead adorned the room's panelled walls, the oak having been imported from England by Joan – I suppose she wanted the décor to resemble that of her ancestral home, now so far away. On the main feature wall were two large portraits, one of Maria's favourites being the oil of her great-grandmother Anna-Maria Holdford, resplendent in some rather grand jewellery: an emerald and diamond necklace and matching earrings fit for a queen. What happened to those baubles was unknown – they were certainly no longer in the family's possession. But Anna Maria's husband, Joshua Walker II, although a religious Methodist, had allegedly had a penchant for gambling with his friend Beau Brummel. Perhaps he had had to dispose of the jewels to cover a debt. Joshua and Anna-Maria had seven surviving children, so perhaps they went to their eldest son and thereon down *his* family line.

The artist, George Dawe RA, had painted Anna-Maria seated, holding a book in her gloved hand. She was wearing a fashionable high-waisted, Empire-style, silver-grey evening gown with square décolleté and small, close-fitted puff sleeves. Her ensemble was complemented with matching elbow-length satin gloves. She looked wistful and serene. Hanging next to this eye-catching portrait was another depicting her husband, 'Gentleman Josh', as the family referred to him. He looked as gallant and handsome as she was elegant and beautiful.

Over the fireplace was a great buffalo boss, a trophy from one of Allen's hunting safaris, now blackened by wood smoke from the fire below. When the wind blew in the 'wrong' direction the smoke had a tendency to billow back down the chimney into the drawing room, much to Joan's consternation, thus over the years staining the chimney breast and the trophy above. There was many a night when a roaring open fire was lit to combat some of those cold African evenings when the sun went down promptly at six o'clock, with only a few minutes of twilight. The fact that Kenya was situated on the Equator meant there was equal daylight and darkness.

In the dining room, which housed a large dining table and chairs, also brought out from England, were more family paintings, along with Victorian silverware, complementing a pair of huge willow pattern soup tureens which, for some reason, stood on the sideboard between a pair of silver candelabra and a rather splendid silver spirit kettle used by Joan every afternoon for tea. These were but a few of the treasures from the family collection which had been shipped out to Nanyuki.

During the hours of darkness the house was mainly lit by Deitz hurricane lamps, which were fuelled with paraffin and had a tendency to smoke if the wick was too long. The drawing room and dining room were illuminated by Tilley lamps, a brand of pressure lamp, lit using methylated spirit, which produced a bright but soft light from the mantle inside the protective glass globe. In later years, whenever I used meths, the smell always reminded me of those lovely old brass-stemmed lamps and the gentle hiss of pressurised air which emanated from them during the long cosy evenings spent sitting in front of the fire playing cards or dominoes. It was many years before generators and electricity were installed.

Outside, Joan worked on transforming the gardens, designing beds and borders that were filled with exotic flowers. These took a few seasons to fully mature, but over time, picturesque ultramarine blue agapanthus flourished beside red, pink and yellow cannas, bird-of-paradise flowers and red-hot pokers, to name but a few. It was astonishing how such beautiful plants grew so lavishly in this part of the world, thriving in spite of the heat and dry sandy soil.

When the jacaranda trees came into bloom towards the end of the year, their soft frond-like leaves having fallen and been replaced by an abundance of pale smoky mauve fragile flowers, they too contrasted dramatically with the bold burnished red of the Nandi flame tree to the east of the garden – only in Africa could you find this assortment of colours mingling so harmoniously. Beyond the lawn a path lined with tall eucalyptus led to the plains. Their fallen leaves would crackle beneath one's feet, releasing a fresh, slightly medicinal scent. Their trunks were a curious mottled flesh-like pink, which made them look as though they had suffered an attack of sunburn, resulting in the blue-grey bark peeling away leaving tender new skin on the bare trunk beneath.

Added to all this beauty, the snow-capped mountain stood majestically in the distance, forming the perfect backdrop. The local Kikuyu people believed that their god, Ngai, resided on the peak and one could understand why, since it was a most fitting and imposing place for a god to dwell and survey his realm.

*

Maria and Grizel loved the outdoors, becoming very keen riders, roaming the plains, investigating and enjoying Mother Nature at her best. Days were warm and carefree, full of interest and fun. They used to spend most of their spare time on horseback accompanied, when children, by a *syce* (groom) who was responsible for their well-being. He would guide them down game tracks through the bushes to the open savannah on their locally bred, strong and sure-footed skinny Somali ponies explaining how to care for themselves and their mounts whilst keeping an eye out for predators. The ponies were hardened to this harsh climate and would happily travel long distances so that the girls could visit friends on neighbouring farms, sometimes many miles away, or just spend a day soaking up the beauty of the land and its flora and fauna without a care in the world.

In their very young days, as soon as breakfast was over the two girls couldn't wait to don their large-brimmed floppy felt hats, which their mother insisted they wore 'to protect their complexions' from the harsh rays of the searing African sun, before heading for the plains. In those days there was no such thing as a hard hat or riding helmet and certainly no high-factor sunscreen. They wore baggy shorts as it was too hot to wear jodhpurs or slacks, often ending up with the inside of their legs chaffed raw if they spent too long in the saddle. The *syce* would saddle up the ponies and they would set off, in their rather strange attire, riding down to the track beside the furrow, an offshoot dug from the river which ran through the farm and from which the fields were irrigated, before heading on out to the plains, accompanied by the family's dogs.

Their brother, meanwhile, being too young to go with them, kept himself busy following his father around the farm, 'supervising' the construction of the cattle dip and riding proudly on the new tractor, pretending to drive it under his mother's watchful eye.

Although the plains were scorched and arid most of the year, they were not as bleak as they first seemed and it was not long before the children fell in love with their new home, learning all about its flora and fauna from Raymond, who was such an authority with an endless knowledge of all things Africa. The sun-bleached land had a beauty of its own in spite of the appearance of being just a barren and colourless expanse of scrubby grass with a smattering of acacia bushes and whistling thorn trees struggling to exist under the scorching sun. The plains were home to a multitude of animals, insects and the most beautiful, brightly coloured birds.

There was always an abundance of game to be seen on those days when they took to the saddle. They would particularly keep their eyes peeled for delightful little dik dik, Africa's smallest antelope, standing little over twelve inches at the shoulder, which could often be found in a twosome nibbling grass in the undergrowth beneath the trees and bushes. The dik dik formed permanent mating pairs, unlike other species of antelope which grazed en masse with some, such as impala, forming separate female and bachelor herds. Dik dik were so enchanting, with small tufty topknots of fur between their minute horns, their tiny

Top: Fionn and Joan on the McCormack Deering tractor, 1926.

Grizel, Fionn and Maria on the running-board of the Model T Ford.

faces bearing an attractive little black patch at the lower corner of each eye camouflaging a small scent duct with which they marked their territory. They were not always easy to spot due to their size and the fact that their tawny coats blended so well into the bushes and dry grass on which they fed. Sadly they had many predators, which also added to their shyness.

Unlike the dik dik, most other antelope usually had a dominant buck presiding over a herd of females, leaving the remaining males lurking hopefully nearby in their own separate group. Thompson's gazelle and their slightly larger cousins, Grant's gazelle, were numerous. These sleek, taupe-coloured antelope with a distinct black flash across their flanks formed large and abundant herds and were always to be found grazing lazily on the open grasslands, their short tails swishing nineteen to the dozen in a vain endeavour to keep away the ever-persistent biting flies. It was a shame that these lovely creatures were also 'dinner' for most of the plains' predators: leopard, cheetah, lion, hyena and wild dog. Even the baboons would take a calf or an adult when there was nothing else to eat during the very dry season. The baboons were such loathsome creatures and the girls soon learned never to trust them, avoiding them where possible, as they could be aggressive and unpredictable, particularly towards the dogs. They would take on anything or anyone, hunting without fear like packs of wolves.

Occasionally Maria and Grizel would come across a herd of oryx or eland grazing peacefully amongst zebra and giraffe out in the open grasslands and they wondered whether the giraffe, with their long graceful necks and large dark eyes surrounded by lustrous black lashes, acted as lookouts for some of the smaller game which grazed alongside them. Certainly they were the first to signal the alert if they suspected or spotted any threat approaching.

Then there was always the chance of seeing an ostrich or two. Their ridiculous long featherless legs, sporting huge powerful muscular 'drumsticks', somehow gave them a strange, almost prehistoric look. As soon as they spotted the riders they would stride away at great speed, fluffy plumage ruffled by the wind as they sped off across the plain. It seemed they did not have many predators and, if attacked, their strong legs and lethal toenails could inflict serious damage. Amongst the many things they learnt from the *syce* was that during the nesting season, in order to keep the eggs at the correct temperature and to camouflage the whereabouts of their clutch, the sandy-feathered female sat during the day, leaving this job to the black-feathered male after nightfall. The speckled down of newly hatched chicks provided a perfect camouflage, enabling them to blend unseen in the undergrowth until they were large enough to fend for themselves.

The warthog families which rooted about the scrub were particularly amusing. They were such comical little animals to watch as they had a curious way of eating, getting down on their knees to gnaw away at miserable offerings of weed or grass. Even the tiny babies would do this, and on seeing the horses they would scamper off with their little tufted tails straight up in the air like an aerial. The adults were aggressive and ugly-looking with nasty curving tusks protruding from either side of their hairy cheeks, and the girls always made sure the dogs didn't chase them as the adults could turn vicious, particularly if they had piglets in tow.

There was little shade out there on the plain, where a heat haze would appear in the middle of the day when the sun was high and beating down. Birds of prey soared above in the hope of spotting the remains of a kill on the ground below. The distant pale blue hills and herds of animals would appear out of focus in the shimmering mirage. This was such a contrast to the river banks, where the bush was thicker and greener. It was there they used to stop, sometimes meeting friends for a picnic and giving the ponies a much-needed drink.

It was cool under the trees and the riding party would often be greeted by numerous species of butterflies, hovering on clusters of pink and yellow or red and yellow flowering lantana bushes which lit the undergrowth like bright little beacons: nature's endeavour to decorate the edge of that harsh landscape. Herds of graceful, sleek chestnut-coated impala, the males with their splendid lyre-shaped horns, could often be found grazing in the shade of the trees by the river. They were one of Africa's most stunning species of antelope and one of Maria's favourites.

The streams, home to both brown and rainbow trout, were fast moving, crystal clear and icy cold, their source being the snow-capped peaks of Mount Kenya, unlike the rivers further out in the savannah which ran thick and reddish brown, especially after the rains when the eroding soil would get swept into the swirling waters. It was out there that the giant yellow-barked acacia trees, locally known as 'fever trees', grew. The 'fever' was actually malaria, which could be contracted from mosquitoes breeding in stagnant pools at the river edge and was nothing to do with the trees themselves. These trees grew alongside tall doum palms on the sandy banks of the river where crocodiles could be seen basking in the sun or wallowing in the muddy water in the hope of snatching an unsuspecting antelope or zebra foal approaching the water's edge to quench its thirst. It amazed them how the hippo, also living in these murky rivers, and the croc, two of Africa's most dangerous beasts, seemed to coexist without causing undue harm to one another. These rivers were to the north and much more than a day's ride away from the farm, in an area where the family used to travel for camping safaris during school holidays.

Bird life on and around the farm was abundant – an ornithological paradise. Secretary birds and Kori bustards, the largest flying bird native to Africa, strutted the plain catching mice and grasshoppers; superb starlings, their iridescent plumage glinting blue-green in the sunshine, were always scratching around in the garden by the house. Masses of black and yellow weaver birds could be heard chattering high in the thorn trees where they wove their intricate nests. Hoopoe and lilac-breasted rollers scoured the sandy earth for their daily ration of the many insects harboured in the scrub. Partridge and guinea fowl would take dust baths in the warm sunshine and, on being disturbed, they would scuttle off into the undergrowth clucking noisily to themselves, returning to the dust as soon as the coast was clear.

The plains were not always dry. There were brief occasions, after the rain fell, when the shimmering heat haze above the bleached grass and cracked earth would be replaced by a short-lived carpet of bright green shoots and scattering of delicate little wild convolvulus, which looked like a sprinkle of stars made out of tissue paper. The rains: how one remembered the smell of the rain coming. The first cool breeze, carrying a fragrant and fresh earthy scent, would cleanse the air dispelling the heat before the rain started to fall. It seemed that only in Africa could one actually smell its impending arrival.

Over the period of a few weeks, thunder clouds would start to accumulate and the sky would become overcast and heavy, eventually darkening to inky black. Thunder would roll and lightning would flash, illuminating the deep indigo skies, forking down to further sear the earth, sometimes splitting trees as it tore into the ground. On occasion these lightning strikes would start massive bush fires destroying everything in their wake: terrifying for the animals and tribesmen caught up in the fast-moving flames, usually stoked by the high winds which came with wet weather. The scorched earth and the trees revived quickly following these downpours, and the horror of the flames was forgotten for another year.

Rain would lash down. Rivers would swell. The swirling greasy torrents of muddy water brought back life not only to the thirsty land so in need of sustenance, but also to mud fish, toads and other aquatic creatures which had lain dormant in a cocoon of sludge deep beneath the cracked surface of the dry river beds for so many months. One could smell the clean freshness which followed a storm and almost hear the earth breathe a sigh of relief. The countryside and its inhabitants seemed to take on a new energy and spring. The air would become cool and clear. The countryside would be revitalised, and the heat would vanish for a while. It was a time when the wild beasts calved and foaled, taking advantage of the lush new shoots of grass and leaves to feed their newborn offspring and nourish their own emaciated bodies. Interestingly, in the case of impala, it is believed they are able to delay the birth of their offspring for up to a month to coincide with the start of the rains.

In the early 1930s, when the children were older, Raymond gave them a beautiful young cheetah, whom they named Pong. He had been reared and handled until he was gentle enough to live with the family as a pet: although not a small cub, he still had a fluffy ruff round his neck, somehow making him even more endearing. He was a delight, a sweet and loving animal with a purr like a tractor, which if one didn't know better almost sounded like a growl as it was so deep and rasping. He enjoyed being petted and loved to go out riding with the girls and the dogs, staying close to the horses, never straying too far away in spite of originating from the plains across which they rode. When back home he was content, often playing with his ball on the front lawn, larking around either on his own or with the dogs.

His diet had to contain bones, fur and feathers to support his digestive system and keep him healthy, ensuring strong bone growth, and in view of Pong being kept in captivity and therefore unable to hunt for himself, he had to be fed chicken, game birds and small wild animals, shot by Allen or Raymond. The girls, however, used to take a quick look into the hutches of the farm rabbits to reassure themselves that no special favourites were missing.

Pong was one of Raymond's many captured animals, some of which he used for cross-breeding; zebroids – a zebra crossed with another equine, either a horse or a donkey – being among his more notable hybrids. Raymond was renowned for trapping and taming cheetah which were subsequently transported by sea to zoos in Europe and America, also to India where they were used for hunting by rich Maharajahs. As a consequence, and sadly for Maria and her siblings, in 1936 twelve young cheetahs were shipped to England by Raymond following an approach to experiment with racing them against greyhounds at the White City, Harringay and Romford greyhound tracks. This was not a successful venture, and it is believed that poor Pong, who was unfortunately one of the group of animals sent to England, may have ended his days confined in an English zoo.

Raymond had decided that Pong, being so tame and easy to handle, was one of the most suitable specimens for the racing project. He persuaded Allen and Joan to return Pong to him, so a heart-breaking decision was made to part with their very special and beloved pet. Maria and Grizel always remembered their cheetah with such affection – a beautiful and exotic creature who had certainly become one of the family. It was such a privilege to have owned and enjoyed him for a short part of his young life, although in later years they both felt it was wrong to have tried to domesticate and tame him only to abandon him to live in a zoo for the rest of his life.

Even as adults Grizel and Maria continued to enjoy roaming the plains on horseback. Africa is a place which becomes part of a person's soul, remaining there for ever. As the saying goes, 'you can leave Africa, but Africa never leaves you'. Maria left. Grizel didn't, but Maria always remembered it vividly and with deep fondness. What a wonderful childhood they had.

*

Maria's formal education, at Limuru Girls' School near Nairobi, a boarding school attended by most of the children of the farming families, ended when she was sixteen. Further education for girls was rare at this time, no matter how bright they might be; most married young and few entertained thoughts of a professional or long-term career.

As soon as she and Grizel could drive, they would use the farm car to go into town, to the Sportsman's Arms or the Nanyuki Country Club, which were the main social spots for the local farming community. Grizel used to tell the story of how when she and Maria were driving back home one evening after spending the day at the Club, the car broke down and they had to walk some considerable distance in the dark. They were convinced that they were being followed by a lion, and although they were well accustomed to the presence of wildlife, they still found it rather unnerving.

It was during one of these visits when Maria was in her late teens that she met her future husband, Peter Pilbrow, who was working at that time for the Kenya Police Force. The clubhouse was located beside the racecourse and polo ground where Peter and all the young men used to either play polo or race ride, most weekends, both on the flat or over cross-country jumps. Maria also played polo, although not seriously as, in those days, polo was more of a man's game. In the main she stuck to cross-country and other gymkhana competitions which took place in the grounds of the club, or on a nearby farm which had its own separate jump course. Weekends were very social affairs, often with

Top: About to head off onto the plains: Grizel (left) and Maria.

Riders gather for a paper-chase at the Sportsman's Arms, Nanyuki.

long lunchtime drinking sessions, at which good old pink gin or John Collins were the favourites.

These sessions inevitably continued into the evening and were frequently followed by dances or parties. It was here too that Maria first met Arthur Atkinson, a shy young man from northern England who had been posted to Kenya with the Colonial Service. He subsequently joined the army at the same time as Peter and they were both posted to Ceylon and then to India together. Arthur was to remain a good friend throughout the war years.

Peter was an accomplished and confident rider and a competitive and dashing polo player, playing with great panache and skill. The eyes of all the girls followed his every move. Not only were women attracted to him, but men also. He had an abundance of charisma and charm which appealed to both sexes. He could tell a great story and would make people laugh. Maria fell for him in a big way. Grizel, much the more sensible of the two, tried to rein her in but Maria was having none of it: she was determined that Peter would be hers and nothing anyone said could dissuade her from accepting his proposal of marriage when it came. Grizel had also met her future husband at the club and both sisters became engaged in October 1938, Maria to Peter and Grizel to Vernon Schalch, who was also in the Police Force. They were married within a month of one another the following year, Maria on 2 May and her sister on 1 June.

The circumstances of the two weddings were very different. Allen and Joan did not approve of Maria marrying Peter, who had a reputation as something of a womaniser, in addition to which they were not comfortable with the fact that he was a Roman Catholic. Maria could not see why this should matter. It certainly didn't bother her, nor any of her friends. Always strong-willed, she had set her heart on being Peter's wife come hell or high water, and to follow him to the ends of the earth if necessary.

Consequently, although Allen consented to give her away, her wedding was a very small affair when compared with her sister's a few months later. Only a few family and friends attended the church service. She had no bridesmaids, and the reception which followed was a decidedly modest gathering held in a neighbour's garden. Grizel's, in contrast, was the full-blown affair, with two bridesmaids, many more guests and a reception held at Killean, the family home.

Nevertheless, Maria herself looked radiant at the ceremony, in a full-length Victorian-style gown of frothy white tulle, with a long train of fine white lace, which was designed and made by Maison Max, Nairobi's French couturier and bridal shop. As a wedding gift Peter gave her a delicate pair of natural pearl earrings and her gift to him was a monogrammed gold signet ring. Her parents gave her a dinner service and a Singer sewing machine, which in those days was a very essential item to have, there being no local dress shops or drapers, with most girls making their own clothes from patterns and cloth ordered from Nairobi. Other family members and friends were very generous with cheques and household items which they would need for the home they would create together after their short honeymoon at Lawford's Hotel in Malindi.

On their return they settled into their new lives in Nanyuki, but four months later war was declared and Peter joined the King's African Rifles (KAR). The KAR had fought with distinction in the First World War, but between the wars had been much reduced, so much so that before September 1939 it numbered a total of less than 3,000 officers and men. Recruitment ran at such a rate, however, that by March 1940 its strength had increased to more than 800 officers, 1,300 NCOs and 20,000 men.

Kenya was bordered in the north by Italian East Africa, where Mussolini had been pursuing an expansionist policy since 1935, when Italy had invaded and occupied the independent sovereign state of Abyssinia. Although Mussolini had not yet committed his troops to the Second World War, the fear was that if and when he did so, Kenya itself would be under immediate threat.

When Mussolini declared war on Britain and France in June 1940 his immediate target was British Somaliland on the Gulf of Aden, already surrounded by existing Italian colonies and less well defended than the Kenyan border country. By August 1940 the territory had been overrun and the small British garrison, together with several thousand civilians, had to be evacuated via Aden.

A well co-ordinated Allied counter-attack launched in January 1941 succeeded in re-taking British Somaliland and driving the Italians out of Abyssinia, forcing their surrender by the end of May. Peter was active in this campaign, as was their friend Arthur Atkinson, who had joined the Royal Corps of Signals.

After he joined up Maria took a succession of jobs, some of them local to Nanyuki and others less so. Work was a necessity, as she and Peter were never well off. Later, she wrote in her journal that they had found it difficult at first to make ends meet:

Ever since we got married my husband and I had been hard up, and we both had the beginnings of extravagant tastes – the only things that put me off mine were the bills coming in monthly and seeing those that we could not pay and had to leave over until the following month. I used to have nightmares about them, as possibly did Peter – there's only one good thing to say about lack of money and that is that one does so enjoy oneself if one has worked for, and looked forward to, either going out or buying something; there is something so satisfying in it all. Maybe it's a sort of halo one feels glowing.

Her first job was in what she describes as 'a small store or slightly *Alice in Wonderland* shop in the little village in Kenya where I lived'. She writes that her salary was 'terrific, fifty shillings a month and my lunch, although that was not always awfully good'. Within the store, she seems to have turned her hand to a bit of everything:

We sold anything from food, tinned and fresh, to needles, toys, a few clothes and odds and ends. We did up baskets of vegetables and fruit and eggs to send up to the troops in Abyssinia or thereabouts; we priced goods, dusted, did accounts, wrote dunning letters and did the filing, checked each others' invoices and hundreds of other things. As you can imagine, it sounds very Heath Robinson and it was! And we all

*seemed to suffer from mental aberration when it came
to adding up thirteen articles priced at different costs.
What wouldn't I have given for a Ready Reckoner like
the ones we had later on with the Wasbies.*

After that, for a short time, she went to work in Nairobi
as a switchboard operator. Telephones were still a fairly
new means of communication at that time in East Africa,
and not everybody had one, particularly people living on
farms many miles from the capital. This was not a happy
experience, as her journal makes plain:

*Don't ever be a telephonist! I was once, and didn't keep
the job longer than a week. Have you ever worked a
telephone exchange? I had never seen, or rather used
one until I took this job in Nairobi, and I was quite
frankly scared stiff of it. No one seemed to want a call
unless at least ten other people were using the line;
my nightmare was all the little yellow taps flopping
up and down and ticking, and the 'language' that
was used, and the trunk calls that were put through
to the wrong people. There should definitely be a law
that people should learn to enunciate over the air, as
they either bellow so that the receiver has to be held
at least a yard away or else they whisper and one just
can't hear; and then there are the mumblers: they are
the worst, and the one in a million, the polite callers
… Needless to say, I wasn't really sorry when I was
handed my envelope of pay at the same time as my
discharge or dismissal.*

In June 1940 she signed up as a VAD (the Voluntary Aid Detachment, civilians who supported medical staff in the field and in military hospitals) in the Nursing Division of the St John Ambulance Brigade who were attached to the Kenya & Uganda Casualty Clearing Station at Kabete, on the outskirts of town. Work started at eight o'clock and she was required to report for collection, by government transport, from Memorial Hall in Nairobi town centre at six o'clock each morning – not a good hour for her. Of this brief assignment she wrote:

I went, after many nights of dreaming of thousands of bedpans and various other things, all starched up and ready for the worst. However, my tasks were merely tidying up, bedmaking, squeezing orange juice and cutting sandwiches for the doctors' and sisters' midmorning tea. I think that I was sent round one day with mugs of eggnogs, soup, custards and other slops with directions as to who should get which, but I think that no one got their real lunch as all the patients disliked the eggnogs and lied like the proverbial troopers when they were offered them.

Once as a great concession I was allowed to take three blood slides; the first poor man had the needle literally stabbed through his thumb until it nearly got buried, but he was really very good about it and didn't tell on me!

This CCS was later handed over to the Rhodesians and most of us moved on. The new orderlies were in many cases West Africans who knew far more about nursing than we did, many of them having worked in

hospitals for years before the war started. So it would
have been ludicrous for untrained girls such as us to
stay on.

Maria left the VAD in August 1940 just as the evacuation from British Somaliland was in progress, and when Peter returned he persuaded her to leave Nairobi and go back to up to Nanyuki. 'I think he thought I would be much safer up there,' she wrote, 'away from the temptations and wildness of the South African troops that had come into the colony. Little did he know that they were just as much a menace up country as they were in the towns: those who are menaces always will be wherever they are, and although not all of them were difficult or bad, there were many who were troublesome.'

There, she occupied herself with 'the inevitable canteen work' for the soldiers and the airmen who were stationed in the area and later, she found employment on a nearby farm as a clerk/typist-cum-book-keeper, occasionally having to mind the baby for good measure. The work was mundane, but as she was later to write in her journal, the skills she acquired were to stand her in good stead during her Wasbie years.

In the latter half of 1940 Peter was in Aden and in 1941 took part in the Allied counter-offensive against Italy which regained British Somaliland and liberated Abyssinia, entering the capital, Addis Ababa, on 6 April. Still, he was close enough to come home on leave, and in late 1941 and the beginning of 1942 he seems, as far as can be established from her photograph albums, to have been back in Kenya. In April 1942, however, he was posted first to Ceylon and then to the staff training college at Quetta in

Northern India, now part of Pakistan. She must have felt this separation even more keenly, with her husband now thousands rather than hundreds of miles away and, given the scale of the threat posed by Japan in South East Asia, more than likely away for the duration.

Consequently, when he suggested that she should join him in Quetta for the length of his training period at the staff college there, it is hardly surprising that she should have jumped at the chance. His telegram arrived on 12 July, followed by another on 4 August and a third on 13 August saying 'Permission granted military India, military Kenya informed'. On 27 August she received confirmation in the form of a letter from the Assistant Adjutant General's office at East Africa Command Headquarters in Nairobi, stating that 'a signal has been received from the HQ to whom your husband is attached to the effect that permission has been granted for your entry into India for the duration of the course which your husband is to attend.'

There was by this time little to hold her in Kenya. Allen and Joan had left for England, where Allen served initially as commanding officer at the Driving and Maintenance School at Bovington in Dorset, and then spent the rest of the war in Scotland, where he organised ground-based air defence. The only immediate family member still in Nanyuki was her sister Grizel, who was looking after Killean in their parents' absence.

At the beginning of October she left Nanyuki for Nairobi and then on to Mombasa, from which Cooks the travel agents had booked her passage to Bombay. She did not know it at the time, but this was to be her final farewell to Kenya, and the journey she was about to embark on would change her life.

PART TWO

From Kenya to India

1942–1944

This is where Maria's journal fully begins. Other than a few brief notes, the narrative from this point onwards until the end of Part Five on page 268 is almost entirely written in her own words.

6 October 1942

With tears in my eyes and a very forlorn and frightened feeling in my heart, I leant on the rails of the SS *Talawa* and watched the port of Mombasa fade into the distance, and wondered whether I had made a serious mistake. Years later I often thought of how different my life would have been had I stayed in East Africa, or what sort of a person I would have turned into – as it is, I have now learnt to stand on my own feet, as well as how to make a few decisions for myself without being too reliant on other people.

This was the first time that I had travelled alone – both my siblings and I had journeyed several times between East Africa and England after the family had emigrated, but we had always been chaperoned by our parents. People can be so negative about upping sticks and moving and they certainly were about my upheaval, as everyone thoroughly disagreed with it on every principle they could come up with. There must be a streak of obstinacy in me somewhere I think, as the more they said the more determined I was to leave. Added to this there was every foreseen and unforeseen obstacle put in my way – permits to leave Kenya and permits to enter India; innumerable injections to have; and then the problems of clothing and money – never have I been so thankful for the days that I had sat and sewed dainty garments for other people, saving the proceeds in the bank for a rainy day.

When I had said goodbye to Peter nine months ago I never thought I'd be travelling out to India to rejoin him in so short a time – indeed if ever, so it was a most terrific thrill I got one Sunday afternoon, sitting in Lola's garden at Naro Moru entertaining a lot of RAF lads when a telegram turned up for me laconically saying 'Join me Quetta earliest'. *[Naro Moru was the location of the farm where Maria was working. There was an RAF station at Nanyuki which was home to an OTU – an Operational Training Unit where crews could hone the essential skills of navigation and accurate bombing before they flew full combat missions.]*

So like Peter not to have foreseen any difficulties or anything – it sounded so easy, too, but not until I had made a few enquiries did I realise that it might take me months to get out and it did – three, to be exact. There was severe petrol rationing which made things very troublesome, the post took a long time to arrive anywhere and it was all most unsatisfactory! Then everyone assuring me that the shipping losses were so great that it was a certainty I should never be heard of again, and that Peter had no right to put me in danger, and so on and so forth – which only added further fuel to my desire to go. I knew too that the future for me in East Africa would be, until the end of the war, one long dreary existence, and I longed to go and see places and people and do things – real things, though quite what 'real things' meant, I didn't know at the time. Alice was the person who cheered me up by saying, when she met me in the New Stanley Hotel and had tea with me the day I left Nairobi, that she envied me my adventuring into a new world and a new country. Poor Alice – life had its trials for her in a large way I think. [Alice was an old school friend. What it was that made her life so hard Maria doesn't say.]

Anyway, I got myself on the boat although had I only realised it, there was waiting for me at Cooks – except that I didn't go there to collect it – a wire that would have set me by the ear and put me in a spiral of indecision. My husband, thinking I would never reach him in time before he left the Staff College, had wired me to say, 'on no account come', and that was his first remark to me when I arrived at Quetta. Many people who knew about it thought and still think that I 'turned a blind eye' just as Nelson did at Trafalgar. One wonders what one would have done [if she had known that he had changed his mind about her going].

The *Talawa* was full up and I and two other women shared a three-berth cabin somewhere near the aft end of the ship not far from the galley. There were only about ten European passengers on board; the rest were Indians and the smell of curry cooking seemed to linger and infiltrate through everything. I used to sleep on deck at night as the heat below was intense, owing partly to the need to black out all the windows and portholes. My fan, poor thing, was on so consistently that it almost set itself on fire.

We were travelling during the month of Ramadan and many were the times that we stumbled back down to our cabin just before dawn at 5.30 a.m. to find rows of Muslim passengers on their knees in the corridors saying their morning prayers to Allah. Once finished, they would hop into their respective cabins, not to be seen again until next morning. The women and children in particular never seemed to come up for fresh air.

We had apparently, so I heard later, been followed by a Japanese submarine, but for some reason best known to herself she decided not to sink us. Thank God she didn't, it would have been most unpleasant. The deck passengers would have been almost certain to have panicked wildly and there'd have been scant hope for our little group of George the chemist, the two merchant seamen, Auguste [not identified] and me.

October 1942 – Arrival in Bombay

Our arrival into Bombay, the gateway to India, was rather subdued. We had all had a large party the night before and had the most frightful hangovers. So in the morning, as we began to pass land – usually the period for hanging over the railings and making inane remarks – we were drinking Horse's Necks [brandy with ginger ale and Angostura] in the hope that the 'hair of the dog' might make us feel better before we actually docked, which we eventually did at 5.30 in the afternoon.

Customs and Immigration formalities had to be processed, with the disembarkation authorities asking the usual idiotic questions. It was rather like the 'animal, vegetable or mineral?' game we played as children. It struck me as vaguely ludicrous when I was given a form to fill in that asked my nationality, name, age, etc., then I had to state whether I was male or female. Couldn't they see and recognise gender by my photograph, name and title which were all clearly detailed in my passport? The thing I found most unpleasant was the way in which all my personal letters were read by extremely nosey and slightly gloating officials in the arrival kiosk. Foolishly I had brought some of my husband's letters along with me and I think that they went down big-time with their readers. However, I was through and had made it to India unscathed.

No sooner had I left the docks than, as was only right and fitting, I was 'had for a sucker'. All the coolies carried boards with 'Free Coolie' written on them, so I thought that must mean no tipping. Alas I took none of their numbers and by the time I had left the customs shed, I had a string of screaming dervishes following me, no doubt attracted by the foolish Memsahib who appeared not to know the drill. In desperation I dispensed fifteen rupees and was then able to tell the taxi driver to proceed, which he did very hastily. There was, however, much yelling on our departure and I came to the conclusion that insufficient largesse had been distributed and that the howling crowd of blue, red and yellow-clad Indians was going to haunt me for ever. I never did find out what I had done to cause such a commotion.

Although the immigration procedure had been easier to pass through than I thought it would be, it wasn't until seven o'clock that we finally reached the Taj Mahal Hotel and I was able to wire Peter to let him know I had arrived.

The next worry was how to change my traveller's cheques and convert my money from East African shillings into local currency then get up to Quetta as soon as possible. Quetta was located in the foothills of the Hindu Kush mountains of North West India, and having been told that it was cold and snowy up there, I was concerned because I didn't have suitable warm attire with me, having not experienced such low temperatures back home in Kenya. So, I had to scout about for some new clothing before I went north.

My East African money was the hardest stuff to get rid of. I tramped up and down the streets for a couple of days with various people looking askance at me when I tried, in vain, to find out how to exchange it, feeling at times as though I was some sort of bank robber trying to change phoney ten-pound notes or something.

Thankfully I remembered that one of the girls who had travelled out with me had given me her brother-in law's address and had told me that I was to contact him if I was in any difficulty at all. Consequently, with much relief, I did and although he was a banker, even he had to send out to a dubious money trader to change my cash. The problem was explained, but to me it was very complex and I have since forgotten what it was all about; I was just relieved that the conundrum was resolved.

The next few days were passed wandering about gazing in amazement at the local sights. The situation that astonished me more than anything was at night when the Indians slept quite happily, and seemingly comfortably enough, on the pavements. It appeared that even the higher classes, who obviously did have beds indoors, moved outside their shops to sleep, joining some of those who clearly did not have a roof over their heads. I suppose that it must, in their case, have been due to the fact that it was a lot cooler outside as Bombay certainly was extremely hot and humid.

The main roads seemed clean enough, but it was extraordinary how many cows mooched aimlessly along the streets and in between the traffic without any apparent supervision. They were very gentle, pretty beasts with a slight hump and frilly dewlaps, floppy ears, dark eyes and shiny black noses and appeared to come in a number of soft colours. I was to discover that in the Hindu religion cows were considered to be sacred, even to the point of being decorated with bells and garlands on festival days such as Diwali.

However, the alleyways off the main streets, which initially appeared so enticing with their colourful blend of shops and merchandise, in fact tended to be indescribably filthy and smelly and on asking what all the 'blood' stains were on the pavements, I was told that it was betel nut which the locals chewed then spat out leaving these red marks splattered on the ground. There was a great deal of hawking and spitting, which I have to say I initially found repulsive, but before long I had ceased to notice it at all.

On my first visit to the Metro Cinema, *the* cinema house in Bombay, a home-made bomb was thrown into the lobby just as everyone was leaving after the film show. It made the most hair-raising noise and was frightfully alarming to me, but nobody else seemed to take much notice and no harm was done. I was later informed that it was quite a frequent occurrence during the '42 Riots when Gandhi's Congress Party was pushing for Independence. Apparently bombs were taken into a number of the cinema houses and other venues frequented by Europeans, then left to explode. Luckily they seldom caused much in the way of damage.

There were practically no taxis about, and everyone seemed to travel in very old and dilapidated Victorias [horse drawn carriages], in most cases drawn by ponies which were positively skeletal and looked as though they had never had a square meal in their lives, poor beasts. This aside, the Victorias were actually a most romantic conveyance and one felt that a high-neck crinoline or bustled frock, accompanied by a dainty pearl-handled parasol and bonnet, should have been worn for the occasion.

There was not much in the way of luxury or fancy goods in the majority of shops, as a lot of ships were being diverted from Singapore just before it fell and, as a result, shelves were cleared pretty quickly by the numerous passengers passing through the ports. I think most local people realised that unless they made hay whilst the sun shone with regard to acquiring the little there was, in later years they might kick themselves for not buying imported items whilst stocks were still available. Finding a bottle of Peggy Sage nail varnish and a pot of Pond's face cream lifted my heart tremendously.

Quetta – 22 October 1942

All this time I had unsuccessfully been trying to get hold of Peter at the Staff College in Quetta. The River Indus had flooded its banks and had breached both the rail and the road which meant that travelling up there was, I was told, impossible and that telegrams would not have arrived, so for three nights I endeavoured to get him on the phone. I realise now that it was a hopeless thought as he could never have taken the call, he lived too far from the main mess where the only telephone was located.

Eventually, after four days of luxury in the Taj Hotel, the like of which I had never known before, I finally received a wire from Peter telling me how to get to Quetta. I was seen off on the train by several of the people who had come out on the boat with me. I travelled north in an air-conditioned coach, in which I simply froze to death. Not having been told that they could be so chilly, I had neither blankets for the night nor a jersey for the day. All my warmer clothing was packed and stowed in the luggage van. Consequently, I had to nip out at every station where the train stopped to get warm. The countryside was dry and dusty but we were able to keep clean because we had a 'pull-over' blind across the window, whereas the less fortunate passengers travelling in the second- and third-class coaches looked very dirty and dusty by the time they reached Delhi and 'Pindi [Rawalpindi].

I must have appeared a complete and utter half-wit or something, as I was looked after the entire way up by everyone travelling first class on the train, in particular by a charming old colonel who took me under his wing when we reached Lahore two days later. I had to spend the whole day there before catching an onward train in the evening, and he let me use his hotel room which had its own bathroom. He gave me breakfast, provided a friend to take me shopping in the morning and then again in the afternoon. He himself took me round to Phipson's, the wine merchants, to supervise my purchase of an ample supply of whisky and gin to take on my journey. He had heard that drink of any kind, and cigarettes as well, were impossible to obtain in Quetta following the breaches of the river and resultant transportation difficulties.

That dear man put me on the train in the evening under the charge of six young officers who were also on their way up to Quetta. They did their best for me in no mean way, especially when it came to my baggage having to be removed from the train and taken across the flooded areas in little local boats.

Early the following morning the train arrived at a place called Rori, which I can remember little about, except that we had a very excellent breakfast at the station at six o'clock, then hung about until nine o'clock that evening when we were all taken to an army transit camp for the night, having somehow managed to miss the country boats which would take us across the flood. Later on, in my Wasbie days, it would have been a very ordinary occurrence and we would have thought nothing of it, but being new to this sort of predicament it did amaze me somewhat, particularly as nobody was overly bothered by the situation.

I must say the Colonel had advised me well, as I think

the arrival of the booze was almost more welcome to Peter than I was. People had resorted to drinking crème de menthe in the evenings due to the lack of anything else being available. A few lucky people had a bottle or two of rum, which we were reduced to eking out in the form of a punch before Peter's training course was over. As I had been warned, Quetta was engulfed in deep snow and a warm and cheering drink was very welcome when one was frozen to bits and stiff with cold.

My first three months in India were enjoyable: the newness of it all, the beautiful snows of Quetta, the parties and the thrill of being with my husband. However, all good things come to an end and, despite the initial fun, I began to be aware of a slight coolness on Peter's part, which led me to fear our relationship was becoming a little fragile.

Bombay and Kodaikanal – 1943

Peter completed his term in Quetta early in 1943. I returned to Bombay, made arrangements to stay on in India, and spent the next six months assisting with Army Canteen work. Peter was now away with his battalion in Ceylon and strictly speaking I should have returned to East Africa [as her permission to stay was only for the duration of his training course at Quetta]. But, having only just arrived in India I hadn't the slightest intention of leaving, besides which I was labouring under the illusion that if I stayed on I might get to see more of my husband than if I went back home.

How little did I know. I was headstrong and always wanted my own way, although I didn't always succeed in achieving it. However, I had made up my mind. I was going to stay whatever the consequences.

Although swelteringly hot and humid, Bombay, in common with any big city in which one lives alone, seemed large, unfriendly and cold. Following the Japanese invasion many evacuees had arrived from Singapore, Burma and Hong Kong, causing a severe shortage of accommodation. As a result, when I first arrived back, I had to scour the town for somewhere to stay, initially having to resort to a shared room.

It was here that I first encountered a rather nasty form of creepy crawly: an infestation of those unspeakable creatures, bed bugs. I was woken up by an agony of burning irritation, switched on the light and to my horror found the bed alive with the filthy things, not just the odd two or three or even ten, but hundreds, so I ended up spending the night on the floor, much to the consternation of the 'boy' who brought in my morning tea! The next night was not much better in spite of the 'going over' which the beds were allegedly given by the woman who owned the accommodation. The pesky creatures left their normal happy hunting ground and followed me to the floor. I was quite sure even more remained in the bed hoping for my return, so I stuck it out where I was. Alas, I was so bitten that I couldn't go swimming as it looked as though I had a nasty attack of chicken pox or measles.

After a few days I managed to find lodgings in a boarding house, in a bed-sitting room that smelt vaguely of disinfectant. No more bed bugs, although this accommodation was alive with cockroaches – big ones – and their multitude of infants. With the exception of the hungry locusts which used to swarm over the landscape in Kenya some years, I had never come across an insect so voracious. They even started nibbling on my clothes in the wardrobe, and absolutely nothing would deter them.

Army pay tended to be intermittent which made life very difficult, so a strict rationing regime was decided upon. After my board and lodgings had been paid every month, I allowed myself a maximum of ten rupees (just under £1 sterling) per week for pocket money. Needless to say it was very difficult to keep within my limited means. Marine Drive, where I lived, was a long way from the centre of town and from where I worked in the Army canteens. Soon all bus rides were curtailed, and having a couple of good sturdy legs, I resorted to 'Shanks's pony', resulting in copious extremely painful blisters. As Damon Runyon once wrote, 'Boy, oh boy, were my puppies [feet] fatigued.'

Letters were cut down to a minimum. This was of course no big hardship as I always loathed writing them, although I often wondered how my family reacted to the lack of news. I imagine they thought I was busy enjoying myself and couldn't be bothered to write, and to assuage my guilt I pretended it was part of my economy drive.

It was here that I first made the acquaintance of that chap called 'loneliness'. I knew nobody and for the first three months I missed Peter enormously. I used to sit in my room looking out of my window in the evenings, watching the Indian women clad in bright, rainbow-coloured saris enjoying walks with their children along the Bombay seafront. It made me think, wonder and wish, what did the future hold for me? Would I ever enjoy such happy times with children of my own? I made use of this 'lonely time' by trying to brush up on my typing skills in the futile hope that it might get me a better job. It has never got me a good job, although it did get me sacked from one once.

I was very worried and didn't know how to cope at all. I couldn't bring myself to tell anybody how I felt as I had after all brought the situation upon myself. I certainly couldn't discuss it with Peter. He knew by now that I hadn't returned home but I felt he had enough on his plate without me adding to it, and I couldn't help feeling that our relationship was continuing to deteriorate, so I just worked hard and tried to keep my mind busy. Being hard up had its trivial amusements, and I found it fun to see how long I could make six anna last – an anna being only one-sixteenth of a rupee which certainly wasn't very much. I had never been good with money and it definitely did me no harm to try to economise. I discovered that even toothpaste could be made to last longer if the finished tube was split open, but one had to have a penknife to do this, as a nail file was not up to the job.

After three months, during which time life was getting rather dim, a girl I worked with asked if I would like to share her flat. I accepted her offer, settled in and started to enjoy Bombay a little more. I met new people and began going out and about. Having someone to share things with made a big difference. No further lonely evenings or ghastly Sundays in an empty town with nothing to occupy my time. I remember there was a family with a charming little child who were also living in the same house. The child was a source of constant amusement and great enjoyment to us both.

Regrettably, this situation lasted only a short time as it was far too expensive and I could not manage on my allowance. So, after a bit of investigation into other possibilities on the job front, I decided to take the long journey to Kodaikanal, a hill station in the Tamil Nadu region of Southern India, where I felt life might be more congenial. However, if I thought I was lonely before, it was here that I was to learn the true meaning of the word. Things got to the point where I wondered what life was all about and what had possessed me to leave Kenya.

From Peter's letters it was now even more evident that things had started to go very wrong between us, and he was looking to call it a day as far as our marriage was concerned. I couldn't write or talk to anyone; it was too personal and too painful. I felt empty, frightened and at a very low ebb. There was just nothing to live for and a big black cloud seemed to totally envelop me. I suppose it was just the circumstances which go with young marriage and war. I knew I had been terribly lucky, as during the four years of our marriage Peter had made me so happy and I had met quite a few people who had not had a tenth of the happiness we enjoyed.

Looking back, Peter seemed to have distanced himself from me since leaving Kenya and coming to India. I felt I no longer had a place in his life and I couldn't accept or understand how or why this situation had come about. It was all so hurtful and I felt desolate and confused. What had I done wrong? For a long time, I wondered what might have been had our situation been different. Initially his cooling attitude to our relationship caused me enormous heartache, although strangely enough no bitterness or ill-feeling towards him. How I wished I could find out what he really thought; it was still all so unbelievable. I'd have given anything to see him again even if it was only to confirm to myself that our marriage was beyond redemption. I supposed there would be a certain amount of awkwardness if we did ever meet up. I considered going back to Kenya, however difficult that might be, but couldn't face the inevitable 'we told you so …'s. Surely marriage couldn't end just like that? Not if I could help it. The thing to do was to work hard and get away from the artificiality of life at Kodaikanal.

Anyhow, trying to put my unhappiness behind me, my great wish was to go as far forward with my work out here as I could, although secretly still hoping that Peter might realise what he had done and perhaps change his mind about our relationship. At the same time, I was determined not to let him see how much he had hurt me. Dear God, how I hoped all would go well with him, that he would keep safe and that our life together really wasn't completely over.

Coimbatore – November 1943

It took me a few months to pull myself together then I moved on and found myself another job in Coimbatore, a hill station further south, with the Royal Navy Fleet Air Arm. Having decided to leave Kodaikanal I applied for, and had been offered a job as a TWA [Temporary Woman Assistant]. I was advised at the outset that I was not to consider my position a permanent one, as a contingent of WRNS [Women's Royal Naval Service] were due in the near future, and as soon as these girls arrived I would have to look for something else.

In all keenness I had sent in an application saying that any work would be considered, but when I reported for duty I discovered to my horror that I was to work in the Pay Office. A large heavy tome, with very small print, was pressed into my somewhat weary arms and I was told to read and digest all I could about the naval accounting system. My eyes rolled, my brain reeled and I am ashamed to say very little sank in for the first few days. However, after the initial bewildering week I settled down, developing a kingly disregard for handling large sums of money. We dealt in such enormous multiples (tens of thousands) of rupees on a daily basis that the value of money became rather meaningless. My seemingly paltry salary of only Rs.140 per month was such a pittance in comparison to the sums we were handling.

My boss was an amorous old devil who hadn't an 'aitch' to his name, and although he had a kind heart he did have a distinct fondness for young ladies. We all teased him remorselessly.

We used to have the most wonderful arguments in which everyone in the office would participate; they never seemed to lead to anything, but everyone had their say and felt happier. As far as I can remember it was always about our salaries, as we all thought we were underpaid, and I think that we were; but the powers that be worked on the assumption that as officers' wives, we didn't really need the money – how wrong they were.

Six months passed working with the Fleet Air Arm. Accommodation was a continual problem, especially for me as a single girl with no immediate family and very little means. I was reluctant to dwell on personal circumstances and was desperately looking for something more stimulating to keep my mind occupied. It was either another job or, alternatively, return to Kenya to sit on my parents' farm waiting for the war to end. I hadn't any intention of doing this unless I was forced to, and I was still hoping against hope that my marriage to Peter wasn't over, so when I read a notice that said the Women's Auxiliary Services (Burma), a small group of women operating mobile canteens attached to our troops in India and Burma, urgently required suitable recruits I got quite excited.

The caption on the notice read: 'Come and help us to help the Fourteenth Army'. It detailed what the WAS(B) actually was and what qualifications were required to join. I felt I fitted the bill quite well as recruits needed to be physically fit, willing to turn a hand to anything and able to rough it when necessary. It was suggested that a knowledge of typing and accounts and an ability to drive would also be useful.

The thought of working with the Wasbies fired my imagination more than a little and I immediately applied to join, directing my request to their Commandant, Mrs Ninian Taylor. To my amazement and thrill, my application was accepted. When I received Mrs Taylor's positive reply to my request to join her team of ladies, I tendered my notice to the Fleet Air Arm. There was a nasty moment when there was talk of me being indispensable, as no one else could be found to do my job. This was strange, because when I was recruited I had been told my job would be redundant when the Women's Royal Naval Service personnel arrived. Thankfully, the predicament was resolved, and after spending three days hectically packing the things that I would not take with me and would need to be stored, I was ready to depart from Coimbatore at the end of March.

I had to travel back up north, this time to Assam: a marathon journey of approximately 1,400 miles. I was sent a railway warrant to travel from Coimbatore to Shillong, where Wasbie HQ was situated, and was told that if I wanted to upgrade to first class that would be at my own expense. Sadly, this was beyond my means. I was to join the Wasbies as an auxiliary and promotion to the rank of sergeant or subaltern would be on merit.

Admittedly I was not without qualms as to whether it was a good idea or not to join the Wasbies, but I couldn't ask my parents what they thought as they were in England and besides, it would only worry them unnecessarily if I asked their opinion. I made the decision myself and never regretted it. Needless to say once again some of my work chums thought I was mad and said goodbye to me as though I was going off to certain death, or worse, which was all very cheering!

It was at this point that I decided to start keeping a detailed record of my life as a Wasbie.

PART THREE

Women's Auxiliary Services (Burma)

India and Arakan
1944

Journey to Shillong, Assam – March 1944

As the steam train pulled out of the station at Coimbatore, laden with my luggage plus a pile of papers, sweets, cosmetics and bottles of gin, I thought about what one of my friends had whispered in my ear just before leaving, that perhaps I should take some poison with me in case I fell into the hands of the Japanese, so very comforting! My own thoughts on the situation were, I am afraid, nil. I hadn't a clue what I had let myself in for, it just sounded exciting and I felt sure it was going to be an adventure. They were quite possibly correct in thinking that I was being a bit reckless but I was game for pastures new – other girls had joined, so why not me?

I settled down into a corner seat, made myself as comfortable as possible in the train carriage and fell into contemplation wondering how I could occupy myself during the three-day train trip. The journey was via Madras, then onward to Calcutta before reaching my destination of Shillong.

Having done very little train travel purely on my own, this long journey across India frankly terrified me, but I told myself I should just jolly well get on with it and stop being such a namby-pamby. I had never been good at asking anybody for assistance, which reminded me of my father, who would rather get lost than stop to ask someone the way, but now I would probably have to pluck up courage and ask for advice or guidance, as the thought of getting lost was not a good one. Later on I discovered that once I was a Wasbie there would be endless such journeys, and these turned out not always to be in the same civilian comfort as I was now enjoying.

I broke my journey in Madras where I spent a marvellous two days with Arthur 'Flags' Atkinson, so called because of his service with the Royal Corps of Signals. Flags, by this time a Lieutenant Colonel with the 19th Indian Divisional Signals, was our old friend from Kenya.

I was able to talk to him about all my worries and troubles. He was a good listener and gave me sage advice. He managed to instil a little more confidence and faith in myself, as did Jacky, a colleague of his whom I also met during those two days in Madras. Jacky's naïveté and simple attitude to life did much to restore my sense of proportion about my immediate future and the route I had now chosen to pursue.

The ongoing journey from Madras up to Calcutta was very hot and uncomfortable. My travelling companions were a mixed and motley lot, but all women, so I suppose I was lucky as this was not usual. It often happened in India that men and women who were strangers to each other travelled together, sharing a compartment. One girl I knew travelled for a number of days with three men in her carriage. She said that the only compensation for her discomfort over sleeping arrangements was that due to the unlimited supply of Scotch whisky they consumed, she became a bit tipsy and therefore able to cope.

I was met in Calcutta by some army friends who showed me around before taking me to the Tollygunge Club for the afternoon. The large station complex had a striking Deco façade, leading on to the road and the thronging city centre with its imposing Victorian-style buildings. My first impression of Calcutta, in the few hours that I spent there, was that it was a more attractive city than Bombay, with larger and wider tree-lined roadways. These were criss-crossed by busy trams, operated by smart uniformed drivers, carrying hundreds of people to and from their place of business in either first- or second-class carriages. Some of the trams bore bright advertising placards on their sides, adding to the colourful atmosphere. In amongst the tram cars there were Dodge buses, dozens of rickshaws and bullock- or hand-drawn carts, carrying all manner of folk or goods around the shops and bazaars. The buzzing city was also a good deal cleaner than Bombay and some of the other towns I had visited in India.

The *maidans*, a local name for town squares or parade grounds, were larger and there were more of them, although they were rapidly being built over by the army. Had it not been for some of the hunger-stricken local people who were begging for food at the station and who were difficult to ignore, I would have found Calcutta to be an attractive place. I learned there had been a famine in '43 following a cyclone which resulted in failed crops, with thousands of people and animals starving to death. This ghastly situation affected a great number of poor souls: they were so pitiful and I found it extremely upsetting, it just wrung my heart to see them. Some were also horribly crippled with others too emaciated even to be able to walk. It was a scene which haunted me and remained in my mind for some time.

Following the bombing raids to which Calcutta had been subjected, vast barrage balloons, sometimes called 'blimps', had been strategically placed around the city in an endeavour to deter aircraft from being able to fly low enough to be accurate when dropping bombs. It was the first time I had seen any of these and I thought they looked strangely attractive hovering noiselessly above the ground against the intense blue of the sky. They were gas-filled, tethered to the ground by thick steel cables which could be extended or shortened as necessary; and were effective against the Japanese air attacks.

Having been shown around the city I was driven to the Tollygunge Club, which was slightly reminiscent of the Hurlingham Club in Ranelagh Gardens in south London where I had stayed with my parents on trips to England from East Africa. I was treated to a splendid tea during the horse race meeting that afternoon. After the races I was given a very good dinner in the Army Mess before being taken to an 'hotel'– more like a girls' hostel – where I was to spend the night before continuing my journey north.

On arriving at the location where I was to stay it was a little unsettling, as at the entrance to the premises, gates had to be unlocked to allow me in and it felt as though I was going to prison to serve a sentence, particularly when they were noisily clanked shut and relocked behind me. I gathered next morning at breakfast that this was normal security procedure. I was the only European girl staying there that night. In addition to me there was one Burmese girl and the rest were either Chinese or Indian.

After inspecting my allotted sleeping area, and swearing under my breath at the clumsy person who had dropped and broken my precious Thermos flask, I undressed and climbed into bed, turning the light off quickly. There was nothing inviting about my cubicle at all; it rather reminded me of an attic room that might have been allocated to the lowest of 'tweenies' from a Dickens' tale. The bed itself looked uninviting and suspect, possibly harbouring creepy crawlies the like of which I had experienced before and certainly did not want to encounter again. Sleep did not come easily, and when it did, of all things I dreamt that I was in an opium den. I had been told they were quite popular in the city, not that I had ever been in one of course. This was possibly because all the rooms had a sort of greenish hue about them, dark green paper having been placed around the lights in an attempt to make a 'brownout'.

Cleve, Shillong – 10 April 1944

On the road trip from Calcutta up to Shillong, a beautiful hill town in Assam in the north-eastern region of India, there was little of note. The journey up to Assam was long and tiring. Between reading and talking to fellow passengers, my thoughts drifted back to Rudyard Kipling's tales, read to us as children, about Indian wild animals. These bore the same names as ours in Africa but were a different species and also differed in appearance, in particular the rhinoceros and the elephant. Indian elephants were smaller than the ones at home, their ears were a different shape and their grey skin was frequently mottled with pink, unlike the African elephant. They were more benign and easier to tame and train for domestic and agricultural work. The local people used them as a means of conveyance and also to carry large loads, fell trees and haul logs in the forest areas where there were few roadways.

I felt I would be unlikely to see Indian rhino which mainly inhabited the forest areas of Assam and Nepal. I had seen pictures of them: they had a single horn and more pronounced 'armour-plated' warty hides than the African species. Monkeys were plentiful and as always were cheeky and could be a pest. On the big cat scene, would I ever be lucky enough to see a tiger? Again probably not, but to see one of these spectacular creatures would be memorable.

The lengthy trip was like so many journeys I was to undertake in India. It was scenically interesting and tolerably comfortable, with the exception of the final seventy-six miles from Gauhati to Shillong. Gauhati is the largest city in Assam, lying between the great Bramaputra River and the foothills of the Shillong Plateau. This final sector of the journey had to be undertaken by car. The drive up into the mountains was a rather sick-making experience with the vehicle constantly pitching and swaying as we climbed steadily upward round the endless hairpin bends encountered along the winding, heavily forested and picturesque road to our destination.

I arrived at 'Cleve', the house which was the WAS(B) headquarters, in a state of nerves, but I received such a wonderful warm welcome from all the girls and, in particular, the Assistant Commandant, Lois St John. I shall never forget it. It felt almost like being welcomed home by my mother. Mrs St John was middle-aged, gentle, and certainly the sweetest and most kind and thoughtful person I had met since leaving Kenya. It was clear she was a 'mother' figure to all the girls.

I soon realised that I had definitely done the right thing in joining the Wasbies. I enjoyed more peace of mind and was certainly much happier since moving away from Bombay and Coimbatore with its raw unhappy thoughts which were now no longer constantly at the forefront of my mind. There was a terrific atmosphere at Cleve; all the Wasbies were friendly and helpful, and any fears and doubts I had were quickly dispelled. It was not long before I began to feel young and gay once more and certainly part of a great team.

My spirits were raised even further by the receipt of a heart-warming letter from Flags, who quite rightly felt that upon arrival at a strange destination, I would appreciate knowing that somebody, somewhere was thinking of me, and that there was no need to feel lonesome or to experience the hollow emptiness one often felt when far from home, friends and family. He said how marvellous it had been for him to spend a few days with me in Madras and chat about our lives in Nanyuki and the times Peter and I had with him and his wife Judy on the farm. He went on to say how my visit had brought a little magic to his days, how much he admired me for what I had done in leaving Kenya and how he was already missing my company. I felt a little saddened at his reminder of what we had all left behind, but also uplifted by the warm feelings he expressed for me.

Cleve itself was a large house situated in lovely grounds surrounded by pretty gardens and wonderful flowering trees and shrubs. In the complex there was a scattering of bungalows where new recruits stayed when they first arrived or when Wasbies were on leave. Shillong was a hill town high in the tea-growing area of Assam. It was an area of cool climate with rivers, lakes, pine forests and tea plantations, added to which there was a very social 'hill station' lifestyle. There was an active Country Club, golf course, polo ground and gymkhana racecourse with numerous events which were always well attended and greatly enjoyed by all who visited or lived there.

Before the war Shillong was a place where some of the English families came to spend their holidays or if they needed a short bit of R&R. Those who were working in some of the hot areas further south, where the summer months were steamy and humid, holidayed in Shillong. Since the outbreak of war the small town was being used by large numbers of transiting and recuperating troops.

It was a grand surprise when, not long after my arrival, Peter Hook, one of my mother's cousins, came up to stay for a few days during which time we had dinner at the Club, and he updated me with news from home. Having been on the move I hadn't been in touch with the family for a while and correspondence from them had not yet caught up with me. There were dances held in the Club twice a week and Peter stayed on for a few days with his friend Pat with whom I got on very well. We all had an enjoyable time during which I discovered they were both jolly good dancers.

First day as a fully fledged Wasbie, with the mobile canteen at Shillong.

The first few days as a Wasbie recruit were a whirl of learning the ropes. I was to stay in Shillong for approximately three months before being posted to forward areas of the Fourteenth Army, as most needed. It was explained to me that Wasbies were moved around from place to place so as not to have to spend too long in difficult climates. Initially our tasks consisted of selling in the canteen, a certain amount of office work and accounts, plus the supervision of IOR [Indian Other Ranks] cooks and canteen staff.

In the case of mobile canteens there was a team of six. Usually four girls would go out each day to visit isolated units, one would stay at base to do the routine work and the sixth member would have a day off. We were taught that canteen itineraries had to be planned and prioritised in detail and swift decisions made on the many problems connected with establishing a welfare service, particularly in busy transit camps coping with the influx of thousands of troops moving in and out of battle zones.

Whilst in Shillong we were permitted to wear mufti on days off and in the evenings, but in the forward areas uniform had to be worn at all times and, because of the mosquitoes, we had to wear uniform trousers in the evenings, even when it was hot and humid. I was allocated the necessary field equipment: camp bed, water bottles, tin hat, cutlery, mosquito net and a mass of other camp kit. I was measured for my uniform which then had to be made. Name tags and numbers had to be painted or sewn on all the items which had been supplied to me. I was quickly kitted out and ready to start my new life as a full-time recruit, awaiting allocation to a team which naturally I hoped would be soon.

Mrs Taylor, our Commandant, was adamant that as she was petitioning Area Command to allow WAS(B) Canteens to move into forward areas, the operation she was representing should be professional in all ways. The women's comportment was intended to reflect the discipline of the Army Ranks they were serving.

In addition, I was issued with the following official information:

WOMEN'S AUXILIARY SERVICE (BURMA)
Mobile Canteen Establishment

————————

Summary of Terms of Service

1. The W. A. S. (B) Mobile Canteen Establishment has been formed to provide personnel to operate Mobile Canteens placed at the disposal of H. E. The Commander-in-Chief in India, for service in India and Burma.

2. *Conditions of service.*

(a) Enlistment of women will be for general service in India and Burma for the duration of the war and for so long thereafter as their services may be required.

(b) Officers and auxiliaries will be subject to Military Law to the extent set out on the detailed conditions of service.

(c) Officers will be appointed and the appointments will be held for so long as the services of an officer are required.

Auxiliaries will be enlisted under the general rules applicable to British soldiers.

(d) If a husband or relation, on whom an officer or auxiliary is dependent and with whom she normally resides, returns to India from service overseas or from a theatre of operations in India, for duty in India, she may, if the exigencies of the service permit, be transferred to the unemployed list without pay up to a maximum of six months, but subject to recall at short notice. If on the expiry of six months, the officer or auxiliary has not been recalled for active duties, she may, if an officer, be called upon to resign her appointment, or, if an auxiliary be discharged.

Subject to the exigencies of the service, an officer may be permitted to resign her appointment, or an auxiliary be discharged, on compassionate grounds on the recommendation of the Commandant of the W. A. S. (B).

3. *Ranks and rates of pay will be as follows:-*

Senior Commander, ranks as Major	...	Rs 380/- p.m
Junior Commander " " Capt	...	Rs 220/- p.m
Subaltern " " Lieut	...	Rs 175/- p.m
2nd Subaltern " " 2nd/Lt	...	Rs 150/- p.m
Sergeant	...	Rs 120/- p.m
Corporal, L/Cpl and Pte.	...	Rs 100/- p.m

4. *Promotions.*

(a) Candidates for appointment as officers, unless possessing special qualifications, will normally be selected after six months' service in the ranks.

(b) Promotion from the rank of 2nd Subaltern to Subaltern will be admissible on completion of six months' full pay service as an officer subject to the officer being classified as fit for promotion.

(c) Promotion to higher rank than Subaltern will be in an acting capacity only and to the rank suitable to the appointment held. On vacation of such appointment, or on becoming non-effective, the officer will revert to her substantive rank.

(d) Auxiliaries. All promotions to higher rank than private, will be in an acting capacity only   and to the rank suitable to the appointment held. On vacation of such appointment, or, on becoming non-effective, the auxiliary will revert to the substantive rank of Private.

5. *Accommodation* as available, rations and messing service will be provided free of charge, or, when either rations or messing arrangements, or both, are not provided by the government, allowances in lieu will be admissible at the following rates:-

(a) In Lieu of rations and messing	Rs, 2-0 per head per day
(b) In lieu of messing service when rations in kind are provided by Government	As. 8 per head per day
(c) In lieu of rations when messing service is provided by Government ...	Rs. 1-8 per head per day

6. Uniform and clothing

    (a) The following are admissible:-

      (i) Initial uniform allowance-

Officers	Rs.	200-0
Auxiliaries	Rs.	140-0

      (ii) Winter clothing for officers and auxiliaries,

        when authorized ... ...   Rs.   40-0

      (iii) Upkeep allowance :-

        (a) Annual allowance for replacement of

          uniform ... ...   Rs. 80-0 p.a.

        (b) Cleaning and repairs allowance

          for auxiliaries only ... ...   Rs.   10-0 p.a.

      (iv) Free issue of certain items of clothing and

        equipment as laid down in authorized scales.

(b) When an officer or auxiliary leaves the service for any reason, she will be required to return to Government all items of Government clothing and equipment which she received as a free issue, and will be required to refund $1/10^{th}$ of the total initial uniform allowance she has received for each month by which her service fall short of 10 months.

7. Leave

    (a) Leave may be granted to officers and auxiliaries in accordance with the leave rules applicable to British personnel, *vide* Special India Army Order dated the 26th November, 1941 *(i.e.,* subject to the exigencies of the service, war leave may be granted up to a maximum of 28 days in any one year; station leave will be limited to three periods of 10 days in any one year; and sick leave as recommended by a medical board).

    (b) Should the husband of an officer or auxiliary return to India from service overseas or from a theatre of operations in India further leave up to a maximum of 28 days may be granted, if the officer or auxiliary has not sufficient leave due under *(a)* above.

8. Medical treatment, dental treatment, and free conveyance are admissible under the conditions applicable to corresponding ranks of the British Army, with certain modifications.

9. Disability pensions and gratuities. The provisions of the Royal Warrant dated 29th June 1940, published as an appendix to A.L. (I) No. 4 of 1941, insofar as applicable to women members of the military forces, and as amended from time to time, will apply.

10. Organisation. The W.A.S.(B) will be organized on a fixed establishment of ranks as sanctioned from time to time.

11. Applications for enrolment will be submitted in manuscript to the Commandant, W.A.S.(B)., Cleve, Shillong.

12. Further information may be obtained A.G's. Branch (Bur.Sec.) Simla or from the Commandant, W.A.S.(B) Cleve, Shillong.

LIST OF CLOTHING AND EQUIPMENT TO BE MAINTAINED BY PERSONNEL OF THE WOMEN'S AUXILIARY SERVICE (BURMA) MOBILE CANTEEN UNIT.

Numerals..............................1 Pair (from W.A. S. (B). Q.M.)
Bag - with shoulder string............1 Pair (from W.A. S. (B). Q.M.)
Shies Black (no Toe Caps)......................................2 pairs.
Boots, Gum...1 pair.
CapsForage..1
UniformDresses(Khaki)..4
Slacks (Khaki Drill), no tum ups...................3 pairs. (minimum)
Bush shirts (Khaki) Cellular.......................3 pairs. (minimum)
*(b)*Jersey,Cardigan...1
Socks ankle................................3 pairs. Socks mens... 3pr.

Aprons, Khaki Drill..4

(a) Greatcoat..1

(b) Mackintosh...1

(b) Blankets, Barrack..2

(b) Sheets..2 pairs.

(b) Pillow-cases..2

(b) Pillow..1

(b) Mosquito Net...1

(b) Valise with Straps..1

(b) Towels..2

(b) Kit Bag..1

Holdall (containing Knife, Fork, Spoon)

(b) Enamel Mug..1

(b)   "   Plate

Torch...1

(b) Bottle, water...1

(b) Brace without Buckle...1

(b) Carriers. Water Bottle...1

(b) Haversack, O. S. 1

(b) Bucket, canvas..1

(b) Ground Sheet..1

(b) Bedstead, Camp Portable and Bag..1

(b) Washing stand, Collapsible with canvas

Basin, Bath and Bag. 1

(b) Camp Chair...1

(b) Camp Mirror...1

Notes

(a) Greatcoats will be issued free to all personnel if serving in places where the climate in the opinion of the local Military Commander necessitates their use. They will be returned to Government on discharge.

(b) Free use from Ordnance.

1. Materials for uniforms can be purchased from the W. A. S. (B), Quarter-master, at wholesale prices.

2. Now that price control has been established recruits should buy their own material, if possible olive green, and have uniform made before reporting for duty.

*

We were also issued with supplies of Mepacrine, an anti-malaria prophylactic to be used in infected areas of India and Burma, plus a supply of potassium permanganate crystals to disinfect water supplies, treat cuts and sores and in an emergency, if there was nothing else when in the jungle, it could be used for snake bite – one was told to cut the bite in a Union Jack-style cross then apply the permanganate.

*

11 April 1944

After the awful weeks of wondering if I had done the right thing and whether it was for the best, I was now a fully-fledged Wasbie. The past must be put behind me, and I was now settling in well and ready for the challenges ahead. I knew it would be hard work and very tough, but it would be a good life and I gathered from the other girls that our efforts were very much appreciated.

There were many new faces and names to remember – Prue, Pat, Audrey, Fleurette to mention just a few. One girl in particular, Elaine Cheverton, who had joined up in 1943 came across as the perfect Wasbie example. She was one of the most popular girls in Shillong and I hoped I could take a leaf from her book. She was so efficient, cheerful and friendly with everybody, a truly lovely girl, much admired by the men who thought she was the cat's whiskers.

Initially our uniform was khaki, our emblem was a *chinthe* [mythical lion found guarding Buddhist temples] embroidered in black on a square scarlet background. The uniform was by far the smartest that I had seen amongst any of the women's services, with the exception of the bush tunics and slacks which we had to wear in the evenings as a deterrent to the malarial species of mosquito in this area. I defy anyone who does not have the tallest and slimmest of figures to look their best in these ghastly garments. Later on we were kitted out in jungle green.

For the first few days after my arrival somebody had to lend me a uniform until I could get my own made up. I was then put to work in a mobile canteen operating around Shillong itself. The mobile canteens consisted mainly of specially converted Chevrolet vans with sides which hinged out to form a canopy where the girls stood to serve from stores contained within the truck. Other times, when busy, we served from the rear of the vehicles as well.

Needless to say I was totally confused over prices of all the goods we sold – soap, cigarettes, hair oil, needles, threads, shoe laces, razor blades, toothpaste and a thousand and one other different items which the troops bought. The mystery of Indian currency, with all dealings in cash, was hellish, but worst of all was my inability to speak or understand even a smattering of Urdu or Hindustani, the local dialects spoken in this area. How the girls working with me coped with selling goods and helping me with the language, which they understood having lived in the country for many years, was astonishing. Everybody was so patient, and nobody ever complained of wrong change, which I am sure must have happened regularly. The queues of men visiting the canteens in Shillong were every bit as long as those we were to encounter when we moved to the Arakan and later on the Northern Shan states in Burma. Troop numbers in each Division ran into the tens of thousands – a daunting thought.

The intricacies of stocking up the canteen when it came home empty in the evenings, the making of sandwiches and baking of cakes, buns and tartlets, replenishing dry goods and fruit squash and how to keep the accounts, etc. were all explained to me prior to my posting, but it took time for it all to sink in. There were hundreds of things that had to be learnt and my head was in a whirl with all the information. Nevertheless I was loving it, every moment of it.

The chief topic of conversation was postings. We were all so envious of those who had been issued with theirs, and we enjoyed the stories of teams already working with front-line troops near Imphal. We heard about the notices that were being left on trees entreating the Wasbies to 'Please call'. An amusing story was that of a very deaf elderly Wasbie who was serving from one of the canteens. She was attending to a shy young man who came and asked for a cake of soap. Completely mishearing his request, she gave him one of our home-made currant buns instead. He was too shy to say that was not what he asked for, so he bought it, only the story did not end there. Poor fellow, when he bit into the bun he broke one of his teeth on a stone that had somehow been mixed in with the sun-dried fruit in the cake. He had to be rushed off to a medic to have it dealt with. All for something that he didn't want in the first place but was too bashful to refuse.

These were tense times, because the Japanese were making a ferocious drive on Imphal and Kohima in north-east India, as well as in the Arakan region in Burma further south. The fighting in these theatres was very fierce and we were hearing upsetting news of many casualties. Frantic messages and signals were coming through about the Wasbies who were in the northern region and were having to be evacuated as it was considered too dangerous for them to remain in the area. Our Commandant, Mrs Taylor, did some terrific work up there by calmly and efficiently commandeering trucks to bring the girls back to a safe base in Jorhat, along with a large quantity of CBID [Canteen Bulk Issue Depot] stores which would otherwise have fallen into Japanese hands. She was the most amazing person, with an enormous amount of vitality and energy, and she commanded the complete respect and devotion of all the Wasbies old and new.

One of the most notable moments of being a new Wasbie was going down to the town in uniform for the first time to get a pay-book photograph taken. The pay-book, a scruffy affair, was tied up with a bit of bright candy-pink tape. We later found out that this style of pay-book was the same for everyone irrespective of position. My photograph was ghastly – I looked rather like a female gorilla as I had a sort of 'I'll get you whatever happens' look on my face.

When in uniform we were supposed to salute all officers, and that was another thing that used to fill us with shy pride. My first attempt at a salute was on reflection quite amusing, but at the time it was a great disappointment when it wasn't returned by the officer it was directed at. Either it took him completely by surprise or wasn't as smart a salute as I felt or hoped it to be. Maybe he thought I was just flicking off a fly or something. I would have to practice in front of the mirror to get it right.

Life was certainly full of fun in Shillong. Apart from going out in the mobile canteen and doing the usual things required to maintain daily operations, another of our duties was to organise tea parties for the officers and men from the Convalescent Depot. There were never less than three or four tea parties every week, along with dances twice a week. I only hope they enjoyed the teas as much as we did. Some of them said they loved the homely atmosphere and to me, not having been back to England for so many years, these afternoons reminded me of the tea parties we used to have in the late autumn, when the evenings drew in and it was cold enough for a fire to be lit and often for the lights to be switched on making for a very cosy atmosphere. These gatherings often used to end up with a number of us going down to the Chinese restaurant for supper, where the food was reasonably good and also relatively cheap.

The company was always very jolly and carefree. We all had a sort of infectious and careless cheerfulness, little things appeared outrageously funny and we never seemed to stop laughing. Looking back, it was probably due to the amount of alcohol we all seemed to consume. There was one memorable evening at the restaurant when we were each given half a chicken to eat, which quite surprisingly we all managed, after which we could hardly stagger home. As taxis were frightfully expensive and difficult to find, it was just as well for our figures that we had to walk, no doubt sobering up a little at the same time.

24 April 1944

Went to the races yesterday with Prue Brewis, one of my new Wasbie friends, where we made a spot of cash backing one or two of the horses. It was most exciting and great fun with both of us thoroughly enjoying ourselves. A dance followed in the evening where we met up with some of the other girls. It was a very mixed crowd and I didn't enjoy it much, but hoped I'd given a little pleasure to some of the troops who attended, as there was a distinct lack of women at these parties.

Earlier I had a phone message from one of George Hirst's minions. George was a friend of Flags. I wondered why he was being so thoughtful but no doubt Flags had asked him to keep an eye on me. I knew that if ever I wanted any help I'd always get it from George. I felt so lucky as I was now making some very good new friends.

25 April 1944

There was a great commotion this morning with a sudden fall of debris down the chimney in our cottage, followed by a bird landing at the bottom amidst a cloud of soot. Elaine caught it and exclaimed, 'Look, it's got a blue backside,' whereupon the terrified creature promptly laid a pale blue egg right in the palm of her hand, before she popped it outside and let it fly away unscathed. Just typical of what happens to Elaine, and after the initial surprise we had a good laugh; the poor thing must have been frightened out of its wits.

Went out with Pat Wilcox in a 15cwt truck; she had just got her licence. I was due to take my test the following day, only I didn't, for some unknown reason. It was another day of pouring rain which was pretty dreary. Spent the morning in the canteen and in the afternoon went into town to try to find material for my own uniform; succeeded too, although finding a *dherzi* [tailor's shop] to make it up quickly was the next problem.

Later I spent a most amusing evening in the bar of an 'hotel' of the worst description, in the company of Elaine, Audrey and some chaps from the Convalescent Depot. One of these, Bill, was much admired by Audrey but sadly the feeling was not reciprocated. What a pity we girls make such fools of ourselves over men. I suppose we all do at some time or other, but I certainly hope that I don't again. Once bitten twice shy, although there is no doubt about it that men do attract me. One of them, Pat Williams, took me out for a drink having only just arrived after the long tiring journey from Calcutta. I do feel so at home with him and hope he writes as he promised to. He is one of the nicest types of men I have met: no silly nonsense.

Looks like Pat Wilcox has eyes for an officer called Toby and I feel I may have to talk to her about it, though I don't suppose it will do any good as she appears rather besotted. It seems we are all fated to be hurt these days which is something I personally am going to have to accept and cope with.

26 April 1944

We have had such fun and foolishness once again this evening. I feel sure that we should perhaps be less carefree in our general demeanour now that we have a serious occupation in which we hope to be recognised as helpful to the war effort, yet we behave like the gayest and most carefree of youngsters. It is, though, a relief to feel happy again, in spite of what is going on around us, not to mention what lies ahead of us all. For my part it is good to try and forget my personal problems.

Later in the day two of Fleurette's officer-chums turned up at our house in a Jeep. It was the first time we had seen one of these vehicles and whilst they were busy chatting, Pat and I took it upon ourselves to take it out for a spin, driving it at speed round and round the compound, which I might add was an exceedingly small area. Then having driven it up the hill and out of the front gate the only way to get back in again was to do a tight three point turn around on the narrow driveway. However, we decided it would be much more amusing to reverse down the hill back into the compound, rather than try to turn the vehicle round on such a narrow track. How we didn't kill ourselves I shall never know because we couldn't find the brakes. Perhaps there was a special saint who looked after idiots such as us that evening. I still hadn't taken my driving test so could have landed myself in a bit of hot water.

As there was a shortage of bathrooms in the complex, five of us decided that we should bathe together. Alas, the bathroom floor soon became flooded and some boxes which had been stored in the middle of the room were awash under inches of water, resulting in a hasty mop-up operation with our bath towels, having nothing else suitable immediately to hand. We never found out what the contents of the boxes looked like when they were finally opened up. In Cleve, it was always referred to as 'that flood'.

Following this little episode, we all went to a BOR [British Other Ranks] dance at the Club which was great fun, although quite exhausting as every dance was a tag with only about two minutes between each one. Plus of course, there was the usual shortage of women, making for a pretty hectic evening. Many of the BORs were very jitterbug-minded too, much preferring this fast music to a more sedate ballroom tempo. I got entangled with an American Physical Training Instructor who insisted that jitterbugging was the easiest dance in the world and he was going to show me how it was done, but in my heart I was very nervous about managing it. I saw Pat trying to cope, with her head of blonde hair flying around as if it would take off at any minute. I think my PTI decided I was pretty hopeless as he kept yelling, 'Loosen up sister', at the same time shaking me until my teeth nearly dropped out. I was then flung towards some other unfortunate man, and so it went on into the early hours: quite exhausting but great fun and extremely good for our figures.

That evening we heard that Monica's husband had been killed at Kohima, which sobered us up instantly. It was just too sad for words and she was trying to be so brave about it. It just wrung one's heart, how must she have felt? That was the second Wasbie it had happened to since I had joined up. Lord, how we wished all this fighting and consequent unhappiness would come to an end. We heard that there was very little left of Kohima with many casualties on our side.

27 April 1944

We took a mobile canteen out to the Assam Rifles depot in the afternoon, and it was such fun. The Gurkhas were so amusing although some were very naïve and surprisingly lacking in discipline. The locals climbed all over the canteen in the hope that they would be served quicker, which was extremely irritating to say the least. They seemed not to be able to understand the meaning of queuing and didn't like it when we endeavoured to explain the system to them. Their motto was free for all and all for free, with the first man in line getting a better chance to help himself to the best of what was on offer. To them it was no doubt all quite normal to push and shove, but it did make for an immense amount of muddle and aggravation and it was most certainly not quicker. I was starting to learn a few of the local words for the things we sold and was therefore a bit more help than I had been two days previously.

Only two of us went out to the Rifle Club with provisions solely for the BORs. We didn't serve tea and cakes to the IORs: they wouldn't eat the food we made. I didn't understand why to begin with, but it was explained to me and had something to do with their religion and caste system.

Went to the Club again in the evening and thoroughly enjoyed the party which turned out to be rather rowdy in the end. Nine officers joined our party of four and they were all very 'happy'. The Assam rum and gin was really frightful stuff and made one either very sick or very drunk, possibly both, especially Lily brand gin. Makes me shudder even to think about it, and they had obviously had their fair share that evening.

Just heard that a troop ship went down off Ceylon a few days ago, what a ghastly business that was, and I had a horrid feeling that a cousin of mine was on board. It made us even more aware that there was a war on. It seemed to me that in some parts of India, people were not yet really touched by the war in any real sense, and what I found difficult to understand was that some hadn't seemed to grasp that allied troops were having a ghastly time in places like Kohima and Imphal where things were very nasty indeed. [The ship Maria refers to was the SS *Khedive Ismail*, which was sunk by a Japanese submarine on 12 February whilst en route to Burma, with many casualties including nurses, FANYs and Wrens. Information about such disasters was often withheld in order not to affect morale.]

29 April 1944

Hurrah! I have just received my posting orders and am off to the Arakan on 1 May. It is strange how everything of note appears to happen to me between the first of the month and the third. I was so thrilled that at last I was off. It was all too exciting for words. Pat Wilcox was to come with me, and I knew we should have such fun although she was, I believe, staying in Chittagong whilst I was to go on to Dohazari. Great excitement getting everything packed and being issued with a mysterious thing called a 'Movement Order' which outlined our next destination.

30 April 1944

Very serious business today stocktaking, and though it should be undertaken in a sober and organised state of mind, I am afraid that the three of us who did it were anything but staid. I think it was the 'leaving tomorrow' excitement thing. Neither Pat nor I realised how hard it was to count correctly when we were faced with masses of items like buttons, sewing kits, soap, MacLeans and Phillips toothpaste, Brylcreem, shaving cream and razor blades, writing paper, pens, pencils, ink, envelopes and, dear God, those blasted cigarettes: even worse, gross after gross of black greasy leather bootlaces which smelt strongly of rancid bacon. On this note I have to admit I was smoking and drinking far too much. This was not helped by the generous cigarette and booze rations we received – usually two bottles of spirits per month plus beer and an endless supply of cigarettes.

Departure from Shillong – 2 May 1944

My wedding anniversary today and I don't suppose Peter even remembers. We arrived at Chittagong, three hours late, feeling rather strange and a little at sea. We almost felt as though it wasn't us sitting there wondering what to do next. It was terribly hot and incredibly filthy. Being on the coast, like Mombasa, the air was thick with humidity. There was no refreshing sea breeze, we were pouring with sweat having had to manhandle our assorted baggage out of the train with no help. Our uniforms were sticking to us most unpleasantly and we longed for a cool wash. I felt I didn't travel well.

We had been lucky to wangle a lift in an army 10cwt truck for part of the journey as far as Sylhet, from where we then caught a train onward to Chittagong. What a difference it made to travel by road for the first section of the journey south, and this time thankfully neither of us felt sick during the twisty drive, not even when Pat, who was taking her turn driving, took a corner too fast and we left the road, ending up in a deep water-filled ditch. We were very much more comfortable and the road journey enabled us to see more of the lovely scenery before boarding the crowded train.

Thank heavens Pat and I both have a sense of humour because where the train journey was concerned it was certainly a necessity. To start with, there were no coolies for our luggage and we had a lot of it, including stores and a couple of cases of honey, one of which was dropped and the bottles inside broken with honey flooding the carriage, resulting in a horrible sticky mess which was pretty well impossible to clean up due to lack of sufficient water or a suitable mop. There were no fans, no lights and the heat was stifling.

I still don't know how we managed, but we did. The last change of train was the final straw as it was by that time past midnight and we were pretty tired and longed for a wash. We piled into the least full-looking carriage with all our stuff. There were already five officers in it, together with all their equipment and belongings. There was nowhere to walk about, with boxes piled in every available space and by the time we stowed our stuff, even the lavatory was stacked to bulging. We just about expired as a result of our efforts to load and locate a corner for all our paraphernalia, and cursed the amount of stores we had been asked to transport.

One of the officers had brought a motor car seat in with him, quite why we never found out, probably for use in his tent as a chair. Anyhow it came in very useful to sit on when placed on a pile of baggage. Congestion was somewhat relieved when, in the early hours of the morning, four of them got off the train, leaving us with a very nice RAF padre and at last the ability to stretch our legs and move around a little.

Later we stopped at the smallest of sidings, with barely a hut on it, and were told that if we were snappy we could get off to collect some food. The train only stopped for about five minutes, so there was an ugly rush. I quickly bagged a fried egg on a piece of toast before running back to the train closely followed by Pat, who was likewise encumbered, amidst loud cheers from the troops on the train who seemed to take a great deal of interest in us. They were even more entertained when a filthy great crow came down and pinched our food just as we were climbing up the steps back into the carriage. An hilarious moment for the onlookers but we were left cursing furiously. There was no time to nip back for more sustenance, so we had to continue our travels very hungry.

The train journey to Chittagong had been a revelation to us, and by the time Pat and I finally climbed out of the carriage we were exhausted. We hung around like Tweedledum and Tweedledee laden with our tin hats, water bottles, haversacks, handbags and all our other belongings. Fortunately not for long though. There was one thing that we had already discovered: no matter how busy the Wasbies were, new arrivals were always given a terrific welcome and made to feel at home straight away. It was the same here. Gay Tucker, who was in charge, greeted us with, 'Duckies, how grand that you have arrived safe and sound.' She quickly shepherded us onto a truck and we sped away to the mess, all the while wondering whether we should be saluting so grand a person as the 'Area Commander'.

Chittagong wasn't what I expected, but then I don't know what I did expect, except that I thought it would be acres of tents, and it wasn't. I particularly noticed the many flowering shrubs, including lots of beautiful yellow laburnums which were in full bloom. However, the town itself was desperately grubby, scruffy and smelly which could not be masked by the pretty vegetation. We both felt as though we had been on the go for ages, yet it was only yesterday that we had left Cleve.

We were soon given amended marching orders by Mrs Tucker, and were now both due to head for Dohazari, which was further south, the following afternoon. I decided it was most essential that I obtain a hurricane lamp to travel with before I went another step. The RAF padre's lamp had saved us all the previous night and I was determined to go no further without one of my own.

Dohazari – 3 May 1944

After another two-and-a-half-hour very crowded train journey last night we arrived in Dohazari, which was close to the Arakan border of Burma. I had an idea that we were probably to work with one of the most forward canteens serving troops who were operating in the Arakan region. We were to spend the next four months here.

Antoinette Willis, who was the Wasbie in charge of the canteen we were to be allocated to, met us in a Jeep. She drove us at breakneck speed to our lodgings, where she effortlessly lifted our heavy tin boxes from the Jeep, stowing them in our new abode. I couldn't lift mine and consequently felt a bit pathetic. It remained a constant joke between us during our travels together.

Pat and I were sharing a small room with a lean-to bathroom the walls of which were constructed of bamboo matting. We spent a silent few hours, or so it seemed, putting up our beds, basins and mosquito nets, the latter with endless bits of string and a few bent and rusty nails. Not surprisingly there was no furniture as such but we salvaged a box or two from the store room and made a table and a sort of storage cupboard out of them.

The heat, which could reach temperatures over 100

deg. F, and especially the choking dust were unbelievable and, as used as I was to the dusty roads in Kenya, they had absolutely nothing on the ones here in Dohazari. Here the dust was not just a sprinkle. In places it was nearly a foot deep. Later during the monsoon rains this was to turn into deep mud making the roads almost impassable, adding to the misery and difficulties facing our unfortunate troops who were already having to cope with combat in difficult mountainous terrain and thick jungle.

Initially our mess was a shambles as we hadn't organised ourselves particularly well. A table had been set up, on one end of which there were piles of accounts journals, documents, papers and God knows what else. The other end seemed perpetually laid for some meal or other. We had just been introduced in no mean way to the much talked of 'soya link', which were meatless, vitamin-enriched sausages said to 'meet all human needs'. They were utterly revolting and loathed by everybody. Of course we still had that good old standby, bully beef, which was always our mainstay and very much on the regular menu.

The constant flies were a pest and we sweated all day in the unrelenting heat. Our faces were plastered with dust, leaving us wondering vaguely if we would ever look white or be clean again. But with so much to be done we got down to work straight away, hoping that we would soon get used to the conditions. Everyone seemed very nice here, especially the sergeant, Cecily Campbell, who was a girl after my own heart – easy to get on with and liked by everyone.

4 May 1944

Spent all day in the canteen yesterday and enjoyed it enormously. Four of us were to go out most days, as there were so many people to be served, two for the canteen shop and two serving tea, lemonade and cakes, commonly referred to as 'char and wads'. We didn't get back much before six each evening, after which we endeavoured to stock the canteen with as much as we could, so that we didn't have so much to do before setting out the following morning on our rounds of the transit camps, airfield and gun sites.

Sitting exhausted after our first hectic day, we realised that the Wasbies really did create quite a sensation amongst the troops: as soon as the canteen arrived, all heads turned in our direction. Not only were the men eager to buy stores, they were equally keen to spend time chatting with us. One of the gunners later joked that if a canteen arrived during routine drill there was nothing else for it but to dismiss the men.

We did, however, shortly become aware that there appeared to be a terrific officer complex here amongst the BORs as far as the Wasbies were concerned. Some officers appeared to think we were there to run the canteens specifically for their benefit. We had to be careful in a way, as of course this was not the case. Sometimes comments were thrown at us by some of the BORs that we were, 'always with the officers, that's wot', making us feel that we didn't care about them, which we found upsetting as we really were trying to spread our canteen facility fairly amongst everyone and also chat and socialise wherever and whenever possible. Anyhow, we had little or no time during working hours to talk with anybody except the people we were actually face to face with at the canteens.

Jack, who had been allocated to us as our driver, had been a costermonger from Covent Garden in London and had a very pronounced Cockney accent. He was most amusing about what he called our 'flies' referring to them as 'officers buzzing about like flies round a honey pot, blue bottles, great big ones ...', and then he ended up muttering '*bzzzz* ... dead crafty!' shaking his head at the same time. We did have to laugh at him which inevitably broke the tension slightly.

5 May 1944

My poor aching feet – they were puffy and swollen from the hours of standing. The day had been long and busy, but it really had been such fun and so rewarding.

I was rather embarrassed this morning. I was sitting in the back of the van bumping along at a couple of miles an hour over a track running through a very dusty paddy field, when suddenly what seemed like hundreds of BORs appeared from behind the bushes and ran after the canteen shouting to each other, 'Canteen's coming, boys, and there is a real white woman sitting in the back.' Some of the men stared at us in total disbelief, obviously not expecting to see girls. I assumed that after a while I would get used to being a woman in these parts and cease to feel embarrassed by all the attention from the men. I did wonder how they could guess I was white, as being covered in a thick coat of red dust I felt I was a more than delicate shade of the fashionable fake body colour 'London Tan'.

Our temporary sleeping quarters, a small dwelling called a *basha*, was now looking a little more habitable as we had purchased a couple of brightly coloured *lungi* [sarong] lengths at great expense from one of the local shops, and had covered our beds and boxes with them. My side was blue and white, and Pat's red and black, with the rest of the boxes covered in white, green and petunia purple. It looked very much like Joseph's 'coat of many colours', but it was jolly and cheerful and certainly brightened the place up enormously and made it feel a bit more homely. There was still a problem with ants which had bitten me to death, curse the beastly things.

I drove one of the mobile canteens today having just got my licence. Initially I was still not too confident with the gears; I didn't seem to have the feel of them and there was a bit of crashing going on when changing down without double declutching, which was something I hadn't quite mastered. However, practice makes perfect and I soon got the hang of it.

We did have the most pleasant site for our mess tent, in the shade of two large mango trees. We were keeping an eye on the ripening fruit, as fresh produce could at times be a luxury. The site was right on the bank of the Sangu River, which when we first arrived smelt to high heaven and was too repulsive for words. How the BORs bathed in it I have no idea. Although the river remained absolutely filthy, the smell disappeared and it turned into an agreeable and intriguing spot to sit and relax when we had a few spare moments. We watched the little country boats or *khistis*, as they were called, float gently and slowly by on the current. In each boat a little figure crouched in a tiny 'cabin' under a matting roof, working the primitive-looking rudder. They seemed happy going about their daily business.

Bamboo and teak logs were brought down the river in rather the same way as I imagined wood was floated down the rivers in Canada, all bound together into a raft, with the locals who accompanied them appearing to live on top of the floating bundles for days on end until they reached their destination down river.

Dohazari was, in the main, used by the US Army Air Force as their base from which they organised supplies for the troops fighting in Burma. The town itself was a one-horse sort of station with a British medical unit, an anti-malarial unit, workshops of sorts plus a transport depot all under the charge of an Admin Commandant, who was known to us as 'Uncle Grimes'. In addition to this were the Wasbies and our BOR driver, Jack, who remained almost impossible to understand, so much so that one day a youngster from Manchester walked up to him and asked if he was speaking Urdu. Jack was much aggrieved and felt most insulted, but just made some remark about how he 'pitied chaps who couldn't understand the King's English', after which we dared not tell him that we couldn't understand half of what he said either. He referred to his wife, who he told us was a lovely girl, as the 'old ball and chain', and he never asked for a slice of cake, it was always 'Joe Blake'. What's a girl to do? We did know, however, that should he end a sentence with 'dead crafty', we should laugh as he had said something which he thought was amusing.

The heat, combined with the humidity and flies, was quite taxing. We had never sweated so much before. There was certainly no question of 'gently perspiring' as a lady should, it was honest-to-goodness sweat and it just poured off us all day long, leaving us drained and exhausted.

I had been put in charge of the store room with Pat and was going to be shown how to handle the accounts and money arrangements – what a thrill. Why did I always land this task? I was amazed at the amount of stores that we dealt with after leaving Shillong, it quite made the head spin. Here, lemon squash was ordered twice a week and not by the odd dozen, but by the 50 dozen, which made one realise just how many men we were catering for. In addition, Pat took over the running of the kitchen which was turning out hundreds of cakes each day. I hoped that I didn't get landed with that side of it all as it looked horribly complicated. At this time a lot of our stores were coming down by road from Chittagong.

6 May 1944

11.30 p.m. or thereabouts. There was still a lot to record, but so much noise and activity going on outside that my endeavours to write a bit more were somewhat thwarted. A whole crowd of people came into our quarters and we ended up having a picnic supper on the river bank. Somebody had brought along a concertina and there was a lot of sometimes not very melodious singing going on as he played. In addition to this we also had a gramophone and a good selection of records which everyone had pooled.

It was here I heard the hit song 'Paper Doll' by the Mills Brothers for the first time. I thought it was an odd little song; apparently it had held the top chart spot in America for twelve weeks the previous year.

I didn't particularly like eating supper outside as there was too much dust and so many ants crawling about that one didn't really know what one was eating half the time, but as it was only good old bully beef I suppose it didn't really matter much. I was unable to sleep as my legs had been so badly bitten by ants and mosquitoes that the itching drove me mad the moment I got into bed. It was odd they didn't seem to have bitten anybody else, only me. To them I was obviously very tasty fresh blood.

There was great excitement this morning when Antoinette announced that she had received a love letter last night from one of the West African chaps next door. Apparently he had climbed the fence and just 'dropped in'. Fortunately she woke up, yelled at him and he ran off, dropping his letter as he went. It was signed 'your friend Sam'. She never did find out who he was, so her yelling must have well and truly frightened him off as he made no further attempt to contact her.

No family mail since I joined up and I was so wishing and hoping I could receive some post very soon.

7 May 1944

Those pestilential ants: no blasted sleep again last night and my legs and arms were an awful sight, not to mention still itching like mad. I was just hoping they didn't go septic which could so easily happen in the dirty and humid environment in which we were working. Open wounds could turn into painful infected sores quite easily, so I ensured they were kept clean and disinfected as much as possible.

We went to the railway station early this morning to see the KOSBs [King's Own Scottish Borderers] off to their next combat area with cigarettes, tea and wads. Following breakfast we went to the transit camp as usual and later sorted out a new consignment of stores, after which Cecily Lumley, Antoinette and I were desperate for a cold drink, but as always we only managed to find a mockery of one. It was such scorching weather that none of the drinks were particularly thirst-quenching – they were lukewarm and therefore never refreshing.

8 May 1944

First thing I had scheduled this morning was coping with the new *Dhobi* [laundry man], and this before breakfast – I am not my best in the morning. We had been through quite a few unsuccessful ones. However, this one looked as though he might be a good candidate. My Urdu was still atrocious and when I spoke, he merely stared at me with a blank and pretty vacant expression through the most bloodshot pair of eyes I have ever seen. Fingers crossed for success with him.

Uncle Grimes, who had a very rich and rare complexion, dithered around all the morning. He obviously didn't have enough to do to keep him occupied so wandered over to us for a chat. I did wish these people would not come at a time when we were so busy trying to sort out the schedule and stores for the day. They can be a bother but one couldn't really show them the door. I simply must try to be more tolerant and patient, willing to see other people's points of view rather than arguing all the time when I don't agree with someone's opinion.

It was another hectic day. We sold everything we had on board the canteen so had to come back to restock before finishing our rounds. Selling out did give us a very satisfactory sort of feeling as we felt we had accomplished a good day's work and that our presence continued to be needed and appreciated by the soldiers. I spent the rest of the late afternoon and evening with our Sergeant, Cecily, doing the most hated job – sorting sweets. They arrived in 25lb tins and had to be weighed and approximated into quarter pounds, then wrapped up or put into little boxes ready for sale. It was a filthy job as the heat did the sweets no good at all. Invariably they had melted into a glutinous sticky lump and had to be prised apart individually which was an exceptionally messy business. Cecily got the hammer and I had the chisel and between us we managed to get the job done without personal injury. The men loved their sweets and at times when these were not available and we had the necessary ingredients, we taught our local cooks how to make fudge and served this to the weary troops. It always went down very well and was another little comforting treat we could offer them.

In the evening I had a long talk with Pat. She had guessed the situation between Peter and me, and said she was in the same boat and was in a real tizz-wazz over Toby. Men can cause such misery sometimes, poor Pat all choked up and unhappy and me in a twist about Peter. What a pair we were.

12 May 1944

Goody goody, some letters at long last, plus a box of fudge and grand letter from Flags, bless him. Such a treat, he certainly did spoil me whenever he could.

I noticed I hadn't written in my diary for a few days as we had been rather busy seeing off troops, and with so many people turning up in the evenings, there just wasn't the time to catch up. Our new static canteen was now finished and we were due to open the following evening. We had been told it was to be located by the railway station so we expected to be kept pretty busy.

We were paid a terrific compliment last night by Charles Hayes, one of the officers for whom we had thrown a birthday party. He was delighted with our efforts and said that even if he had had a choice of how and where to celebrate, he could not have asked for a better evening. We were all very pleased that the party had gone so well.

I was learning a fair bit about our bookkeeping from Antoinette and I did hope I would make a success of it, move up the ranks and perhaps get a 'stripe'. Once again reminded myself that I must try to be more tolerant and see other people's ways of looking at situations, also be a bit more tactful. The Wasbies have such a good reputation, which is most heart-warming, so I must keep myself in check and keep up the standard.

Another visit from Major Boenisch, a Pole, whom I

had got to know quite well: he came down several times from Chittagong where he was stationed. I did enjoy his company; he was such a nice person with very strong ideals and wise opinions. He visited the static canteen which I was operating in the evenings.

14 May 1944

This morning's question was, 'would breakfast be a soya link meal?' Almost certain to be. They really were the most frightful things and certainly not at all popular with anybody who had been confronted with them, and it was Sunday too, so anything else would have been so much better.

The US Army Air Force P-38 Lightning aircraft, which flew over us continually, did make the most frightful din. We could hardly hear ourselves speak above the noise but as they looked so exciting racing across the sky we could forgive them. I could have watched them for hours. We often wondered just what their mission was and where they were going. However, like everything this was all kept very secret. They were a most distinctive-looking plane with twin engine booms either side of the central nacelle where the pilot was located. We were told that the Japanese referred to them as 'two planes, one pilot' aircraft.

The new static canteen was not to remain open after 7 p.m. as we couldn't cope with the lighting arrangements. It had been hopeless the previous night, just too dim for words with only five lamps, making it impossible to see what we were doing half the time. The paraffin hurricane *butties* we were using were worse than useless and it was all very frustrating after an already long, sweltering day. We were supposed to remain open until 10 p.m. serving both the BORs and the IORs. The latter really were the limit, they were not the least bit appreciative or grateful for anything we did and it made me so very cross. Here I go again, but they seemed to have a 'thing' about women and their place in life – well not me.

15 May 1944

Stopped work very suddenly yesterday hearing screams coming from the direction of the river, so we dropped everything and tore down to the water's edge where we discovered some unfortunate Indian had tried to swim his horse across. It had stumbled and fallen, become frightened and thrown him, kicking him on the head in its panic to find its footing. He had been under the water for some time before they could get him out and in spite of Pat giving him artificial respiration it was too late, poor man. All his own people just stood on the bank and watched, leaving it to us to try to rescue the unfortunate fellow. It was enough to make one's blood boil. Pat ended up having to go to a Court of Inquiry to explain the incident to the 'powers that be'.

At lunch time today Uncle Grimes came along and asked to look at our hands. We wondered whether the Brigadier, who had been inspecting the canteen earlier in the morning, had complained about our grubby hands or use of nail polish which although given to chipping remained, together with lipstick, one of our few feminine indulgences. It was something completely different. We discovered that an officer in Chittagong, who had met one of the Dohazari Wasbies, wanted to take her out and was unable to ask her as he didn't know her name. He had remembered that she wore a sapphire and diamond ring – very observant chap. He had asked Uncle G to find out who she was and it turned out to be me. I did give him a call but he had lost his nerve so that was that.

There were a lot of troops going through Dohazari on their way to Burma, so we were being kept very busy. The static canteen was going great guns and it was always packed. Our arms were so tired with all the lifting of huge kettles to pour out endless mugs of tea. The queues seemed to be never-ending and the light of the hurricane *butties* was so poor that it was difficult to see the colour of the tea, but nobody complained so we assumed all was well.

Pat and I were on duty together that evening; her sparkling personality and pretty blue eyes won her a *kukri* [Gurkha knife] from a most amusing young officer, Rupert Roland, when he came round to the mess for supper before leaving – he ended up missing his train as a result.

17 May 1944

Late again last night. Sometimes I wish we were able to avoid some of the parties. However, without being rude, we can't and today there is a party at the rest camp which Pat Wilcox, Joyce Irwin and I are scheduled to attend. We had agreed between ourselves that one of us should always act as chaperone at social functions. On this occasion it was me which was quite amusing as I was the youngest.

These parties were still so odd to me, soap boxes for seating or the most dilapidated chairs, dusty hurricane *butties*, either hung in a tree or standing on another soap box, and a crowd of strange men with plenty of drink and us few girls. On this particular night we had a batman who had once been a barman and he shook us all a very tasty but pretty atomic sort of cocktail. The only funny incident that night was the plentiful arrangement of dugouts known as 'funk holes' which everybody seemed to disappear down without warning when they wanted a break from the party. These 'funk holes' were normally used if there was an air attack and one had to get under cover quickly.

A very busy day what with covering the hospital and the rest camp followed by checking in the stores, which involved opening and counting the contents of endless boxes of provisions – another loathsome and, in the heat, draining job. However, on the upside, the much-waited-for mangos were now ripe. We had to constantly chase off the monkeys to get our fair share of the fruit but we managed to pick a good supply of the lower-hanging mangoes and made complete pigs of ourselves on these – too delicious for words.

Poor Antoinette, she had received bad news about her son who was apparently very ill and I hoped she would get some compassionate leave to visit him. We could manage without her, despite the busy days which lay ahead of us. Cecily and the rest of the girls were all very good and we worked extremely well as a team.

18 May 1944

Another busy and hot day, cutting hundreds of sandwiches ready for the troop train leaving in the evening. I don't think the aroma of tinned salmon and slightly mouldy army bread will ever be forgotten by any of us. The mess table will clearly never be the same again, its surface having been severely battered by our bread knives.

Thankfully a couple of men from Signals had surpassed themselves with the new lighting arrangements and we were now lit up as if we were on a stage, enabling the canteen to operate successfully after dark. All the sandwiches went like wildfire and the tea only just lasted out that evening. When we were finished we went and spoke to the lads boarding the train and eventually got a community sing-song going, which was grand fun, and the train left with everybody singing loudly. Poor chaps, we felt so sorry for them as there was little for them to look forward to, just the misery of the front line.

Later in the evening we heard a noise and went out to see what it was, only to discover that a couple of the native boats which travelled up and down the river on a daily basis had brought down from the Kaladan region some wounded West African troops and some Indian sepoys. They had no idea where the medical facility was located, so whilst the ambulance we asked for was on its way, we talked to them and gave them tea and cigarettes. Some of them were in pretty bad shape, having been caught up in a nasty battle.

The wounded men had travelled in those mouldy, stuffy little boats for five days and it must have been hell. We probably looked pretty odd to them, as we were all on the river bank overlooking the boat landing wearing our nighties and dressing gowns, having not had time to change and with little idea of what we would find at the riverside. Antoinette, looking rather like Florence Nightingale, was standing on a little hill at the edge of the river holding a Petromax lamp which was the only light we had to work by.

I have to say the garb we were working in was not the most suitable for climbing in and out of those awful little vessels, trying to lift, but ending up dragging, those poor men out of the boats onto the shore. It seemed so dreadful that no one with any authority, medical experience or knowledge of the hospital's location had been available to accompany them, but anyone who might have come had their hands full tending to further casualties at the battle front. All was finally sorted out and they were soon on their way to the medical unit for much-needed treatment at the CCS where the medical staff did their best, not helped by the constant flies, heat and humidity – this, along with 'hospital smells', took a bit of getting used to at first when we visited the men with supplies we were able to provide from the canteen stores.

21 May 1944

Jack and a cocky little MP [Military Policeman] had had a terrific scuffle and as a consequence Jack could hardly see out of one eye and his face was very swollen. Although we had no idea what it was all about it was clear that tensions were running high as a result of their set-to. The men were all tired and under immense pressure and it wasn't surprising they were a little edgy at times.

The predicted monsoon had started at last, and on the dot too. The rain absolutely lashed down in torrents and did all our *bashas* leak! As a result of the heavy rains the dusty roads turned into quagmires, making the mobile vans difficult to operate. With such sodden conditions the heavy vehicles just wallowed like whales in the glutinous mudbaths that the roads had now become. There was mud and flood water simply everywhere and this curtailed most of our mobile operations.

Fleurette Pelly, although very young, was one of the longest-serving Wasbies. She and Pat Boyd came through on their way to Tumbru, stopping for lunch with us, so we were able to catch up on the gossip about Cleve and what the other Wasbies were doing. They also brought along a large box of chocolates, a present from Mrs Taylor. These were delicious and a lovely surprise. Mrs T was such a thoughtful person. Luckily, now that the heat had abated, they had not melted so I suppose the rain did have its merits.

22 May 1944

We had been hard at it for the past few days and were very short-handed. Antoinette obtained permission to go to Darjeeling to see her son, and Elaine Cheverton went back to Manipur and was thrilled about this, but it did leave us rather stretched. There were so many convoys going to and from the combat areas, where ferocious battles were being fought with an awfully large number of casualties on both sides.

Late again last night. Gordon and Chris the culprits once more, they always stayed so long. They did seem to love talking, and as so often happened, the conversation turned into a psychoanalysis, which was interesting but it did get embarrassing at times. However, it was better than endlessly discussing the war.

Gay Tucker arrived the day before yesterday and was to stay until Antoinette came back from compassionate leave. Cecily was supposed to go to Chittagong; she hated the idea and I didn't blame her as our little 'happy family' was getting split up. Maybe it was a good idea not to get too attached to the same people. I didn't know. I felt it just made things much easier when we all got on well. It was sad to be parting. We had gone through a great deal together, all giving each other so much support when things became difficult or uncomfortable.

Heard last night that Peter would be coming down this way. I wondered whether it was a good thing or not. I felt like running away from it all but it would not help and would only drag things on. Anyway, although I was afraid that there was a packet of hurt coming to me, I had to accept it. I just wished I didn't still care for him so much … ah well, what was the use?

Took the mobile canteen to the gun sites round the airstrip today. The chaps were as always so cheerful and pleased to see us. We loved it when it was their turn to be visited, but what a soul-destroying and boring job it must have been for them, especially as there was no excitement at that time with the airstrip closed because of the monsoon rains.

However, on this occasion one man infuriated us somewhat as he managed to diddle us out of four rupees which we didn't pick up on until we had left.

Jack got very upset when we drove past the American camp where we saw one of their lads having a wash 'in the altogether', completely oblivious to the fact that three ladies were driving by. It shocked Jack so much that he nearly steered us into the ditch with his startled remarks of, 'Look, t'aint right 'ow 'e's washing on the roadside like that, it's no' proper', and, 'Wouldn't like me missus to see 'im.' Jack looked and sounded so indignant which merely sent us into paroxysms of helpless laughter. Poor Jack, he was so 'proper' and he did try very hard to protect us from anything which he felt was 'not for the ladies'! Despite Jack's indignation, we girls never failed to be impressed that the men managed to retain an element of pride in their appearance and, after returning from a battle, took the first opportunity to wash, shave and attend to their battle kit.

24 May 1944

Big mail today which was marvellous, almost the first letters I had received in any great number since leaving Cleve. It was, however, difficult to answer these as we were constantly being told that we must say nothing about our work and where we were or what we were doing. Rain continued pouring down so the mobile canteens were still unable to get along the roads. The vans were so un-roadworthy when it was wet. This gave me plenty of time to read and enjoy my letters in peace and quiet, whilst eating and savouring some of the remaining ripe mangoes.

Heard that some East African troops had arrived so rushed off to see who was there, only to find that on this occasion it was actually the West Africans. I spent the rest of the day counting money ready for stock-taking on Wednesday.

Once more Major Boenisch turned up from Chittagong and stayed for dinner which again, was an unexpected but very pleasant surprise for us all.

28 May 1944

Antoinette arrived back with a horrible cold and looked simply awful, so worried about her sick child and her husband's injuries which he had sustained whilst fighting in the north.

We had a rather frightful dinner party with the RAF lads the night before they left. They were most ill-mannered and drank all Gay Tucker's whisky ration which annoyed us. Still, they had been in combat for some time so perhaps in the euphoria of being back at camp for a few days they had forgotten their manners. Added to their strange behaviour they then wouldn't leave the mess until after 2.30 in the morning by which time we were quite exhausted, not helped by the fact that we had to get up at 6 a.m. or earlier, with long days ahead of us. One of the group was moderately funny when he made a joke then tried to imitate a hen laying an egg, but after about the tenth time it ceased to be amusing.

1 June 1944

Pat and I operated the canteen at the railway station for the RAF departure the next night until after midnight. What with the rain and shortage of wood, it was pretty difficult to keep the fire going to boil sufficient water for tea. However, with the help of the MTO [Motor Transport Office] staff, who were wonderful, we managed to keep going.

After the RAF train left, we were told another troop train was due in at 3 a.m. but needless to say it was late and didn't arrive until 4.30 a.m. This time the train was carrying a large number of East African troops, approximately 800 of them; anyway it was estimated that about 800 cups of tea were doled out.

It was a lovely surprise when up popped Willie Spur, an old family friend, together with a number of other East African people that I knew. It must have really shaken some of them to see me operating the canteen, as they had absolutely no idea I was there.

How everything lasted that night and how the water ever boiled in large enough quantities is still amazing, as we only had a few little camp kettles and a small petrol drum of hot water into which we kept dipping our jugs in an endeavour to fill the endless queuing mugs. It was a miracle how we managed until 6.30 a.m. when the water cart finally ran dry and it started to pour with rain yet again.

Back at 'home' we gave succour to some recently arrived wounded African and Burmese troops. Thankfully the little local boats they travelled in were unloaded before the rain came down, although there were no ambulances or doctors to take care of them as they disembarked. Some of the Africans were so thrilled to discover I spoke Swahili and had come from East Africa, so we ended up having a long natter together about Kenya and the days before the war. Later I went down to the hospital to see Willie to take him some of the bits and pieces he had asked for – razor blades, soap, toothpaste and the like. I also took a couple of the newspapers with which we were regularly supplied. Although a few days out of date the news was still of great interest to us and I liked to try and keep track of the whereabouts of Peter's regiment. Despite our strained relationship I continued to worry about his safety.

The more I thought about it the more apprehensive I was getting about Peter's impending arrival. What would his reaction be? The cat would be out of the bag as to where I was and what I was doing and that I had not in fact gone home as he had requested. Then, dear God, give me strength enough to deal with the situation without making a fool of myself and matters worse than they already were. Would our relationship be helped by him knowing what I was doing out here or would it make matters worse between us? He had expected me to go back home to Kenya. God, what fun our life could have been had we not been estranged. I still wondered what I did wrong; the sheer doting I suppose, or maybe he felt I was too dull. I shall never know, but it did not stop me wondering and wishing things would get back to the way they were before the war.

15 August 1944

It has been weeks since writing in my diary. Things became so difficult and we were terribly busy in Dohazari, with vast numbers of troop movements to cater for on a daily basis. I just couldn't write as I was far too tired, and really had no time or inclination to do so. One day was much the same as the next – long, hot and busy. At night we all just fell into bed completely exhausted, with throbbing feet having been on them all day.

We met trains every night, running our static canteen and the mobiles as well. How we did it with only five of us I just don't know. No sooner had trains stopped coming in than they started going out again, moving the troops who had just arrived on to other locations after a bit of R&R.

Some of the girls had to have their hands dressed by the medics because they developed so many blisters from cutting sandwiches and opening tins, and in the heat and filth in which we operated, these often ended up going septic. We met huge numbers of battle-weary troops coming in with harrowing stories of the jungle and mountain warfare they had faced trying to push the Japanese out of Burma and northern India. Some of the men hadn't eaten for twelve hours or more and were very fatigued and hungry on their arrival. They were clearly so extremely grateful and appreciative of our efforts that it made our toil even more worthwhile, and our exhaustion of the previous day was quickly forgotten each morning when we started all over again.

We also had to go up river to the East Africa camp twice a week, which was terrific fun in spite of the enormous additional workload. All the stores had to be packed the night before, ready to stow on the boats early in the morning to ferry us up river. This took an hour or more. On arrival we had to unload and reload everything into Jeeps ready to drive five miles inland, only to have to haul all the supplies off again, stacking them into tents before selling until there was nothing left. We never had enough stuff and we never got back until dusk; our takings were terrific and it was grand, especially for me as I knew so many of the men.

One day I met, walking down the road, the *Askari* [African guard] who had been Peter's orderly in Abyssinia and he greeted me like a long-lost friend, congratulating me on becoming a corporal like himself and for having joined what he thought was the KAR [King's African Rifles]. I didn't try to explain what I did as he was just so pleased to see me and actually it didn't really matter what he thought I was doing. His delight at meeting me was rather touching.

It was here that Peter and I finally met up by chance. At the time I was not aware that he had arrived, and one day when I was handing out tea from the mobile canteen I looked up to talk to the next chap in the queue and it was Peter. Naturally he was astonished to find me there and later on a lot of explanations and discussions took place relative to our relationship and why I had not gone home. Sadly, his presence did not make for an easy time. It became clear that our marriage really was over, although Peter continually refused to be specific as to his reasons for leaving me. I was left feeling even more bewildered, hurt and upset and still none the wiser as to what had really caused the breakdown of our marriage. I have to say that being as busy as we were helped me cope: moping around was just out of the question – there was far too much to do.

At one stage in early August, the monsoon rains came down with spectacular violence, raising the water level of the river over thirty feet in a 48-hour period, leaving the main traffic bridge in danger of being washed away. The river was a mass of swirling debris with bodies of dead animals and drowned natives, tangled with torn-down trees and wreckage from their fragile homes. They were probably caught unawares and were unable to escape. They would have been quickly swept away by the raging torrent which was leaving such havoc in its wake. It was very upsetting to see, but we ourselves were in such a state of high alert that we didn't have time to dwell on the dreadful plight of those poor people, many of whom probably couldn't swim. We did, however, manage to go out with a mobile canteen to serve hot tea, laced with rum, to the West African troops who were called in to clear away the mass of detritus from around the bridge supports. They were soaked to the skin and a hot drink was the least we could offer them whilst they undertook yet another dangerous task.

As the day passed and darkness set in, the water level still crept slowly higher towards our mess so we were told to pack up our stores and equipment and be ready to evacuate at short notice – all this by the light of hurricane lamps. Thankfully, by dawn the rain had eased and the river had started to subside, with immediate danger over. However, the bridge did give way which meant we then had to get our supplies ferried across the river in local boats and on rafts.

It was whilst we were hard at it in Dohazari that I met up with and got chatting to George Kinnear, a war correspondent for *The Times*, who had originally been based in Nairobi. He had been travelling through Burma and had pitched up at the back of our canteen, weary and bedraggled after a long, wet and exhausting journey from Burma to the Bengal railhead at Dohazari where we were running our canteen. Whilst listening to his tales of what was going on in the war zone, I recounted the story of meeting up with a very shocked Peter, also mentioning the hair-raising night of the flood, about which he wrote a column for his paper.

The piece he wrote about the Wasbies was most touching: he described how his world was wet and gloomy until somebody said there was a Wasbie canteen in the *basha* near the railway track. So he set out to find us and wrote:

There, placid and unruffled, surrounded by a swarming mass of British Tommies, were girls, real genuine white girls, handing out steaming tea in mugs with wads of cake and a smile. And among them, strangest thing of all, was a girl from Kenya, from Nanyuki no less! Mrs Peter Pilbrow, one of the Holford-Walker girls. Thereby hangs a more than ordinarily interesting tale. Peter Pilbrow is a Major with the East African Force which had been sent to Ceylon, and months ago had been at Training College in India where he was joined by his wife. After returning to his unit, she became a TWA [Temporary Woman Assistant] with the Navy in Bombay or somewhere else. Then in about March or April this year she joined the Wasbies and was posted to Dohazari where, one day, a tired officer stepped from the train and she gave him a cup of tea. Just like that. Neither knew the other was anywhere near.

He wasn't aware, of course, that at the time Peter and I were in the throes of a marriage breakdown.

The article went on to recount the story of the flood and how Pat had struggled with the heavy awkward case containing the blasted soya link sausages. How she struggled and struggled to get it nailed up and to high ground, stating that next to the cashbox the infernal sausage was given the tenderest regard. When Kinnear looked at Pat reproachfully on behalf of the whole Fourteenth Army, she replied: 'Yes I know, but it was stock, and we had to save everything we could.' 'Me,' he said, 'I would have let the darned thing drown!' The notoriety of the soya link sausage spread even more after it featured in his article. George, along with the rest of us, had been subjected to this rather unpleasant 'delicacy' on his travels through Burma and could not believe the trouble we had gone to in trying to save it from being swept away in the flood waters.

I can't imagine the reaction of my family if they had picked up the paper in Kenya and read this piece!

After the drama of the flood our work slackened down enormously and during the remaining monsoon season we read or alternatively wrote long-overdue letters from the static canteen area. The mobiles hardly ever went out, as they were impossible to drive on the muddy roads which were now almost impassable. If we tried, we ended up getting stuck. We then had to get hauled out by vehicles which were needed for more important duties and they themselves found it equally difficult to cope with the road in such appallingly muddy conditions.

In spite of my personal turmoil during this period my spirits were lifted a little by some of the fun parties that took place. But, like so many things, our time in Dohazari came to an end with the almost complete collapse of our Wasbie team. Some went on leave, some were taken ill and on one famous day I was the only Wasbie available to open the static canteen in time for the outgoing troops. As far as I can remember, they got bully beef stew that night for supper. Poor Pat was in bed with a bad mastoid [ear infection] and I felt near to breaking point myself.

A few of the girls went back up to Chittagong, others to Cox's or Shillong. This brings me to one amusing incident when some of the girls were leaving. We had been issued with a batch of hens to produce fresh eggs for the mess whilst we were in Dohazari, and when they stopped laying the unfortunate creatures had been handed over to the cooks. However, one of the girls – a bit of an animal lover – was not having this and nurtured and protected one of the birds which subsequently started to lay again. When she was transferred up to Chittagong she insisted it went with her, so it was crated up and relocated along with the Wasbie team.

For me personally a lot of water passed under the bridge during this period, all far too painful and personal to write about.

4 September 1944

I moved up to Cox's Bazaar on the coast for six weeks, and what a hectic six weeks that was. The eggs went rotten, the butter rancid and most of the other fresh stores perished rapidly due to the extreme heat. Although the high temperature and humidity continued to sap our energy, we coped with the endless troops coming through from the Arakan Region and once again worked long days at a flat-out rate. We had the usual problem of poor lighting and insufficient lamps at night. It was a very trying period to say the least. However, our efforts were worthwhile, and it was in a way enjoyable in spite of the difficulties. Once again I felt the girls coped cheerfully and did a great job.

3 October 1944

After my assignments in Dohazari and Cox's I was sent up to Shillong for three weeks as I was so exhausted and needed to get away from the debilitating coastal climate for a while, but we seemed to work even harder, with hundreds of troops up there.

The journey back up north was quite one of the worst we would ever have to encounter. It was usually a 24-hour trip between Chittagong and Shillong but this time it took 48 hours, on a goods train in a third-class carriage with no food and no water. Every station we came to we all hopped out, ever-hopeful of finding some form of sustenance, only to find that there had been a troop train through before us and they had polished off every bit of available food. We finally arrived in Shillong at 3.30 in the morning, then had to hang around until we were picked up by Jeep at 7.00 a.m. I don't think I had ever been so tired or hungry.

There were two canteens operating in Shillong, a mobile and a large static which was allocated to me to manage. From this we dished up hot meals for the men as well as serving tea, cake and sandwiches and sundry other essentials and personal bits and pieces which the men were in need of.

The climate was miles more tolerable with less heat and humidity than Cox's; such a relief, and so much less draining to work in. Unfortunately, I did not find the girl I was teamed up with very easy to work alongside, so had to try hard to be tactful and tolerant knowing it was not going to be for any length of time. The exception to this somewhat tricky period, and my saving grace, was my ability to go out riding, which I was able to do early every morning before breakfast with an Australian officer who was nice enough to let me ride the better of the two horses he had borrowed for us. My heart really warmed to him. He was a devastatingly attractive man and certainly lifted my flagging spirits enormously!

2 November 1944

Shortly before leaving Shillong and returning to Cox's Bazaar again, I received my sergeant's stripes with the promise of a commission very soon. I ran No.14 Canteen in Cox's for ten days only. I was then promoted to Second

Lieutenant and was sent back to Shillong to prepare for a flight to Burma, which was to be my new and more permanent posting. The British forces had now switched from defence to attack against the Japanese in the Northern Shan State of Burma, and we were to be attached to the 36th Division.

This British Division comprised 29th and 72nd Brigades, and although under American command, the Division was led by Major General Francis W. Festing, DSO. 'Front Line Frankie' Festing was a giant of a man, not only in stature but also as commander of his men, who were all extremely proud to serve under his leadership, and it wasn't long before we learnt that he and his troops were greatly feared by the Japanese.

'Front Line Frankie': Major General Francis Wogan Festing.

PART FOUR

Women's Auxiliary Services (Burma)

Northern Burma – 36th Division
1944–1945

20 December 1944

I received my commission and, on 18 December 1944, full of excitement, journeyed back to Shillong from Cox's via Chittagong. I was heading up a team of my own and we were going to be flown into the north of Burma. Everything was very rushed and hectic as I was given about twelve hours notice and only just managed to catch the train in time from Chitters, with literally a few minutes to spare.

I had the good luck to travel on the same train as an Australian mission group this time. They told me they were touring the battle grounds and what I would have done without them I just don't know, as VIP treatment had been laid on for their journey and I felt very privileged to be asked to accompany them. They were not only extremely kind and generous in letting me travel on their special train, but they also gave me a lift up from Sylhet in their private cars and provided me with a meal prior to eventually dropping me off at Cleve twelve hours earlier than if I had wrestled alone with the usual mode of transport. They later sent me a wire at Christmas, bless them.

My team and I spent a hectic two days sorting the stores and equipment which were to be flown into Burma with us, in addition to which we purchased a number of *lungis* for the Burmese. These were to represent payment and gifts in case the local people would not accept money for any help they extended to us. Eventually we set off on 20 December, at the ungodly hour of five in the morning – Mrs Taylor, who was overseeing our trip and would stay with us until we were settled in and running smoothly, plus three other girls, and me.

Our attachment to the 36th Division was a great moment for us and must have been an even greater one for Mrs Taylor, as it was only recently that the Wasbies had been permitted to be attached to a Division instead of operating in the usual Line of Command sub-area. Even more of a thrill was that we were to be amongst the first women, and only the second loaded plane, to land at the newly repaired Indaw airstrip in northern Burma which had only very recently been made serviceable by the Americans.

We drove from Shillong to Moran, an all-day drive, calling in at Jorhat to collect the fourth member of my team, Barbara Williamson. There was a visible tightening of lips when she floated out wearing a cowboy hat and leading a cat attached to a bit of string which, clearly terrified and wide-eyed, persisted in meowing plaintively and incessantly, poor little thing. That was not all. There was a tame duck as well. However, that was jettisoned very rapidly and was probably eaten for Christmas dinner by the people that she had spent the day with whilst waiting for us to pick her up. I sincerely hoped that they enjoyed their feast. The bird really was the limit. However, in spite of the livestock situation Barbara really was a dear girl. She was very young, extremely pretty and fun-loving, with a radiant smile.

We spent that night in a tea planter's home at Moran. It was such heaven to be in a civilised house with a proper bath, and warm cosy fires. We were well aware that we had to make the most of this comfort as we knew that the time ahead of us would probably be pretty rough, not to mention somewhat primitive.

The following day we boarded a US Army Air Force DC-3 Dakota accompanied by our camp kit and supplies, taking off at 12.30 p.m. having hung about the airstrip for hours. What a party: Mrs T, myself, Vivian Wynn who knew the area, Bubbles Clayton and Barbara, accompanied by her cat, which for some reason we all accepted, Mrs T included. It was the first time that the majority of the girls, including me, had been on a Dakota. It had been an early and cold start, followed by hours of waiting with endless cups of hot tea at Moran airstrip before we eventually climbed on board the aeroplane, destined for Burma, the land of spectacular temples and pagodas.

The flight itself was uneventful. It was a noisy, hot and uncomfortable trip, but we found it interesting to look down on the thick forests and mountain ranges below. Scattered around we noticed glider wreckage, a reminder of the recent battles fought by the Allied Special Force, the Chindits. As we neared our destination the plane circled round and round and my eyes felt they were getting more and more kaleidoscopic. My head ached and I felt nauseous which was probably due to the fact that this type of plane was prone to yawing which could be rather sick-making. I looked at the others who were all a shade of pea-green, so honour was suitably satisfied.

It was a marvellous experience for all of us, especially for Vivian who used to work as a missionary in the district in which we were to land. Although we were all very excited, there was a certain amount of apprehension as well. This time, being attached to a Divisional HQ, we were going to move forward with the troops as they battled south over a distance of around 550 miles in an endeavour to liberate Mandalay, the beautiful ancient capital and religious heart of Burma, en route to Rangoon.

We had on the plane with us dozens of crates of equipment and stores for the canteens we were going to open up, plus of course we had the infernal cat which Barbara absolutely insisted she brought along with her. It nearly went apoplectic during the flight, probably due to the constant loud drone of the two propeller-driven engines. Poor animal, it must have been petrified. This was the first of a number of flights it undertook with us.

We finally landed very precisely on the minutest of airstrips. The doors of the plane were thrown open, an American soldier approached and asked, 'What cargo do you have on board?' and when a slightly dazed and still quite queasy bevy of jungle-green-clad girls stepped gingerly to the ground, laden with haversacks and tin hats, we were met with whistles and exclamations of, 'Gee, what a cargo: women!' Apparently we were indeed some of the first, and certainly unexpected, women the Americans had seen for some time.

We were piled into a Jeep, driven by a vague and rather harassed-looking officer, who had been designated to collect us. Following closely behind was a 15cwt truck with our baggage and supplies, plus the three servants we had brought along with us to help out in the kitchen. We were all driven to a dilapidated building where we were to spend our first night.

Our initial experience in the field was on the way to the main camp area, when we stopped at a clearing on the side of the road where there was a small encampment of men. We chatted and shared a cup of tea with them, before inspecting their dinner which was in the process of being cooked. I have to say it looked and smelt jolly good too, bearing in mind their surroundings and lack of facilities.

It was quite a pleasant drive through forest along the usual dusty road, if you could call it that – it was more of a track really. Unfortunately, we were behind an escort truck which smothered us with billowing clouds of dust. The roadway was at least a foot deep in powdery red earth, and by the time we arrived we were all filthy. I would have defied even my own mother to have recognised me under that coating of dirt.

During the drive we all got stuck one by one in a small *donga* [ditch], and the already extraordinary day was made even more unusual when a ragged rather pathetic-looking little Burman excitedly rushed up to Vivian with a beaming smile on his face, calling out, 'Mama Wynn, Mama Wynn.' He had recognised her from her missionary days in Indaw some years previous to the evacuation. It was very moving to see the tremendous joy and pleasure with which he greeted her. Thereafter, whenever we drove through any of the small villages in the area, some of the local folk who came out to meet us also recognised her and were thrilled to see her again.

The local Burmese had had a very hard time of it following the Japanese invasion and were finding things extremely difficult. They couldn't get seed to start planting their fields again, food was in short supply and there was very little in the way of material for clothing. The town of Indaw was just a splattered mess of bombed buildings and tattered remains of wooden houses, following the American and British action to oust the Japanese. It was in fact difficult to believe that there had ever been a large town there at all. The area had taken such a tremendous pounding.

We spent the night in the small three-roomed house which had been allotted for our use. It had been one of Gay Tucker's little homes prior to the Japanese occupation, and was where the No.12 team of girls had first stayed when they arrived shortly before us. They had already moved on to Katha where we were to meet up with them, working together as two teams. We dined at 'A' Mess where I bumped into a man whom I had met in Quetta when spending time with Peter at Staff Training College, and he updated me on all the news from there. It was a large, and I thought, rather formal dinner, but then we didn't know most of the people and the circumstances in which we now found ourselves, attached to an actual Division, was a new experience for us.

The night was not very comfortable as we had to sleep on the floor with mice or probably worse – rats – scuffling and scratching around the rooms intending, no doubt, to nibble at anything which took their fancy: certainly a very disconcerting feeling. Vivian had ideas that there were snakes as well, so I was kept up most of the night popping into her room to check she was alright, aware that when I got off my sleeping mat I could have been stepping on all sorts of unpleasant creatures.

Katha – 22 December 1944

Today we were driven down to Katha on the banks of the Irrawaddy River: a long, dirty and dusty journey through more beautiful forest thick with tall paddle-leaved teak trees and pretty yellow flowering rosewoods. We were astonished by the width of the river, reputed to be at least a mile across, with strong and swirling currents. It was here where we were to open our first canteen. Katha itself seemed relatively unscathed, and surprisingly offered an assortment of much needed fresh produce.

A quite nightmarish few days followed our arrival. It still seems a dream to me. We arrived there at eleven o'clock in the morning and looked around the large empty shell-splintered building in which we were to live. It was a wooden construction which might once have been a school. Our stores and kitchen equipment were unloaded and we faced the daunting task of getting everything operational as quickly as possible.

However, prior to sorting any of our kit, we had to wash and scrub the place down, as it was absolutely filthy. Armed with brushes, soap and water, we got down to it with gusto, chatting and laughing, cursing the odd broken fingernail, ending up none too clean ourselves. Having accomplished this, we set about gathering a motley collection of tables, chairs and benches, which we found in the shelled remains of houses in the vicinity of the camp, most of which contained very little in the way of intact furniture. The final touch was to hang curtains of bright red and yellow cotton material which we had also managed to find in one of the houses, in an endeavour to make the Mess look as festive as we could. We were now ready for our final task of unpacking hundreds of mugs, plates, knives, forks and spoons, after which we collected firewood for the new ovens which had been built for us by one of the Field Regiments stationed in Katha. The ovens were constructed from empty ammunition boxes and a length of pipe, with mud taking the place of bricks. These were then lit and stoked, ready to be tried out by the very harassed cook and his small staff.

In preparation for dinner the ghastly job of opening countless tins of foodstuff began. We had been briefed that we would be catering for at least 500 men, all of whom were expecting to go straight into action and were eagerly anticipating a pre-Christmas supper on our first day. So we ploughed on regardless of our appearance; hair all over our faces, hands I regret to say filthy, all semblance of cleanliness gone. Case after case of tinned sausages, bacon, garden peas and baked beans had to be opened, followed by dozens of boxes containing tinned fruit which was to be served with condensed or evaporated milk for pudding. The meal was to be rounded off with hot cocoa instead of after-dinner coffee.

The cook, poor man, with a very troubled look on his face, got to work and the canteen opened up at six o'clock, but with no cashbox. I have yet to discover how the girls coped with the money situation. I personally was past worrying about that, either deep in cooking or making what seemed to me like hundreds of gallons of cocoa. Then, dear God, we were faced with the washing up. Had it not been for the help received from a couple of orderlies from the MDS [Main Dressing Station] next door, I felt our girls would have been found dead to the world amidst a pile of filthy, greasy plates and mugs. This was another occasion when some of the girls had to have their hands dressed by the medics because they were so badly blistered and cut as a result of opening all those tins.

Never ever shall I forget that first evening, and neither will the rest of the team – we were all feeling more than a little battered, finally finishing up at eleven o'clock that night and falling thankfully into our camp beds exhausted but happy. Our accommodation was pretty chaotic, our beds and nets having been put up in a hurry by one of the girls who had managed to grab a few moments to do it in between the unpacking etc. But we didn't care, it was a bed and we could finally put our feet up. The men had been fed, we had accomplished our first task and actually we were jolly pleased we were able to cope so well.

23 December 1944

Day dawned next morning and I can't say the challenges ahead concerned us overly, even though there was so much to do and so few of us to do it. We managed to keep our canteen open with 'char and wads' throughout the day, and the girls got down to opening up a little shop with CBID [Canteen Bulk Issues Depot] provisions.

I went round to the supply point and organised the evening meal for the Officers' Mess, and as far as I remember it was chops. It was almost too much to cope with after all that had happened the previous day. However, the worst was yet to come when dinner arrived in the form of a live pig. Our faces must have looked a picture, and eventually two BORs were thankfully sent round to deal with it. I nearly fainted when to my horror the animal was then returned to us in an un-butchered state. The cooks hadn't got a clue how to cope with it, so nothing daunted and armed with a huge carving knife and a cleaver, I proceeded with the dastardly deed of making ribs into chops in what might be described as anything but an expert manner.

Everyone thoroughly enjoyed their meal which was accompanied by a lot of beer and whisky. During dinner we heard that when the pig was 'dropped' from the supply plane, its basket had broken and it had rushed off into the forest and had to be found and caught. One of the Christmas turkey baskets hadn't landed so well either, and one of the birds broke out, disappearing into the undergrowth with its parachute and broken basket trailing behind it.

At this point most of our food supplies were to be dropped by parachute from supply planes, flown by the Americans, as there was no method of overland transportation. Prior to the Division's arrival at Indaw, an improvised system had been devised for the transportation of men, food supplies, equipment and ammunition, using adapted Jeeps with flanged wheels which could run on the unused rail tracks: the rolling stock itself having been destroyed by the Japs.

Christmas Eve 1944

It was lovely that everybody seemed to be getting into a festive mood in spite of being closer than ever to the front line. Most touching of all I think was the midnight service held in a very small and almost completely derelict church, in amongst some Buddhist stupas many of which

Improvised 'Jeep Train' with Jeeps adapted to run on the railway in areas where there were no roads. © Soldiers of Gloucestershire Museum Image No. 5915.8.

remained remarkably intact. The atmosphere is hard to explain, but somehow the candles which had been attached to the walls to illuminate the church did much to enhance the occasion. Their flickering glow gave out such a real feeling of Christmas whilst we sang carols and listened to the padre's sermon. Despite the cold and the bitter wind coming through the broken windows and holes in the shelled church walls, few of us came out with a dry eye. There was something so infinitely ethereal and sacred in that little church, and the simple service somehow brought home the promise and hope of goodness and peace to come to a world currently so ravaged by war.

Christmas Day 1944

This was another of those days we would always remember. Festivities started for us at nine o'clock in the morning when one of the mess sergeants came round laden with beer, an offer which indeed could not be refused, and from then on we never looked back, Mrs Taylor included. One thing just led to another. It amazes me still to think of the amount of drink there was for the troops, not to mention cakes, puddings, mincemeat and nuts to supplement the usual banana crisps. The stores people really did a grand job with these special Christmas supplies.

We all went to a party at Brigade HQ where considerable amounts of sherry and gin were consumed, and it was there that I received my most prized possession, a yellow parachute-silk scarf given to me by the Brigadier. It has since been worn on many occasions. One of the officers turned up wearing a turban and looked so much the part of an IOR that we were initially quite foxed as to who it was.

Later that morning, and with great sadness, we bade farewell to Mrs Taylor who had to return to Wasbie HQ in India, after which there followed a slightly drunken trip across the Irrawaddy River, headed up by Colonel Mackenzie-Kennedy of the 1st Royal Scots. We paddled ourselves across in a small local boat and the greeting and cheers we received the other side made us feel so proud to be there. The officers took us to their mess for drinks and then the sergeants came in force and collared us. We were offered the most marvellous assortment of yet more booze: gin, rum, whisky and sherry, some being swigged straight out of the bottle. Very merry indeed, we crossed back over the river again where some of the girls went on to another sergeants' party, whilst the static canteen was opened by a tipsy me, and was understandably extremely busy.

The rations which had been air-dropped specially for Christmas were so good that we were able to prepare a wonderful festive dinner for everyone, so much so that in the end all they could do was sit and stare at the still laden tables. They just couldn't manage to eat everything the cooks had produced.

Another amusing incident I remember, in addition to the turkey and pig event, was when the two Christmas geese and three ducks, provided by the Ration Sergeant, were found swimming peacefully and serenely on our drinking water tank doing I know not what in the water! I can't recall them being eaten, but feel sure they must have been as they were certainly far too tasty a morsel to be left at large.

The day ended with a shrill scream. My bandeau, which was part of our uniform, had been triumphantly seized by an over-enthusiastic Burman to clean the frying pans. I was furious, but later saw the funny side although it was never the same again and I had to somehow get a new one.

So ended our first Christmas in Burma. What a Christmas. What fun.

No.12 Canteen girls, Gay, Fleurette, Cecily and Janet, who had a springer spaniel called Nell, turned up a few days later and the house was just bedlam, but it was great to catch up with them all before Fleurette, Cecily and Vivian left for a short break in Calcutta, leaving Janet in bed with a horrible-looking carbuncle on her hand, poor girl. However, her husband Jim had arrived and was staying for a while which was good news for her. We now had a cat and a dog.

15 January 1945

The mail plane arrived today with a letter from Peter finally confirming that he wanted a divorce. I've really had it with him and just hope the formalities will all be over quietly and without any more hurt, although I have no idea how, when or where these will take place. What an awful blow it will be to the parents. Myself …? Well, at the moment I'm numbed, and don't feel much, although I suppose I knew it would come to this. I had a vague idea of going to Kenya on leave – I shall have to take some soon, I know, as things are getting me down. On the other hand, the Wasbie team had only just arrived here and I really wanted to take full advantage of this new opportunity. I decided the best thing to do was pull myself together, not dwell on the situation and stay on with my team. We were having great fun and were being kept so busy that I really didn't have time to fret over something which was beyond my control.

17 January 1945

My birthday tomorrow: 28 – what an age! I have to say there are times when I feel much younger. Barbara's boyfriend, Bill, has given us a delicious recipe for a drink called a 'Tom and Jerry'. The girls had it the other night and said it was marvellous so we were about to give it another tasting, in spite of the fact that it did entail using a large proportion of our egg ration. Recipe as follows:

1. Separate yolks from whites of 10 fresh eggs
2. Beat yolks adding sugar until a thick creamy consistency is obtained
3. Whip whites and fold lightly into the above mixture
4. Fill half a container with the mixture, add a jigger of rum and top up with boiling water, stirring continually
5. Finally add a sprinkle of nutmeg over the top and serve.

18 January 1945

My birthday! How odd to be celebrating it out here in the jungle, although I must say everyone has been terrifically kind and I was woken up by a bottle of gin being placed on my pillow; a present from young Barbara, bless her. I did wonder where the child got it from.

What a lovely day, everybody was so generous with masses of little presents dropped in for me. Spent the morning helping Barbara make a chocolate birthday cake, which she insisted on baking herself. There was even a rumour that there were also going to be some candles on it, although goodness only knows where they would be found.

I went for a walk to the airstrip in the evening with Fleurette, who had returned from her brief leave and was now based with us permanently. It was lovely to take a short stroll, having spent most of the day busy in the canteen. Whilst walking we noticed a leaflet lying on the ground. It turned out to be a piece of propaganda from His Majesty's Government assuring the local people that the British would understand if, as a means of protecting their lives, some pretence of cooperation had been needed with the enemy in civil matters.

We met up with some of the girls who had worked at the airstrip during the day, helping with the men who were due to be flown down to join 29th Brigade at a time when they were so badly in need of reinforcements. It was a slow job to transfer the men as it was done by the little Stinson L5 Sentinels, or as we called them, 'Jeep Planes', which carried only a couple of passengers at a time. These little aeroplanes could literally 'land on a postage stamp' so were very well suited to the job here in Burma where they had to use the short, rough improvised airstrips which were hacked into the jungle by the men as they moved forward. On return trips the planes brought back casualties from the front line, dropped them off and turned straight round, time and time again. Often the American pilots who flew these little aircraft used to come and have drinks with us of an evening. They did a phenomenal amount of flying hours, returning exhausted at the end of the day.

It was during our walk that Fleurette was caught with her pants down, literally, and had to go rushing off into the undergrowth at great speed when a GI appeared unexpectedly and out of the blue, finding her in a rather compromising situation. Naturally as she hastily disappeared for cover, she was followed by lots of loud and hysterical laughter. It was the subject of great amusement for all who witnessed it, leaving poor Fleurette very embarrassed.

We had a proper ENSA [Entertainment National Services Association] show scheduled in the evening with Nan Kenway and Douglas Young, who were known simply as 'Kenway and Young'. It was a tremendously entertaining performance, greatly enjoyed by everyone who managed to attend. Because of the incessant heat most of the men, as usual, were shirtless and the girls were all very envious. It was fun to be treated to a show with professional entertainers. Nan Kenway was a giggle; she had a terrific bubbly personality, taking our basic camp facilities in her stride. She amused us all by quite unperturbedly washing and setting her hair in the sitting room of our basic accommodation. A crowd of admirers watched her put it up in pins, with bags of good advice and laughter being bandied around.

The entertainment was held on a makeshift stage in a clearing near the Toc H canteen. We watched the show with Bill, Gee and a few of the other chaps we had got to know well. After the show we all went across to the Toc H building where we provided tea for everybody and the birthday cake was duly brought in 'alight'. What fun, all done by Barbara, such a truly thoughtful young girl. Of course the cake was insufficient for everyone to have a slice so we served up all the leftover canteen cakes and sandwiches, not giving too much thought as to what we would start the canteen up with in the morning.

A typical mess tent, complete with Nell the springer spaniel. Courtesy British Library Ref. 9059c33.

Nan Kenway and Douglas Young performing for ENSA in January 1945 at Katha, Burma. © Soldiers of Gloucestershire Museum Image No. 59152.

The party was very amusing, made even more so by an air raid warning going off in the middle of it. We all sat dead still, although one unfortunate lad got an uncontrollable attack of the jitters and jumped clean out of a window, which was no mean feat as he was on the second floor, but he didn't seem to hurt himself. Fortunately an attack did not materialise and the celebrations went on. After the tea party, we all went over to the mess and ended up in very high spirits. Nan and Douglas stayed on with us and we thoroughly enjoyed having them. They were as amused as we were when a rather less professional item of entertainment arrived in the form of a poem written by a member of the 10th Gloucesters. We were only sorry when Nan and Douglas had to leave. It was such a thrill for everyone and of course it absolutely made my birthday. The poem read as follows:

> *To the WAS(B)*
> *Now this 'ere canteen a short way up the road,*
> *Is run by the Wasbies as most of us know.*
> *You are either served by a blonde or brunette,*
> *Who have never been seen without a smile yet.*
> *I think all the boys with me will agree,*
> *That they always get a good mug of tea.*
> *Only one drawback – not enough chairs,*
> *But we can always sit upon the stairs.*
> *So to the Wasbies who work till half nine,*
> *The boys agree you are doing the job fine.*
> *We wish you good luck and a very big cheer,*
> *And hope you'll be with us this time next year.*

Bubbles then read one of the little ditties which she had written for the Wasbie Newsletter one day when we were not busy and she had resorted to her poetry writing, which she so loved. It was entitled 'Trees', and referred specifically to the various notices posted on them:

I wonder if I'll ever see
A tree that's wholly notice free
A tree that may in summer wear
No mention of the Field Cashier
A tree with nothing to suggest
That Military Police may nest
A tree that doth not know too well
The M.D.S or P.O.L
A jungle where there are no grounds
For 'WAS(B) AREA: OUT OF BOUNDS'
And trunk ne'er carries legend plain
To bring one home to 'HQ MAIN'.

19 January 1945

Fleurette, Gay and I borrowed a Jeep in the early evening after we had finished our day's work, and went for a drive along the banks of the Irrawaddy and through one of the little local villages. The countryside was so lovely and fresh and we welcomed the opportunity to be able to get out and about to relax a little. It was so sad, however, to see thousands of pounds worth of Irrawaddy Steam Ship Company vessels damaged, neglected and quite useless, now abandoned and littering the banks of the river. They all looked so pathetic and forlorn with weeds and shrubs growing out of some of the little steamers which had obviously once been the buzzing centre of life in these parts before the Japanese invaded, driving the local inhabitants out and leaving devastation and havoc in their wake.

In this area and others we would visit the little temples and stupas, so prevalent in most villages and towns, which had mostly been stripped of their contents, and were now either damaged or devoid of the statues, bells and other Buddhist religious artefacts normally found in Burma's temples. In most villages there were very few, if any, shaven-headed red-robed monks to be seen – they had all fled, or possibly some had even been killed by the Japs. On occasion there was the odd tinkling of a bell in the breeze, but on the whole, most of these religious sites were abandoned and unused, making for an even more haunting emptiness.

Whilst out we stopped and watched some of the village lads engaged in a game of Chinlone, the national Burmese game which is played using a hollow wickerwork ball. They were all very agile and as far as we could gather the idea was to form a circle and keep the ball moving, using feet or head (no hands), passing the ball from player to player without it ever touching the ground. One of the youngsters very proudly did a fabulous backward flick of the ball using his heel, much to the excitement of the other players. It appeared not to be a competitive game as there seemed to be no winner or loser. It was certainly good exercise and they were thoroughly enjoying themselves and the audience.

We had been told that a number of Burmese women had become embroiled with the Japs, resulting in them having mixed-race children, leaving them very distressed at being left behind after the Japanese withdrawal. It was such a sad situation. There was also a strong rumour about a small white child hidden in one of the local villages somewhere around there. Apparently the local villagers had looked after the child and protected it from the Japs who were most suspicious and appeared to know of its existence, although thankfully not its location. I suppose the child would eventually be tracked down and enquiries would be made about its parents and their whereabouts, hopefully ending up with a happy reunion. As we moved on so quickly we never did hear the outcome; neither did we get the full story as to who the child was and how come he/she was there and alone in the first place.

What a lot of tragedies there were connected with the evacuation of many families from Burma when the Japanese invasion started in 1942. A number of Burmese got as far as Katha, then the railway ceased to function after the Japs attacked, leaving the Burmese fleeing into the forests on foot, walking many miles through the dense jungle across the mountains in an endeavour to find sanctuary. There appeared to be no trace of hundreds who had been captured during that period. A man came round whilst we were there, having got leave from his unit, to make enquiries about three of his children who were last seen in Katha. He could find no trace or information about the girl of fifteen and two younger boys. It was too sad for words and we sincerely hoped he would eventually find his missing family.

It was hard to believe that this place had been the scene of so much misery and fighting as the countryside was so lovely. In the evening there was a strange peacefulness that settled over the river, despite it being the scene of some fatalities since our arrival. Swimmers would get drawn under the water to their death by the strong currents which could be seen swirling on the surface. I shudder when I think how lucky we were when we crossed at Christmas in a none too clear state of mind.

20 January 1945

Caught a ghastly cold and suffering from neuralgia making life a bit grisly, so I spent most of the day sitting in the sun out of everyone's way. However, I pulled myself together and went with the girls to the weekly Toc H dance in the evening. We always did the tea and refreshment side of their entertainment. In spite of being great fun, the dances are exceptionally hard work as there are only about ten girls at most – ourselves and nurses from the CCS – with numerous men all vying for attention. The Palais Glide always came as a relief after a period of energetic jitterbugging.

I think that night was the best we had experienced so far, as the lights were good and so was the band. Mostly swing music was played as the majority of the men there were American and my gosh, did we jive. My hair, which I wore up, was never 'up' by the time a dance was over. There was a typical Texan cowboy type there who danced with his revolver strapped low on his hip, and as a result didn't 'swing' too much so it was a nice rest to dance with him. I wonder if he realised how popular he was with all the girls. Strange thing; the Americans all seemed to chew gum madly most of the time which I found a particularly unattractive trait.

Some of the BOR lads at the dance felt that they were being ousted by the Americans and it was all rather difficult in the end, but if they wouldn't ask one to dance, what was a girl to do? What a party. Nick Geodani, one of the Americans, was most amusing and thought he had made a hit with me, poor sweet. He was I think slightly miffed over the lack of enthusiasm on my part when he suggested a walk outside. Fleurette and I finally got to bed at midnight which was quite late enough.

Canteen No. 16. Back: Maria, Barbara Williams, Fleurette Pelley. Front: Bubbles Clayton, Gay Tucker and Joan Morton, Area Commander.

22 January 1945

Still felt lousy with my cold, but went shooting with Fleurette and Cecily, along with General Festing's chauffeur, Joe Robinson, Taffy our Welsh driver, and George Westbrook who was in charge of Toc H here. Cecily was a pretty good shot – four bulls out of five and I didn't disgrace myself, I did at least manage to hit the target every time but sadly no bullseye for me.

We thoroughly enjoyed our afternoon and only hoped that if any of our chaps were around and about they didn't think that some dacoits had got loose, as we were shooting with sten guns, revolvers, .303s and a Jap rifle which made for a fair amount of noisy gunfire. I am surprised we didn't get ticked off when we returned to base.

George was a grand person who 'messed' with us Wasbies and spent his time blushing wildly because we frequently forgot his presence and got into a feminine huddle talking about girlie things which of course embarrassed him no end.

Later we went to the airstrip, where Fleurette, Cecily and I went up for a flip in an ambulance Jeep plane. It was only a fifteen-minute flight but it was terrific fun and we looked down on a beautiful temple and pagoda below. We squeezed into the tiny space specially constructed for a stretcher meant for one. I don't know how we fitted in, but where there's a will there's a way as they say, and we managed. It was very good of the pilot to take us up as he had only just finished his day, having started at dawn, fetching the wounded from 29th Brigade to bring them back to the Division HQ hospital facility. The poor fellow hadn't had anything to eat at all that day either. They did such amazing work, those lads.

26 January 1945

Had the most wonderful picnic yesterday with Barbara, Bill and Nick G, driving out to Indaw Lake where we relaxed, cooked Wiener sausages on long sticks over a makeshift camp fire, shot with automatics and a 'jungle carbine', a type of short-barrelled Lee Enfield rifle designed especially for use in Burma. A most enjoyable afternoon, after which I got to drive the Jeep home.

We all met up again in the evening and played jazz music on Barbara's gramophone. Nick was so charming, and Bill, who was a typical college-boy type, was one of the first Americans I got to know quite well. I found it rather a revelation. It was a very chilly evening in my 'office', with its flimsy parachute sides which were somewhat ineffective against the cold breeze. In spite of this, the evening turned into a pretty late session once again.

27 January 1945

Spent most of the morning unpacking stores flown in from Moran and to my dismay found that there was no shoe polish or ink. The latter was needed very badly, especially as we couldn't get pencils at all, so absolutely nothing to write with. Soon we will have to sharpen up some charcoal! Ironically there were many boxes of writing pads and envelopes.

I had to go to the workshop about the water cart which kept forgetting to bring much-needed water to the canteen, and when I was there I was asked if I was a 'married lady' and if so, would it be possible for me to make some pyjama trousers out of silk parachute material for one of the officers. Couldn't quite see where the 'married lady' bit came into the equation, but naturally agreed to the request if a sewing machine could be found in the village, otherwise I would have to hand stitch which would not really be very satisfactory, not to mention time-consuming. The things we Wasbies are asked to do.

Work in the canteen slackened off a lot after Christmas as the Division moved on and there were only the hospital staff and a few other odd bods left along with us in Katha. Didn't think much of the local orderlies; they could be a very rude and undisciplined lot. Strangely, they all seemed to have 'boss eyes'. One never knew which eye was looking at you when you addressed them – all very disconcerting. Work was therefore rather humdrum and boring, which was a pity because we were so desperately needed further down river but were not permitted to move down to Div. HQ yet as it was considered to be too dangerous. I think that they might have been moving forward too fast to cope with our deployment as well.

Barbara spent all the morning playing the game 'Donkey' with some American GIs and BORs in the canteen, and as I passed by I heard a cryptic remark from an agitated BOR who was down to the letter 'E' and looked as though he'd be out next round.

1 February 1945

A few days' gap again since last writing, during which time we received orders to move on to Bahe, so we spent a busy day packing all the stores and equipment, sixteen cases of which I had to leave behind with CAS(B) in the hope that eventually they could be sent down by river to Mandalay, when we regained control there. Suffered a few qualms about this as it was all quite valuable stuff, but as we had been told we all had to travel as light as we possibly could for the next few months it was useless cluttering ourselves up with unnecessary personal belongings.

Bahe – 2 February 1945

Gay Tucker flew ahead and fixed it with Gilbert Longden, the DAAG [Deputy Assistant Adjutant General], to keep Canteens 12 and 16 together instead of them getting split up, with half of us staying behind which would have been very disappointing. I didn't quite know what would happen in the long run, but it was fairly obvious that if one canteen had to go elsewhere it would be No.16, as we were the last in and the less experienced team and therefore it would be likely we would be the team to be relocated.

The Americans had been terrifically kind and promised us space in three Dakotas to fly some of the girls and our stores down to Bahe. Gay, Barbara, Viv and I went by air and George Westbrook and his Toc H team, plus Fleurette, Cecily and Bubbles, together with the two mobile vans and the section sent to guard them, travelled by road, arriving two days after us. The cat came with us – surprisingly it had settled quite well and was now an accepted part of the team. The plane in which we flew was one of those used for dropping and had no door, so we were treated to a good view of the forested countryside over which we flew, revealing just how dense the jungle was and how hellish it must have been for the troops to tackle the enemy in such difficult terrain.

We eventually arrived in Bahe at ten o'clock, to be met with glum faces. On asking why, we were told that things were pretty bad. There was a big battle going on and ammunition was needed urgently. Instead, begging our pardons, it was a team of Wasbies who had arrived.

We were quickly moved on, down an exceedingly rough road through the forest, to a small Burmese village where we were allotted one of the villagers' *bashas* and were told that our stores would not reach us for two days. I was more than a bit worried about this as they were last seen by us in a large pile on the airstrip, completely unguarded and with every prospect of being stolen or at least pilfered prior to being forwarded on to us.

We could hear the sound of the battle raging, and it did make us realise that at last we had achieved that which we had always hoped for – to serve the really forward troops. There was a tremendous air strike the day we arrived and the sound of guns continued constantly from the time of our arrival and throughout the night.

A bombed temple at Bahe, with soldiers of the South Wales Borderers.
© Imperial War Museum Image SE 2138.

Thank the Lord we brought our cook and canteen servants with us plus the odd spot of mess equipment. Had it not been for George's Engineers and his miraculous powers of persuasion, goodness knows how we would have moved with all the equipment we required. However, it was a pleasing thought that we would soon be mobile again. I didn't much care for operating out of a static canteen, as it was not nearly as interesting as working the area with the mobiles. Once our stores arrived we would start operating straight away from a 15cwt van until the larger vehicles arrived.

We got our ovens up and running as quickly as possible after preparing the lower floor of the *basha* for use as our store room, and spent two busy days in the 15cwts selling practically everything that we had on board. In fact, we had to leave one girl behind out of the three of us, to help with cutting and preparing the huge number of sandwiches required. She had to remain at the stores facility to distribute additional flour and other provisions for the cooks to bake extra bread and keep us stocked with sufficient sandwiches throughout the day.

I don't think that I or any of the other girls will forget our first few days either, serving so many men out in the field. We hardly had a moment to stand upright as the queues were so long. Each man in the line had stood very patiently for about two hours before his turn came. Today the sun was crushingly hot and it was pretty exhausting work. We enjoyed it nonetheless, as it was clear the men appreciated our presence and efforts.

When the other girls arrived they were full of pep and vigour, buzzing with stories about their trip down by road. We were very relieved to see our vehicles, and the stores which had accompanied them were intact and untouched. Thank the Lord the CBID [Canteen Bulk Issue Depot] was located close to us, as it was well stocked up with much-needed goods. Both the Chevrolet canteens had experienced trouble on the road and had to go straight to the workshops on arrival for repairs to the suspension.

I had to send Vivian back to Katha the day after we arrived as her poisoned hand took a turn for the worse and the MDs could not deal with her as they were too busy with battle casualties. Poor Vivian, she was upset, but was so doped up against the pain, together with a sleeping draught the doctor had given her, that she wasn't really conscious of very much in the end. We had been warned about the likelihood of infections out here from which many of the troops were suffering – often caused by leech and insect bites or blisters turning septic and ulcerating in the dirty and humid jungle environment in which the men were in combat.

In addition to the two mobiles, we started up a small static canteen in the evenings as Toc H was too full for us to amalgamate with them, and there was need for an additional place for the men to rest and try to unwind. We had masses of games for the troops to relax and amuse themselves with. One evening one of the girls came up with a splendid idea which wouldn't take much planning and ended up a great hit. We put up a notice in the static canteen asking all eligible men to submit photographs of their offspring for a 'Baby Show' which the Wasbies would be arranging. A number of proud fathers produced pictures of their babies which were judged by Gay Tucker, our Area Commander. It was a well-attended, fun gathering and the competition was voted a very popular change to the usual recreational activities available at the end of a day. We always made sure we had a reasonable amount of stores available for sale in the evenings as well, in case the Div. Office staff had not been able to get anything from the mobiles during the day. It was a pokey little space, as usual, which was located about 100 yards outside the perimeter of the camp. This meant that the guards who protected us, armed with their machine guns, had to extend the secure area to include the canteen until we closed at 9 p.m. It was, however, very popular and well patronised.

We were always busy and our old Gurkha cook, whom we brought down from Katha, had great difficulty keeping up with refilling the tea urn. We coped in a very slapdash manner; there were two 40-gallon petrol drums on a makeshift fire outside. These were filled by the water cart each evening, and we just had to hope that the 80 gallons would last out. More often than not it didn't, but everybody pulled together and did their best.

Bubbles was simply grand, lending us her gramophone and we all pooled our records so that we had music whilst we worked. We had a section of men, who were changed every three days, to guard us and they had to accompany us when we went out in the mobile canteens as well. They were all so nice, and a great little man by the name of Snow helped get the static canteen building, such as it was, ready for opening in a matter of only a few hours. When it had paper streamers and red cloth hung on what was left of the walls it all looked fairly jolly. Janet, who was with No.12 Canteen, did a great job there. You cannot imagine how angry we were when one morning we got up to find that everything had been pinched by the locals during the night.

The girls were working really hard and I did wonder if they were overdoing it. It was all extremely difficult as there was so much to do, but they were very keen to get on with it. During this time there were terrific air strikes being carried out by US Army Air Force Mitchell Bombers, and even though they were operating about six miles away from where we were located, our little hut really shook and the noise was quite deafening. There was relentless gunfire, which continued throughout the nights, and it was here that we first saw some dive bombers at work.

I met up with an old friend, James Murray, who added a new red scarf to my collection. We were all allowed to wear coloured scarves, even the men. These were still being made from the silk parachutes which dropped our food and ammunition supplies.

11 February 1945

Just heard we were not allowed down the Myitson road yet, as there are too many Jap snipers about who had taken shots at some of our lads. A couple of our evening guards got it in the neck for straying out of bounds. Those of us who were not out in the canteens spent the morning in the store room tidying up a spilled case of envelopes, sorting them into bundles of twenty-five to save time when we sold them later on. A horrible, fiddly job but it was soon done.

Our rations were still very good. We were getting quite a lot of canned fruit juice which made a lovely change from the endless Mother Hubbard lime juice and orange squash. We were also getting a good supply of American rations which was a pleasant change. These, after the Arakan rations of biscuits, bully beef and soya links were, to me and some of the other girls, complete heaven. I have to say that we were all getting tremendously fat.

12 February 1945

We have all been issued with revolvers and went out with Captain 'Bog-Whistle' this evening to learn how to shoot with them. After our shooting practice we drove out to a Burmese village which had been very cleverly hidden in the jungle. Nobody would ever have known it was there, it was so well tucked away. There we found a dear old man who could speak a little English. He asked if we could get his glasses mended as he was completely blind without them. We gave him some cigarettes which put a smile on his face immediately. He offered one to each of us, and was most aggrieved when we insisted that he should keep them all for himself. However after we managed to repair his specs he was delighted – his day couldn't have been much better.

Came back to find the little American engineer, Gee, whom we met in Katha, had just arrived and what a strange sight he was, as he had grown an enormous beard, rendering him almost unrecognisable. Poor Rajah Bent, the Town Major [an officer appointed to maintain good order in an occupied town during wartime], was sent to the hospital with a fever. Dreadful for him, and he was nearly in tears as it probably meant that he lost his repatriation for a while and permission had only just come through. It was not surprising though as there were so many cases of malaria, in spite of everyone being issued with Mepacrine. A number of the troops were down with dysentery as well.

Had supper at 'E' Mess where some of the company was very much the worse for drink. Fleurette was rather taken with a chap who was a psychiatrist. Personally I don't care much for those types as I feel they are always trying to analyse me, which makes me feel a little uncomfortable.

Another extremely noisy night with constant gunfire throughout; some poor devils were getting it in the neck. How I wished we knew whose chaps they were, hoping to God our men would not suffer more casualties.

13 February 1945

Fleurette and I had tracked down some horses and had managed to go riding. It was enjoyable as there were such lovely rides through the woods, but we had to have an escort of three IOR sepoys with us. I felt really sorry for them as they were by no means horsemen and had to come armed with sten guns and heavy ammunition belts, which were very clumsy to carry on horseback. Looking back, it was extraordinary that we were permitted to do this and it was probably rather irresponsible on our part.

Gee came round at 5.30 this evening and stayed for a while bringing with him some of the photos he had taken at Katha, and we had great fun and a few laughs looking through them all. He was just the same. The photos were pretty awful though, confirming how much weight I had put on.

Not a very busy day, but we were still exhausted as we had been dealing with IORs all day and they were very trying – they didn't seem to know the meaning of the word queuing. One just had to be patient with them, but they could be so annoying – one IOR tended to take so much longer to serve than two BORs.

14 February 1945

Lots of battle noises again last night along with torrential rain. It was also rather chilly. We now attended the 'morning prayer' session which took place daily whilst we were at breakfast. The IO [Intelligence Officer] came round and brought maps detailing the area of current operation in order to ensure we were fully in the picture as to what was happening and who was where. It was very interesting to be included in this information, and today we learnt that General Festing was due to have talks with Lieutenant General Daniel Sultan of the US Army, who had recently taken over from General 'Vinegar Joe' Stilwell. He is due to arrive tomorrow in his special Dakota nicknamed 'The Magic Carpet'.

In spite of the serious battles going on not too far away, we were still able to ride on some days. The horse which I rode when out with Fleurette was much too big and wide for me and was a brute of a puller with a very hard mouth, but he was a lovely jumper and the two of us thoroughly enjoyed our outings together. When I could find the time and when our situation permitted, I tried to ride him most days whilst we were stationed in Bahe as it was such a lovely treat and a break from camp life.

Had a hectic evening last night with Gee, Nick, Pela and Captain 'Bog-Whistle', who was a little astonished by the company the Wasbies kept. Joined later by Joe Maloney, the kindest man ever, with a heart of gold, but with such a pronounced American accent that one could hardly understand a word of what he said. He arrived along with a visiting RC padre who was also American. They galvanised us all by leaping into the room like a pair of whirling Dervishes, bounding up to Gay saying, 'Swell to know you, sister, let's have some jive', the gramophone being on at the time. They sat and chatted, entertaining us all by throwing peanuts into the air and catching them in their mouths as though they did it all the time – perhaps they did, who knows?

I got a bit 'blue' afterwards, wondering what was the use of ideals and things and would I ever find a settled and peaceful happiness again? I did so want children and a home of my own one day. Perhaps what upset me was when Nick started talking about families and home, or I guess it could just have been the rum!

15 February 1945

Due to tight security we had not been permitted to venture down the road for a few days although we hadn't been far away from the front line troops. Our canteen serviced the 25-pounder Battery yesterday, and we were nearly deafened by the din they were making. Barbara and I had lunch at one of the control posts with James and his officers, a good lunch of cheese on toast with baked beans. Afterwards Barbara and I went out and watched the guns in operation, and to her intense excitement she was allowed to fire one. We all had a good laugh at her remark to the gunner whose place she had taken. When he stood behind her and told her what to do, she asked him to put *his* fingers in *her* ears so that she would not hear the noise.

We loved going out to visit those lads as they were always so pleased to see us, and even if we did sell out of the things they wanted they were just pleased enough that we had time to stop by and talk to them.

Since being issued with our revolvers we were referred to as the 'Pistol Packing Mommas' and it was a never-ending joke with the lads who all started singing and making fun when they saw us approaching.

Evacuation from Bahe – 19 February 1945

When I arrived back from riding last night with Joe, we found the camp in total chaos and on full alert. The guards in our mess had been doubled and everybody was told to wear tin hats and carry their guns. The atmosphere was very charged with Wasbies packing frantically, literally hurling stores into sacks and boxes, having been advised that General Festing had sent a message round to say that we were all moving back up the road some three miles. By early evening the mobile canteens were stacked with stores and equipment, the mess was bare of its curtains and parachute cushions that served us as chairs, and Gay was keeping us informed of exactly what was going on.

At eight o'clock General Festing, accompanied by Gilbert and Paul, his No.2, came round for drinks and joined us sitting on the floor. The General was very apologetic and said that he had had to change his mind and he was now having to send us back to Katha as the risk was far too great for us to stay anywhere near Bahe. Naturally this was a little alarming, and after supper we continued our packing, or rather unpacking and repacking, ready for a complete withdrawal.

Most of the stores were handed back to the CBID who were themselves in the process of packing up in order to move back up the road, and the two canteens were filled with what we would need the moment we were able to start up again. Their contents were listed for the stocktaking that would have to be undertaken later, and the keys given to the drivers, Taffy and Neal, who were being left behind with Div. HQ to look after our vans.

Gay and I spent a sleepless night, wondering what was best to do with regard to the remaining packing and moving, etc. However, in the morning Gay had decided that it was time that we split up and Mrs Taylor radioed her confirmation, so we got Gay and Barbara off to the airstrip along with Cecily, who was to go to Shwebo to join a team there. Gay had a long trip back to her area in the Arakan, and Barbara was going on leave. We were all terribly sad to see Gay depart. She was one of the best, so dedicated and easy to get along with.

Having left Gay and Barbara at the airstrip I went back to the house to see Gilbert who was helping the rest of the girls to pack a few last-minute things. The Town Major, now better, turned up to assist as well, and a frightful 'session' resulted as a half bottle of ration rum was left over with nowhere to put it, so it was filled with water and was passed round for us all to have a swig – most unhygienic. Not too sure I like rum at 8.30 in the morning either.

Went to have a spot of lunch with Nick who was in the thick of it, poor soul, as earlier he had been commandeered to go down the road with the two generals. It was an excellent lunch too. Afterwards I drove one of the Jeeps, minus brakes, to drop off the girls at the airstrip, promptly backing into a foxhole as we left. However, no damage and all well. Cecily was at last dropped at the Jeep airstrip and we carried on to the Dakota strip to find that Gay and Barbara were still there, their plane having been delayed. They were a bit frazzled, having been waiting for some time in the scorching heat and dust with little in the way of shade. As we were running late as well, and they were pretty parched, we all went back to the American Engineers' Mess for a bit of refreshment, staying until we all departed at four o'clock, accompanied by Major Harrison. On landing, our taxiing Dakota encountered a soft spot in the strip, got stuck, and had to be hauled out by a Jeep. This didn't take long and away we went, never a more dispirited bunch of Wasbies, and all somewhat weary due to lack of sleep the night before. [Barbara seems not to have returned from her leave, as this is the last time she is mentioned in the diary. We know, however, that she did not leave the Wasbies, so must have been transferred to another canteen. In her absence, the cat adopted Fleurette.]

Katha – 20 February 1945

Well, here we were back in Katha again, all very disillusioned and deflated after the epic evacuation of Bahe. It was the second time that we Wasbies had had to be evacuated at short notice. We learnt there was a fairly strong rumour that the Japs had infiltrated and were coming up behind Div. HQ, hence the necessity for us being packed up and shipped out so quickly.

We were worried that the people at Katha were not expecting us owing to the speed at which we had had to leave Bahe, and we believed the town was practically empty of military so there was unlikely to be transport to collect us from the airstrip. We were also uncertain there would be any accommodation organised for us.

However, we were met and told that we were to move into CASB's [Canteen Army Services Burma] house which meant turning them out of their quarters, which had originally been ours during our previous visit. They were remarkably good about it I must say, and having found transport to send to the strip to collect our belongings, they moved out of the house and into their offices.

After a wait on the veranda for an hour and a half whilst they packed up we eventually installed ourselves, building up a good thirst in the process, so sat down to a couple of bottles of very warm beer which was the only available thing to drink. The cook, as usual, was marvellous and after helping us unpack, produced a very good supper, then off to bed.

Supplies were absolutely nil, so our activities were considerably curtailed. We mooched around for a day or so then tried to do some work helping the nurses at the hospital. We couldn't get stores of any description, and the Supply Point, although willing to help us, had very few provisions that we could use for cakes and sandwiches. However, we went round and chatted to the men and tried to occupy ourselves, keeping open house for any officers or men who came up to Katha. In this way we kept in touch with what was going on and learned that the Hydrabadies and Punjabis were winning the admiration of everyone with their gallantry.

26 February 1945

No news of us moving and we just bumbled along taking about twenty chips a day in the small canteen we had managed to open. With limited stores we couldn't expect much in the way of takings, also not many chaps in the hospital were convalescing, it being too full with more seriously battle-wounded men. Those getting over their injuries and convalescing were flown out every day to make room for more casualties coming in from the front. It was a period when everybody seemed to be rather on edge for various reasons, mainly because there was little to occupy our time and there were so many wounded men coming in which was very upsetting.

In spite of everything the men had encountered, they tried to keep cheerful, even when their exhaustion was so obvious following the hell they had been through. Although our stores were short they seemed grateful simply to spend time talking to us, and when we had insufficient supplies to operate the canteens, we just chatted to them hoping to lift their spirits as much as we could.

We were treated to a couple of picture shows – one good and one a bit of a dud, but it was entertainment and we all enjoyed ourselves. Vivian and Janet were still helping out in the hospital, but were shortly due to rejoin our team – Vivian in a day or so and Janet in about ten days. Apparently her carbuncle had turned nasty but the skin graft was taking nicely and she would not end up with much of a scar.

Gee and Joe Maloney came in last night to say goodbye. The Wasbies lost a couple of very good friends in those two. They had been so helpful to us and always so kind and cheerful. We would certainly miss Gee and his impish humour and what he called his 'negative persuasive' approach to life.

Bill, Fleurette and I went out in a Jeep during the afternoon and I have to admit it was very nice to get away from the camp crowd for a while. This was followed by a good picnic dinner with Peter Buchanan and his No.2, Captain Newbolt.

1 March 1945

Great excitement today as our canteen was to be visited by Lady Louis Mountbatten whose husband had been in Myitson with Generals Festing and Sultan, observing the air attack by British and American planes on a Japanese-held island in the middle of the Shweli River. Lady Louis, who was to meet up with General Festing, was flown into Bahe in her husband's Dakota which also had a nickname – 'Sister Anne'. When advised of her impending visit to Katha, CCS had asked if the Wasbies could possibly make some curtains for their mess to brighten it up for her visit.

I think her visit went off reasonably well, in spite of the occasion being a bit unnerving for us, bearing in mind Lord Louis, known by everyone as 'Supremo', was Supreme Allied Commander of SEAC, the body in overall charge of operations in the South East Asia theatre of war.

Unfortunately, owing to the fact that we had been evacuated back to Katha where there were not many troops and few means of supplies, she was unable to see us actually at work. However, she and the General, together with a number of officers, had tea at the mess and it turned out to be a great day for us all and boosted everyone's morale enormously.

We later learned that on the fourth we would be on the move again, down to Myitson which had at last been taken by our troops. Hurrah!

Planning an attack: Major General Festing and Brigadier A.R. Aslett of 72 Brigade. © Imperial War Museum Image SE 2153.

Admiral Lord Louis Mountbatten, Supreme Commander, SEAC, with Generals Sultan and Festing at Myitson.

Myitson – 4 March 1945

No.16 Canteen moved back to join Div. HQ. We flew by Dakota to Bahe then continued by Jeep along a road by the banks of the Shweli River to Myitson. Our camp was to be located on the opposite side of the river to Myitson itself. Our mobile vans and our stores had already moved down the previous day with Div. HQ.

It was very hot and dry, and for the first six miles we passed through countryside which had been shelled and bombed continuously and had been completely destroyed during the ferocious battle. The forest had been torn apart by the bombing, leaving the trees looking as though someone on a bulldozer had gone on a completely mad rampage. There were parachutes, with their loads still attached, suspended from some of the trees, and an atmosphere of complete devastation and destruction prevailed. The entire area was a total shambles. It was scorched, dusty and ugly and as we passed by, it seemed so abandoned and forlorn.

The stench of death and acrid smell of burning still lingered, making for a particularly unpleasant new experience for us girls. Taffy still insisted it was no place for women and he wouldn't budge on this. I don't suppose for one moment it was; but we loved it and wouldn't have it any other way, and the troops really did make us feel so greatly valued.

Along the sides of the desolate road there were a number of little crosses with tin hats hanging on them indicating the graves of men who had been killed, British, Indian and Gurkha. It was just so ghastly to see; a heartrending reminder of the recent savage battle. The lives of so many brave soldiers had been lost, battling in such challenging terrain in an endeavour to return Burma to its rightful people and out of the clutches of the ruthless Japanese. It was the first time we had encountered battle death so closely and it was a sobering and distressing sight.

After leaving the battle area we continued on to our destination, and all the girls were in much better spirits once we actually arrived. We had obtained permission to bring Janet down with us, so we were now a complete team – all five of us – and I was in sole charge. I hoped that I would do the job satisfactorily, although I was afraid that my new situation would have its difficulties as two of my group were almost twice my age, which might be a bit tricky and require a lot of tact.

When we arrived at our camp site there was a big kerfuffle going on. Some of the men were trying to erect a relatively large-sized parachute tent, with a veranda, for us to use as our mess. At this point normal tents were not carried by the Division, and most of the stores and supplies were still having to be dropped by air.

Initially we lived in our large parachute tent next to 'A' Mess on the banks of the Shweli River, under the shade of tall teak trees bearing the most enormous paddle-like leaves which resembled rather large men's handkerchiefs. One of these trees came crashing down in the middle of the night, narrowly missing the servants' quarters. Parachutes, alas no longer the coloured silk ones, were being used as tents by all of us apart from the General. He had a little caravan arrangement, a converted ambulance, which replaced his earlier adapted railway-carriage quarters which had been nicknamed 'The White Horse Inn', but had been left behind in Katha.

Whilst I was very used to sleeping under canvas, having done many a camping safari during my life in Kenya, for some of the girls this was a new and perhaps even more primitive form of accommodation than the *bashas* in which we had previously been living. The conditions were just as we expected and our new camp kit was quickly put into use, including those horrid little camp baths and basins which we would use whenever Divisional HQ personnel lived under canvas.

I have to say I never really got used to our little folding canvas beds which were only about 2ft 6in wide with a very thin mattress and bedroll. They were far from comfortable. What none of us realised until many days later was that after dark, once a lamp was lit inside the tent, one was remarkably well silhouetted to all those outside!

The local Kachin tribespeople appeared not to have seen white women before and just couldn't stop gaping at us, and this at a time when, unfortunately, we were very much in the open with very little privacy. It was stiflingly hot in the tent at night, so Fleurette and I decided to sleep outside under the awning where it was much cooler and slightly less stuffy. We were, however, woken up very early in the morning when the chaps rose, washing and dressing outside their tents all around us – a bit too cosy for our liking.

As always the first thing to be done after arrival was to unpack all our stores which were then neatly stacked, ready for the two drivers and ourselves to cover them with parachutes, over which we laid a tarpaulin to keep out dew or rain. It was truly a wonder that more of our stores were not pinched, as there was no doubt that a certain amount of petty pilfering had been going on. The kitchen was not far from our tent, with the two cooks and our mess waiter living under another one not far off. Taffy and Neal camped out with the stores to guard them.

Having settled ourselves in, we went for a quick stroll, coming across a phosphorous bomb not far from the mess tent, and Fleurette who found it, and realising how dangerous it was, thankfully stopped herself from touching it, quickly rushing off to find somebody to deal with it. Once checked over it was disposed of in the river where it exploded without harming anyone.

Wash day in the jungle camp. Courtesy British Library Ref. 9059c33.

7 March 1945

Here we were at last, settled in at Myitson, although I gathered that it wouldn't be for long, maybe a matter of only a week or so. The stores situation was bad as the CBID had not moved down with us. They were still at Bahe, and for security reasons I was not permitted to go back up there to obtain provisions, so we just had to manage with what we had. Life was still a little bit ragged and it was terribly hot and overcrowded.

The accounts for the month of February were going to be absolute hell and I was dreading them. What with having taken over No. 12 Canteen as well as all their stock, together with all the losses at Katha before being flown down to Bahe, it was going to mean that I was quite likely be down the drain about 700 rupees if not more. A far from ideal state of affairs.

We got our two field ovens up and running pretty quickly and it wasn't long before cake baking was well in hand. How those poor cooks functioned I just don't know as they had no tables at all, nor any kitchen utensils like those one had at home. All they had were a couple of small tin baths in which they mixed the dough, plus a rolling pin which one of them had made himself out of a discarded piece of wood, and this was used for rolling out biscuits and pastry. Their kitchen table was a large wooden cigarette case, and the tins they baked their sausage rolls and scones in were made from metal taken from the linings of cigarette cases. Amazingly they managed to turn out the most remarkable and very palatable food in those extremely primitive conditions. Their improvisation skills really were astonishing.

I soon realised that the large slab cakes they were making were not economical, because of the shortage of ingredients, so we stopped baking them, sticking to sausage rolls and sandwiches etc., which we usually helped the cooks to prepare. On the whole I felt we were too public with too many people dropping in on us all the time for a chat. However, it was fun, and we knew the men did so enjoy talking to us, even if it was only for a few minutes. It did make life difficult though when we were supposed to be working and had such a lot to accomplish with minimal staffing.

We erected another small wigwam-type contraption for use as my office, in which I hoped to have some peace and quiet whilst I wrestled with the darned accounts. I had already checked and rechecked the stocktaking, but still had to go over the stock sheet extensions once again. All indications were that our takings were certainly horribly down, and I was getting very bad-tempered. What the books would eventually look like I shuddered to think, as the dust got into just about everything and the sheets I was writing up were indescribably filthy; the end result looking most unprofessional.

Fleurette could be very irritating at times, but then I expect I annoyed her just as much, poor dear. We could all get a bit rattled from time to time, but on the whole the girls were all very cheerful and I felt that the move was a new beginning for us. We were to continue now with Div. HQ and no more being left behind. Having received some supplies, we were using both canteens again and started up the usual small evening affair which was so popular with all the men.

8 March 1945

Today we received news of George Westbrook; he was well and was further forward than we were, with the 10th Gloucesters. It was good to get news of him as he had definitely been a favourite with us all.

Bubbles caused terrific consternation by breaking, then swallowing a piece of her tooth, so until something could be done about it, she had to be fed on soggy soft food and doses of medicine for the pain, poor love, and in that infernal heat as well. As always she put a brave face on it.

Trooped our kitchen staff off for their TAB inoculations and was nearly ill at the sight of it. I did hate watching this being carried out as the needles got so blunt with so many lads having to be injected, some of them ending up with blood pouring down their arms. Thankfully it didn't seem to perturb them much.

No letters for weeks – very depressing, but only to be expected in our current circumstances.

Alternate canteens were now being operated, there being no need for two mobiles. Both Indian and British troops were being served. On our daily runs it was made even more apparent that the area surrounding Myitson had been knocked to blazes – it was quite shocking. The dust was thick and heat relentless as always. What hell it had been for the troops involved in that battle. It must have been just brutal. Although they all look dead tired, both the BORs and the IORs were always so cheerful, greeting us as though they really were so glad to see us back again. It was here that the Engineers had built the longest bridge in this theatre of war across the Shweli River: this was referred to as the Mountbatten Bridge, Supremo having been in the Myitson area whilst the fierce battle was in progress.

Stores were getting desperately low again and we were told that until we reached Mongmit we would get no more, so we chatted to the men whenever we could and hoped that female company would lift their spirits and make them feel a little less isolated.

10 March 1945

Finding it increasingly difficult to write in my diary. Life is amusing at times but still full of niggles and frequently stressful. However, what to do? I was sure the debilitating heat, humidity and thick dust didn't exactly improve matters. We looked at our necks a few nights ago and accused each other of being grubby, but it was just impossible to keep ourselves clean. I washed my neck three times in one day and it was still filthy. The dirt, along with the fact that the anti-malarial Mepacrine tablets we were taking had turned our skin slightly yellow, did not exactly enhance our appearance.

I nearly burnt the tent down yesterday when lighting a cigarette. I threw away a match which I thought was extinguished only it wasn't. I flung it aside and *Voila*! – up went the tent. The consequent conflagration burnt a large hole in the side of it before it was put out. Fleurette attempted to beat the flames out with a rug and the others helped with buckets of water, managing to soak all my clothes and bedding in the process. Needless to say there was little sympathy, only laughter. Frank Hunter, an Australian officer with the 9th Battalion, 8th Punjab Regiment, whom I had originally met in Shillong, was now part of the 36th Division and assisting us with our camp arrangements. He was highly entertained by the whole episode.

Fleurette, Janet and I met up with Bertie Hamlin, an old Kenya friend, and another officer called Michael, in the evening for a quiet drink before supper.

Finally received some mail this morning which included another letter from Peter re the divorce. It still upset me, although I knew there was no going back. A little depressed, I once again thought of returning to East Africa in June if I could get some leave. In any case I would to have to break the news to Mummy by letter, as she and Daddy were still in England.

This wretched affair of mine is making me less and less efficient – or I feel it is – and this awful irresolution gets me down too. However I suppose one just grits one's teeth and makes oneself as natural as possible, instead of losing one's grip.

At one point whilst we were in Myitson all hell was suddenly let loose and we were told that there was a group of Japs attacking 'A' Mess near the Wasbie quarters. We all ran for cover only to find that it was actually the Gurkhas having firing practice the other side of the river opposite the mess and nobody had been told. Amusing in retrospect, but frightening at the time.

12 March 1945

We received our moving orders yesterday to go down to Mongmit by road. We had been briefed that the convoy was due to leave at 0430 hrs and we should not under any circumstances be late at the rendezvous. I asked for three x 15cwt vehicles to take what was left of our stores and equipment.

Mongmit – 14 March 1945

What a ghastly day yesterday was – for me at any rate. The dust and heat were frightful, and the road quite the most bone-shakingly corrugated we have been over so far. The suspension on our vehicles took a bashing, and I had a cracking head and felt bloody. Throughout the journey we were all ticked off for one thing or another by the harassed Officer in Charge, who was responsible for the convoy, and the girls became rather upset. I can smile about it now, but at the time, with my small responsibility resting very heavily, I found it hard. Once again the vans had to pay a visit to the workshops on arrival. The bad roads continued to take their toll on our vehicles.

Our little party consisted of our two vans and three trucks, accompanied by a couple of sections of Gurkha guards, one in the lead and another one at the rear. We were travelling in the middle of the convoy of over 100 vehicles and I got the impression things were a trifle disorganised. One of the main problems was that there was no water from Myitson to Mongmit. The countryside was very dry until the road started curling endlessly up into heavily forested hills before dropping down the other side.

We had to stop about four hours out of Mongmit because the road was so narrow, with a challenging gradient and many sharp hairpin bends, making the going extremely slow. The larger trucks kept holding the convoy up, having to manoeuvre back and forth a number of times in order to get themselves round the tight corners. We left our two vans with the remaining Division trucks, gave our water bottles to the drivers and piled onto passing 15cwts. Parting with our water bottles was kind but, as it turned out, rather unwise as we had another hold-up further on, this time for about two hours, when Generals Browning and Festing met the convoy and advised that there was a battle going on up in the hills and it was too dangerous to continue. Poor old Viv lost her temper completely over the lack of water and was u.s. [useless] all day.

There was by this time no shade as we were down amongst the paddy fields again and we were all very hot and thirsty. The unfortunate cat, now known as 'Nausea', almost passed out with the heat as did Janet's springer spaniel, now with two pups. We looked, and I felt, like a travelling circus with all these animals in tow. The one bright spot about our situation was that we all looked odd, covered with red, sweat-streaked dust all over our faces. Janet's lovely white hair had turned an extraordinary colour. It looked as though she had taken a trip to Mecca and had it hennaed rather badly. This in spite of her looking just priceless in her jungle hat with a red veil-like scarf tied over it to protect her face from the sun and dirt.

Further on we were held up yet again at the river just before Mongmit, where the causeway bridge had collapsed under the weight of the 25-pounders rumbling across. It was being repaired by the Royal Engineers, who were moving tonnes of stone to the site in an endeavour to shore up the damage. In that heat the poor fellows, despite stripping to the bare minimum of shorts, boots and bush hats, were just pouring with sweat and looked as if they were going to expire at any minute. After completion of the job, we had a further wait before we could carry on to Mongmit. This stop was to enable the unit and their equipment to cross over to our side of the river, prior to continuing to where they were urgently needed in the combat area.

When we eventually did arrive in the town we found that what had once apparently been a flourishing and pleasant place was now completely ravaged, with most of the deserted buildings just bomb-shattered ruins. The local inhabitants had not all moved away and those who were left said that on the whole they had not been treated too badly by the invading Japanese, in spite of the destruction all around.

Our quarters were to be in an old school building constructed completely of wood. It had no windows or doors and was devoid of furniture, as was normal, but it was otherwise relatively unscathed apart from a few shrapnel marks. As the canteens were not expected for a while we unpacked and settled ourselves in. The building had a large room upstairs which we could use as a sitting room. Outside and adjacent to the lower level of the house we erected a parachute tent for use as our kitchen. On this level there was a very small room which we turned into a bathroom, i.e. we just placed our little tin bath on the floor, cutting a hole in the boards underneath to allow the bath water – often shared – to escape after use.

Upstairs Fleurette and I shared a room with the cat. Janet had one on her own with her dogs. Bubbles and Vivian shared unencumbered by animals, leaving one room for use as an office. There was a large classroom downstairs and this was turned into our store room. It had a very convenient window, now without glass, facing out onto the road. This meant that the mobile canteens could be reversed up to it and stocked up easily through the gap.

It had been suggested we become a sort of rest camp at Mongmit, probably remaining in the area for at least three weeks. One Brigade at a time were expected to come in and we had to have both mobiles going, together with a static canteen, if we could get sufficient stores, as we would be catering for a large number of men. The Supply Point staff were wonderful to us and gave us everything we needed. We were able to make fudge again which was always so popular with the men. This was made using condensed milk, cocoa powder and sugar. Woody, who was in charge, was so charming and helpful, always doing his absolute best for us. Janet really made the mess look grand with some bright curtains which we had hand-sewn from scraps of fabric acquired during our travels.

At this point I had allocated the kitchen operation to Fleurette. She had never handled this side before, and as she was to be promoted to officer status very soon I felt she should know how things worked. The area allocated for a canteen was on the ground floor of Toc H and this location seemed to work well. George Westbrook handled the recreation side for the lads and we did the food. I felt it would be too small. However, we would have to wait and see when we opened up.

Frank Hunter and George Westbrook came round and we had a pleasant lunch with them the day after we arrived.

18 March 1945

Work in full swing and we were all very busy. We managed to get more stores and handed in to the CBID a colossal sum of money which we had been carrying with us. This was an enormous relief. At the same time I handed in the blasted accounts.

The static canteen was, as foreseen, far too small. The first night would have been funny if it had not been so busy. People just poured in, with little room to socialise. Those who were inside were quickly served and moved back out to allow the next batch in. Despite the fact that we had three 40-gallon drums on the go outside with boiling water for tea, they were emptied long before it was time for us to close. Our poor old Gurkha cook was unable to cope, so we had to get three quite gormless, not to mention utterly clueless, locals in to help him out.

It was essential to increase the canteen area, so it was decided to erect a parachute-fabric canopy beside the static canteen with a generator supplying electric light for illumination – a great improvement on paraffin butties which had been used in some of our camps. Under this we placed a large table, made by the Field Company, which enabled us to work and serve the men with plenty of room to accommodate everyone under cover. It was so busy that we now had 5 x 40-gallon drums of water for making tea, which were filled up three times a day by the water cart, but we were still hard-pushed not to run out before closing at the end of the day. I never realised how much tea those men could drink. It was all free issue too. Margarine and sugar were becoming very scarce and we were trying out some of the local stuff, not dissimilar to jaggery, in place of sugar. This came in large blocks looking rather like soft toffee. Apparently it was made by boiling down sugar cane or palm juice which was then cooled and set into square or cylindrical chunks. The men didn't like it much and said it tasted more like a rich syrupy sort of honey with a pretty strong flavour that tended to overpower the taste of their precious mug of char.

19 March 1945

Much excitement amongst the local Buddhists as their spiritual leader, considered to be the second most holy man in Burma, had just returned from a hideout in the hills to resume residence here. He welcomed the General with speeches which were followed by a performance of Burmese dancing.

It was clear that all the locals were delighted at his return to the town, bringing an important touch of normality and stability back into their lives. In return the General arranged for the 1st Battalion Royal Scots Fusiliers to put on a special parade with pipe music, after which they all came and had tea with us in our mess.

Heard that we would be leaving within a few days to go to Mogok, where Burma's largest ruby mining industry was to be found.

20 March 1945

One of the battalions we had with us at this time was the 2nd Bn. The Royal Welch Fusiliers and during some of the evenings they would sit outside on the grass and sing: so wonderful to listen to, as some of them had such lovely voices. They gave a terrific party last night. We all went and it was great fun, but owing to the fact that we had to be on the road at 0430 hrs the next morning, we didn't stay up very late.

21 March 1945

Thank heavens we didn't continue on into the small hours, because when we got up at 0330 hrs we found that the servants were still sound asleep. Despite having been told they were to pack up before retiring, they had done nothing. So irritating! I know I can be bad-tempered early in the morning but sometimes they can be simply exasperating. Notwithstanding this, packing was accomplished at the double, and we were on time at the meeting point, only to find that our escort wasn't there and we ended up waiting until 7 a.m. before we started our move. By that time the unfortunate cat had had to have a number of holes dug for it, can't think why it couldn't do this for itself. Nauseating tea was brought out in dirty mugs with 'God Wot's' [God, what's this?] floating on the surface and we were all decidedly grumpy. There was a nasty silence when our escort eventually appeared – nuff said!

Mongmit had been hotter than hell and none of us really enjoyed it there, in spite of having a number of amusing parties, in particular the last one with the Royal Welch Fusiliers. Consequently, we were glad to be moving on.

Mogok – 22 March 1945

Bubbles was due to go on ten days casual leave. Lord alone knows when we would be able to pick her up again. I hoped that she would manage to get a proper rest. I was worried as no one seemed to know quite where she would be flown to. She deserved a break, poor dear, as she had worked so hard doing a sterling job over the past weeks. She would be much missed by the troops who all adored her and her wonderful humour. She had the best turn of wit I have come across and was always so cheerful, writing a number of most amusing ditties about our travels, some of which were accompanied by a cartoon sketch.

We were told the CBID would not be coming to Mogok with us. They would go straight to the next stop. Consequently, we were to pick up as much stuff as they would allow us to carry to keep us going during our short stay in Mogok.

Very sadly we had to leave our lovely old Gurkha cook behind. He couldn't keep up with us, poor old man. He was just not strong enough to continue with the pressure of work, our constant moving and the huge upheaval involved each time. He had been such a tremendous help to us and we had all grown so fond of him, but he had obviously got something very wrong and had been ill on and off for quite some while, so it was arranged for him to fly back to Katha. We asked the CASB Authorities to send him straight to Myitkyina, the capital of the Kachin State, where he said he hoped to find his brother. It was awfully sad as I felt he would never survive the long journey and might die friendless and away from home: one of the many, poor old chap. It was just too horrible to think about and we were all very upset when we bade him farewell.

We heard recently that when the palace of the Sawbwa, who was the ruler of Hsipaw, was searched, a hidden note was found. It had been written by his wife, an English woman by the name of Mabel who was a friend of Gay Tucker's. She and her husband had been taken from the palace in Hsipaw and held prisoner by the Japanese near Mongmit, but it was believed that as the Shan people were so devoted to him, the Japanese dared not harm either of them. It is rumoured too that Mabel was fearless and in fact the Japs were enormously afraid of her as she was apt to fly into rages and would even box their ears. Gay would be very pleased to hear that she was safe, and would most certainly wish to meet up with her if she could be traced. It is thought that they, together with their family and servants, were moved shortly before we arrived at Mongmit.

The road up to Mogok was spectacular, quite the most beautiful scenery I have seen, so much so that I felt it would be difficult to find another place in the world to rival it. It goes without saying that the road was awful, as are all the Shan roads, full of corners and steep hills, but splendid nonetheless. Tulip trees, with their delicate green-and-white flowers tinged with orange, were in full bloom. These, along with almond trees covered in sweet-smelling blossom, made for a truly picturesque sight, after all the devastation we had encountered thus far. It was certainly uplifting.

We got a couple of 'rockets' again on this trip, given by various officers of Div. HQ who were obviously suffering badly from hangovers – a result of the party the night before perhaps. Both the canteens broke down which meant that the girls who were travelling in them were forced to stop, dropping back out of the actual Wasbie convoy, although they were quite safe as there were hundreds of trucks behind us. Cursing everything, Hunter (our friend Frank) and I looked at each other and wondered where on earth we should travel – move to the rear or stay in our position? All very difficult.

In the end we decided to continue where we were and wait on the road just before we got into Mogok to collect our errant 'family'. When they finally caught up with us we discovered that one of the girls was missing: Fleurette, accompanied by Nausea the cat. It was decided she could look after herself as well as any of us, so we pressed on without her. It would have to be Fleurette; she was just one of those people who managed to get mixed up in any tricky situation. It turned out the vehicle she was in had broken down. Once again both our vehicles had to go into workshops on arrival.

Similar to the other towns we had been through, Mogok must have been lovely before the war. It was situated up in the hills and all the houses we passed would have originally been beautiful, well cared-for homes with gardens full of brilliant bougainvillea and many other colourful shrubs and trees, including the abundant lush yellow rosewood trees which were prolific through the northern and central countryside of Burma, all in flower – it was truly a picture. Our 'home' was a small bungalow on the top of the hill not far from 'A' Mess and 'D' Mess (Dog Mess). It had obviously been a very attractive little place and certainly had a lovely view, but now – we shuddered when we went into it. It had only been vacated by the Japs' Town Major two days before, and was indescribably filthy. The smell was overpowering and an air of gloom settled over us as we knew we would have to set to with the scrubbing brushes again.

But firstly, after unloading the trucks and sending them away to the workshop, we had coffee from our Thermos flasks and ate some K Rations which had come from American supplies. Each packet of daily K Rations bore the following label:

ONE K RATION

BREAKFAST
1 Biscuit Package
1 Small Can Tuna

DINNER
1 Biscuit Package
1 Can Cheese

SUPPER
1 Biscuit Package
1 Large Can Salmon

Packaged by
H. J. Heinz Company
Pittsburgh, Pa.

After this out came the scrubbing brushes once again and by two o'clock we were starting to establish ourselves. The place was clean, beds were up and our supplies were being put into the store room. The Field Company had arrived to install our ovens and Fleurette had finally shown up in a DUKW – an amphibious vehicle better known as a 'Duck'. Needless to say she was looking as perky as be damned with Nausea having some sort of fit in her arms. Poor animal, what it went through and how it survived I just don't know.

We were busy as usual in Mogok with two canteens operating. One was a mobile which travelled long distances each day to where some of the troops were located, the other a static. We also had a tea and cake shop in Toc H, located in a building which, I believe, had once been a clubhouse so was well suited to be a recreational centre. One evening at a party we had organised, General Festing joined us to find that we were in civilian dress, not our usual uniforms, and there was a nasty moment until he said, 'How marvellous to see you girls in mufti.'

Here again all the houses were without furniture, except for the one used by 'A' Mess. I think on this occasion it was not the Japs who had done the looting but the Burmese themselves, judging from the way they hung about when it was time for us to leave. They also poured into the Toc H building and into George's room when they learnt we were moving out. George woke up to find his wireless was calmly being removed from his room by a couple of Shans. He yelled for his orderly who thankfully rescued it, whilst George made a dash for the Toc H Mess where he found a huge number of men, women and children busy walking off with tables and chairs, the curtains made by us, and anything else they could lay their hands on. I know we should have felt sorry for them because they had nothing, but we didn't have much either.

Very little was saved, and all my urns and mugs etc. were stolen along with most of the supplies. We certainly won't forget that in a hurry. This took place early on Easter Sunday morning when we were on our way to church, where we were met by an angry and distraught George telling us the sorry tale. I am afraid it was with a very un-Christian feeling in my heart that I attended the service in the sad little remains of what was once a pretty church. It now had no roof and all the walls were badly damaged following the battle which had taken place there.

Mogok is known for its ruby mines. It is said that the finest pigeon-blood red rubies in the world come from this area, and legend has it that Marco Polo visited Mogok during his travels to the Far East in the thirteenth century. The girls were all very excited about the precious and semi-precious stones being offered by the locals, and I feel sure a lot of worthless stuff was purchased. Many gems were bartered for as money was relatively useless to the village people at this time, there being virtually nothing to buy. All over town troops could be seen bartering clothing, cigarettes and food with Burmese and Chinese artisans in return for trinkets and 'gem' stones for their wives and girlfriends.

The mine owners were mostly Chinese, a number of whom had travelled to England and the Continent to sell their gems prior to the war. Seeing these poor people now in rags, living in hovels up in the hills, it was difficult to visualise them ever having travelled anywhere let alone to Europe. I myself fell for a 'ruby' ring with 'diamonds' either side, for the trivial cost of 100 rupees plus some bully beef. It was a pretty ring, but I had my suspicions that it was either a spinel or a synthetic ruby which flooded the market before the war. The diamonds were probably not real either. However, it was a fine memento which had a wonderful sparkle to it and gave me great pleasure to wear.

Alongside the poverty-stricken local Burmese, there were quite a few Anglo-Indian priests and they told us that luckily they had been treated better by the Japs than the rest of the population.

One evening we had a rather a drunken party with John Sloane, an old friend, and some of his men from 29th Brigade. Fleurette ended up being given masses of jewellery by some of the troops and I was given a beautiful piece of jade. In the morning, once she was sober, Fleurette returned all the jewellery but I am ashamed to say I kept my piece of jade.

Here we got rid of Janet's two puppies and our menagerie was reduced to one dog and the cat. I think that one of the most memorable, but not so pleasant, things about Mogok was the fact that there were more 'pi-dogs' [pariah dogs] around than we had ever encountered before in our travels and they all seemed to live under the floor of our house. They barked and howled all night, and quite apart from the fact that they were homeless and hungry, they were terrified and suffering from what we called 'diver's disease' (they dived under the house at the slightest sound or movement). They were also dreadfully mangy and frightfully smelly, poor things.

After many attempts by the MPs to shoot them and put them out of their misery, we could bear it no longer and got one of our little Gurkha guards to crawl under the house and shoot what he could see whilst another stood outside and shot those coming out. All exceptionally unpleasant, but it had to be done as they were not being looked after, were starving and in pretty bad shape. Poor Vivian was inside the house at the time having not been warned about what was to happen, and she was apparently seen jumping about like a cat on hot bricks, too nervous to come out in case she got in the way.

We were only six days in Mogok before continuing on down to Namsaw via Monglong where we contacted the CBID and asked for stores. Alas they had none and we went on very sadly with not many essentials in the canteens until we arrived in Maymyo, and indeed it was not until we reached Meiktila that we were able to obtain more substantial supplies.

The stores situation was so dire we had to ration cigarettes to one packet per person. There was no ink and no writing paper, no shoe polish, and what was worst of all for the Indians, no hair oil. We even sold them small quantities of our cooking oil which they felt was better than nothing. No sugar and no margarine either. Exercise books and toothpaste were about the only things we had an ample supply of. The nearest airstrip to Mogok was some distance away, hence the difficulty with supplies.

Namsaw – 30 March 1945

This was I think the most fun place at which we camped, but the journey quite the longest. We were getting nearer to the famous Burma Road which we had heard so much about. We left Mogok at six o'clock in the morning and didn't arrive at Namsaw until early evening, filthy as usual.

A very shady area had been allotted to us for our parachute tent, but owing to the fact that our tents were travelling behind us, there was nothing we could do except to wait until the truck carrying them turned up. So with all our personal kit dumped off on the ground we sat about on wooden boxes and waited. Some very kind soul from 'A' Mess, later followed by another one from 'D' Mess, brought us some hot tea which was most appreciated, after which we chose sites for our new homes.

The moment the trucks arrived, with the help of our two drivers, we set about putting up our camp – we owed so much to those drivers and the cooks, they really were indispensable and we could not have coped without their tireless help.

It was not long before we had created some sort of temporary shelter. We had supper with our old friends in 'Dog Mess' and then retired to bed. That night was the first of a kind we were to become very familiar with. It started to rain, and I mean RAIN, in cascading tropical torrents, with wind raging like a mini hurricane. The monsoon had broken with a vengeance.

Parachute tents are cool, functional and all very well until they get wet, at which point they become worse than useless. Within about five minutes of the rain falling on the canopy a thing like an inverted balloon forms inside the tent, followed by many more, which at any given moment can start to leak. So there we were surrounded by hundreds of little water spouts pouring down on us. Oh yes, very funny! Fleurette and I, like the others, spent the rest of the night huddled on our tin boxes draped in our monsoon capes, because our camp beds had turned into small baths. Nausea was the only one who didn't seem to mind and slept the night curled up on Fleurette's lap oblivious to all that was going on around it.

Our area the next morning was a sight, as most of the parachute tents were by that stage down or in a very precarious state. The storm had created havoc. There we were, four very wet, wan and bedraggled Wasbies wandering around in drenched uniforms, hanging wet bedding from trees along with soaking items of clothing. The two drivers who lived in our camp were also hanging everything out to dry, as were the cooks. The tarpaulin mess tent had come down completely with crockery strewn all over the place – what a shambles. However, the Camp Commandant came round, and with the help of five large and strong BORs, our tents were re-erected.

The stores were in a sorry state; the flour had turned to paste, the sugar was like treacle and the raisins had all swollen up and looked like stewed fruit. I could only thank our lucky stars that all the cigarettes and matches were still in the canteen vans. The two drivers weren't stupid – oh no! They had very swiftly evacuated themselves into the mobile canteens when the rain started to come down, remaining dry, warm and comfortable.

The following morning, orders were given for slit trenches to be dug round our camp, and the boys (our servants) and a few IORs were put to the task. Loud screams were heard shortly after they started to dig, so we ran over to where they were working to find that our campsite had been an old cemetery or local burial ground, and corpses (very old ones) were being dug up. One was the trench that Vivian and Janet would have to use in the event of an attack, and I saw them both turn a trifle pale when our little Gurkha mess waiter proudly showed us a very green jawbone and said he would be keeping a few gold teeth from it as a memento – a somewhat macabre fancy, I thought.

It was only possible to run one mobile canteen owing to the extreme shortage of stores, but the tea and cake trade, for which we did have sufficient quantities of ingredients, flourished. Everybody worked extremely hard under very difficult and unsettling conditions, not helped by the requirement to continually move forward every few days from one location to the next.

The Sawbwa of Hsipaw's palace was visited by us several times as it had become 29th Infantry Brigade HQ. The Sawbwa was the princely ruler of the Shan state, and we were all amazed at the extraordinary sort of building the palace was; a mixture of Georgian architecture with a Burmese flavour thrown in for good measure. In the Throne Room we discovered an IO [Intelligence Officer], Staff Captain and DAQMG [Deputy Assistant Quartermaster General] all playing Shuffleboard, with their office desks and maps arranged along the walls. The Japs and/or Burmese had looted and smashed all the fittings and had attempted to burn the palace down, so sadly the place was practically gutted and not in very good shape.

This was the first time for almost a year that any of us had seen ourselves in a long mirror, of which there were about half a dozen still in one piece in the Throne Room. I have to say it shook us somewhat as we had all become rather fat, our hair was dry and straw-like and in spite of Mrs T's endeavours to get Pond's Face Cream supplies for us whenever she could, our skins looked so weather-beaten, not to mention rather yellow because of the Mepacrine we were taking. We all wondered if we would ever get our figures back and look normal again. It made food for thought and a topic of conversation between us all when we got back to camp.

Fleurette and I, though I don't think we should have done, went for long walks unescorted by our guards, and one day we found a lovely clear mountain stream which proved too much for us, so we took off all our clothes and bathed 'in the altogether'. The water was wonderfully cool. There was a small waterfall above us and the beauty of the sun shining through the leaves of the trees, dappling shade on the water below, made us feel carefree for those few moments in our own little secret fantasy world. We did sincerely hope that there were no Japs skulking around watching us.

From Namsaw we went on to Maymyo, which for the 36th Division was a great achievement as it was well on the way to Mandalay. It was particularly special for Fleurette, Janet and Vivian, all of whom had been there before the war and knew the place well.

It was just after we had arrived at Namsaw that we heard Mabel and her husband, the Sawbwa, and their family had been found by the Intelligence people. Unfortunately, they had passed through the day before we arrived so Gay never managed to catch up with Mabel. Thankfully she was well and so were the children. They had not been harmed or robbed by the Japanese. It was rumoured that she had given the men who had found them items of her jewellery, although I can't in any way substantiate this story. Apparently the Japs had not known what to do with the family when the Division got close to Mongmit, so they were given lorries to take themselves and their servants to a cave in the jungle some way from Namsaw where they went into hiding. We heard they had now returned safely to Mongmit.

Not far from Namsaw we finally got onto the famous Burma Road, the main highway linking Burma with the south-west of China. A somewhat disappointing sight. We had heard it was a great highway and an amazing feat of engineering, but it was now very badly in need of repair and had the largest potholes I had ever seen. The weight of the armoured vehicles which had been using the road had taken a heavy toll of its surface.

The drive to Maymyo through the Goteik Gorge was another interesting journey with the most stupendous views from the top. I had no idea how many miles of twisty road it was from the top to the base of the gorge, but I should imagine about five or more. It took us a long time to reach the bottom as we could go no faster than about 5 m.p.h. in the trucks. Every few hundred yards there were tight hairpin bends corkscrewing ever downward and each time one was reached, the trucks had to manoeuvre back and forth to get round. Not a single corner could be accomplished in one movement. I really did take my hat off to the drivers of those trucks. They were dead tired, some of them having done the trip at least three times before, due to the fact that the Division was short of transport, and yet they made not one slip. If they had, it would have spelt disaster.

During our descent, I and the other girls took one look over the edge and then did an excellent job of 'braking' heavily against the floorboards with our feet for the entire perilous downward journey, pointlessly leaning our bodies away from the horrific sheer roadside drop. I personally nearly went through the floorboard of the truck in which I was travelling. It was quite terrifying and one needed a pretty good head for heights too. Vivian and Fleurette were the lucky ones because they had our chums, Taffy and Neal, as drivers. However, after eating our bacon and egg sandwiches at a suitable stopping point on the way down, we arrived safely and in one piece at the bottom of the gorge.

After the beauty of the gorge the roadside became pretty flat and scenically uninteresting, apart from some attractive palm-oil plantations which we drove past from time to time. Otherwise the road was dry and very dusty and as usual oh so hot, making this journey a long and arduous one for everybody.

Maymyo – 13 April 1945

Maymyo, situated only forty miles from Mandalay, was a popular hill station before the war. It was still picturesque, with lush green grass and flowering shrubs in the overrun gardens around once pretty colonial-style homes – we felt we could be back home in England. Best of all was the Botanical Garden, situated around a lake surrounded by a large area of tall specimen trees. I particularly recognised the wonderful pink-flowered Bombax with its strange spiny trunk, and of course there were a number of beautiful mauve Jacaranda. In spite of the gardens being overgrown, they were still breathtakingly lovely. It must have been a truly stunning place before the war. Maymyo was the first large town we had visited since arriving in Burma, and because of its one-time beauty it was even more sad to see that the entire area, and the vast majority of houses, were yet again extremely badly damaged and the town itself was almost devoid of people.

We went straight up to Flagstaff House where we were given our billets. I laugh now, although at the time none of us did. We were allocated the saddle room and *syce's* room [groom's room] at the stables attached to the house. The girls, who were all tired and starting to flag, were furious as we had been promised a house of our own. There were plenty of empty houses in the area but, instead, we had been given this very tiny two-roomed hut, which meant that once more our trusty parachute tents had to be put up.

These were eventually pitched and we all had some K Rations for lunch and did the usual sorting out of stores and equipment ready to start selling cigarettes and other necessities to troops who were on their way through to Mandalay, the ancient royal capital with its 750-odd pagodas and stupas, a fort and the palace of the last King of Burma. We were unsure, however, how much of this had survived as we had heard Mandalay had taken a real pounding and been bombed almost beyond recognition.

After a bit of grousing, and with some help from General Festing, we were eventually permitted to choose a proper house to live in, not that there was much actual 'choosing' as we were told that if we liked what we were offered we could have it, otherwise we would have to stay where we were. It was a very large and roomy place, but as always was in the worst of condition. It had initially been occupied by the Japs, then the Kachin 101 Detachment had taken it over and they were certainly no cleaner than the Japs.

In all the sleeping quarters, platforms had been erected for use as beds and these had to be dismantled before we could establish ourselves. The debris and filth underneath these structures was hard to describe. It was truly disgusting. Out came our well-used scrubbing brushes and it wasn't long before everywhere was clean and we were able to set up. We learned later from the POWs we met in Rangoon that these platforms were what the Japs slept on, and the POWs were made to sleep under the same uncomfortable conditions in the prison camps.

In the evening we all went our separate ways for a walk. It was simply heaven to be in a place that was so very reminiscent of home. Later we borrowed a Jeep and Fleurette, who had lived most of her life in Burma, and Maymyo in particular, showed us round. We saw what utter devastation lay about, so many of the houses gutted and all quite destitute without any sort of personal belongings remaining in any of them. We did discover a swimming pool that looked quite clean, so we earmarked it for future reference, but on the whole it was all rather eerie with nobody about.

Fleurette and I found the remains of Angelo's and the Paradise Restaurant, which she used to frequent before the war when she lived in Maymyo, after which we ended up in the Victory Café, where we found Vivian and our driver, John. After this we spent the evening at a party with some Americans.

Both the mobile canteens were set up in Maymyo, as I managed to get a Dakota-load of provisions flown in from the BCD [Burma Catering Depot]. For this I got into a bit of hot water. It was not easy to get hold of supplies but by using a few gentle feminine wiles, I had managed to obtain what was needed so badly.

In addition to the two mobiles, we opened a large static canteen under a shady tree on the slope leading down to the lakeside in the Botanical Gardens and this operated three times a day so that the troops could relax and come and have buns and drinks after swimming. We were terribly busy here and the queues at the static had to be seen to be believed; so much so that we had to get tickets printed for change because we kept running out and once again the Field Cashier, poor man, couldn't keep up with our requirement for so much small change. We found tables of all shapes and sizes scattered around in some of the less derelict buildings, so we brought them down to the lakeside and decked them out with red and yellow tablecloths, making for a very cheery atmosphere.

It was here that we had Arthur loaned to us. He was an absolute gem, and we would have been totally lost without him. He gathered firewood, helped serve, made tea and delicious fresh coffee which was a treat we had managed to locate. He generally made himself indispensable. He told us his mother kept a fish and chip shop at home, and he said that it was in his mind to open one outside a factory on his return to England, as business would be very brisk in such a location.

There were a few horses around, so Fleurette and I were able to safely go out riding, something which Maymyo was famous for. The rides we went on were cut through the forest and unless one knew them well it would have been very easy to get lost, so of course Fleurette was a great asset here as she knew them all of old. Our ability to go out riding enabled us to relax and enjoy the countryside which was so cool, fresh and beautiful and had such a cleansing effect on all of us.

We had some terrific parties in Maymyo, nearly all in our own mess. We always kept an 'open house' so that anyone who got bored with their mess could come down to ours to relax, have a coffee and chat, or merely just sit and cogitate. I believe it was really much appreciated.

Whilst we were in Maymyo Mrs Taylor and Antoinette paid us a fleeting visit. It was Mrs T's first visit since she had left in 1942, and not surprisingly she found it much changed. There were great plans for making it a large leave centre for service men and women, with the WVS and YWCA already staying over to prospect.

Mrs T was very insistent that we kept the house we were in so that any Wasbies who were fatigued and needed a change of scene for a few days could come up there with their camp kit and have a bit of peace and quiet. The food was by this point plentiful. Everything was fresh, from the sweet cool air to the mouth-watering strawberries – they were huge and delicious and such an absolute and unexpected treat for us all. Apparently the area was well known for its strawberry fields prior to the war.

A number of Wasbies did come up for a rest, and in fact the entire time we were there the house was full up, and great fun was had by all. Indeed, when we sadly had to move on after only twelve days, we left a couple of Wasbies still recuperating.

Kume – 24 April 1945

After Maymyo we moved on to a town called Kume, fifty or so miles south of Mandalay. We were only at Kume for a few days. I had gone down very early in the morning with a couple of officers in an advance party of the RSF [Royal Scots Fusiliers], leaving the four girls to follow later with the main convoy. This time I wanted to be certain that our billets would be ready for us as, despite the short respite of Maymyo, the girls were all showing signs of severe fatigue bordering on total exhaustion, which mainly took the form of irritability and nerves, not that I was much better myself. Good humour was certainly lacking. I had managed to cut my leg on a box and it was not healing well, which didn't help matters as far as I was concerned.

Kume was an extremely noisy spot: the area was overrun with crickets, which never let up night or day. We would need to accustom ourselves to their endless racket, otherwise it would become a constant annoyance. We already missed the refreshing climate of Maymyo and it wasn't long before the heat in Kume once again started taking its toll on everyone. It was even more apparent that the girls were close to breaking point. However, after a delivery of mail, everybody picked themselves up pretty quickly. It never took much to resuscitate our spirits.

We were very busy in Kume, and although we did not have a static canteen, we produced tea for the lads after the evening picture shows. One of the pictures we saw was *The Song of Bernadette*, starring Jennifer Jones. Luckily for us these film shows took place just outside our mess tent, so there was always some form of social gathering afterwards.

On other evenings we sat and listened to music, some memorable, some less so. This was first time I heard Schubert's 'Trout Quintet' – a jolly little composition, which was to become one of my favourite pieces of classical music.

We were all aware that the Division would soon cease to operate in these parts as there was talk of them pulling out and returning to India when we reached Meiktila, which was our next stop.

We were now out of touch with Mrs T as our movements were pretty hush hush and so we were unable to contact her. We did not know quite what the next move would bring forth. All we knew was that the Division wanted to keep us with them which was great news, especially as it would mean that we should go along with them on their next offensive when it came off.

It was at this point that we had to say goodbye to Gilbert. He had been our 'father and mother' throughout our time with the Division, always keeping an eye on us and helping out whenever he could. Dear wonderful Gilbert with such an infectious laugh. We all copied his amusing way of speaking and his pet expression, 'We'll make a *bundobust* of Indian arrangements.' We would miss him enormously.

Meiktila – 27 April to 17 May 1945

Our trip to Meiktila was uneventful, but not so Meiktila itself. I think all the girls have unpleasant memories of the place, along with most other people who passed through this battle-torn area. When we arrived in the morning, we were told that we were to live with another group of Wasbies who were camped the other side of the lake. We were then advised that they were not ready for us, so we were taken to an airstrip five miles away from where we were apparently going to work. We had to get settled in, but probably not permanently, as no plans had really been made.

Dear Frank, who was in charge of our team's placement, did make a muddle over that one. We spent a day and night camping out, sleeping under the stars. Thank the Lord it didn't rain. The next day we trundled into Meiktila itself where we were given the only available empty space, which had no shade. The place was riddled with slit trenches and we were pretty sure that some of the filled-in ones had been used as graves. This was later to be proved correct.

Everybody was fraught and tempers were wearing thin. Mine in particular was, by that time, pretty close to boiling point. We had to put up the parachute tents and the unfortunate BORs who had been detailed for the job had been doing nothing else for the past twelve hours, resulting in most of them also nearing the end of their tethers. The ground was rock hard, and we were all very hot, dirty and thirsty, not to mention disgruntled.

Having arrived so soon after the battle, the place still reeked of death. The lake stank as well. We could not get away from the foetid smell of death. It was horrific. So many bodies had been thrown into the lake that we couldn't drink the water until it was well boiled and chlorinated, and none had been at that point. Even after the water had been treated it still smelt and tasted unpleasant. The last thing anyone wanted was to drink it. Initially we attempted to quench our thirst with warm beer but ended up feeling somewhat sorry for ourselves and still thirsty so had to resort to the vile water. There was nothing else available that was non-alcoholic.

A number of dead Japs were found, their bodies covered in flies and the stench was quite nauseating. I came across two bodies whilst out trying to find a suitable spot for our static canteen. It was all too awful, but along with everything else this just had to be dealt with so we got on with it, and with the help of the men, buried the bodies we found.

The servants were all on the point of packing up and departing, but very wisely Frank Hunter and his minions left us alone and we managed to pull ourselves together by the next morning. It was a wonder nobody broke their legs that night leaping over those slit trenches. It was impossible to fill them all in as there were far too many, most of which were sufficient for only one man to lie in. They had been very necessary during the battle as the soldiers used them for protection during air raids.

Our 'penny house' [lavatory] was always a problem, and this camp was no exception. It ended up with me going out and draping, as artistically and modestly as I could, a couple of parachutes round the hole which had been dug, before arranging the seat on top of a strategically placed packing case. I could write a whole history on this subject and the difficulties we experienced with this particular necessity. The Monglong one was visited by a python, the Namsaw one was located far too close to, and in full view of, the kitchen, and the one here at Meiktila was always falling down, as was everything else. Of course the seat had to be carted around wherever we went, usually resulting in a certain amount of mirth upon packing and unpacking it throughout our travels with the Division. On this occasion we had trouble with the bathroom facility – an arrangement of draped, worn-out tent pieces which during a storm took off altogether, leaving me urgently scrabbling for a towel!

In Meiktila we were the busiest we had been in a long while, and I have a feeling I expected far too much from those poor girls. Yet they were just marvellous and worked and worked and worked some more. We had become an essential part of the men's lives and they appreciated everything we did for them; not only the canteen work but also our company and conversation. There was so much to accomplish, and we couldn't do enough, try as we might.

A large transit camp had been erected near the airstrip where the men stayed until they were flown out. We had a mobile van out there all morning, which was kept extremely busy. There was also the canteen on the airstrip itself which opened at 6.30 in the morning and stayed open until 6 p.m. so that the lads waiting for flights could get tea, in addition to supplying cigarettes and cakes. Some of those lads waited all one day then into the next before they eventually flew off. It was estimated that we sold at least 400 gallons of tea a day at the airfield alone. In the evening we had a small static canteen in the troop lines so that they could get tea and stuff before they went to the pictures. This was always very popular and the queues were never-ending.

At Meiktila we had a little Scotsman to help us out – apparently he was known by his friends as 'Jock Wasbie'. He too did a marvellous job of work. Fleurette was superb as well – she kept the kitchen side of things going at a busy pace, producing a huge supply of the most delicious pies and cakes. How the cooks coped was a pure miracle to us as they used to start cooking and cutting sandwiches at 4.30 in the morning, going right through the day until two o'clock in the afternoon when they rested until six o'clock in the evening, only to have to start all over again.

We used to get through over 200lb of flour a day plus 100lb or more of sugar. Jock shook us all one evening when he looked in and said, 'Do you know how much water we have used today?' When we suggested about 300 gallons he said, 'No, no, no, nearly 800 gallons', which I have to say we did believe as tea here was having to be made in tin baths because our urns were far too small. Each bath held 20 gallons at a time and it was empty within about ten minutes. This situation lasted for sixteen days and I don't think that any of the girls could have kept it up for much longer as they were dead beat, not helped by the fact that conditions were pretty awful because the monsoon rains had started.

We could never have managed without the help of 'Jock Wasbie'. He would light the fires at 5.30 in the morning so they were ready for us at 6.30 and he would stay and help us until we closed at 6 p.m. in the evening. We all looked back at the Meiktila days with horror, and I know now that I over-worked everybody. Vivian and Bubbles were completely knocked out after our stint there. However, in spite of all the nastiness, we did manage to have a few amusing evenings with Frank in Taffy and Neal's tent at the end of a hard day's work.

The monsoon rains were at their height whilst we were in Meiktila, with the rain coming down in torrents. Because of this we had been given proper tents by the army hierarchy, with the instruction that we must dig suitable drainage round them in order to prevent flooding. I, however, had been a bit lax about this and had not been in a hurry to dig a channel around my tent, until I discovered to my alarm that the water from everyone else's run-offs was coming my way. Seizing a spade I tore outside and, drenched to the skin, dug like fury to howls of laughter from Fleurette as she watched, from the shelter of her tent, the rain-water running towards my tent.

The torrential downpours uncovered many more bodies from their shallow scratched-out graves. To her horror, when leaving her tent early one morning, one of the girls nearly tripped over a pair of booted legs which the storm had exposed during the night. Once more, these remains, along with others which had become uncovered, had to be reburied: just one more unpleasant aspect of Meiktila.

Farewell to 36th Division

Sadly, the final day came and we said our goodbyes to the last of 36th Division, returning to our tents feeling rather dejected. Little did I know that this was to be the last time I saw Frank Hunter, to whom I had become quite attached.

I did our stocktaking, returning to the CBID all the stores we had left, handed in our takings and then arranged to send Vivian off for some well-earned leave, which she needed badly. Everybody was tired and pretty drained. Bubbles was completely exhausted, as was Viv. Fleurette and I always seemed to be bickering about something trivial, both of us feeling the stress of the past weeks, so I sought permission from Mrs Morton, the Area Commander, to go up to Maymyo with Fleurette for five days' rest. We drove up in a Jeep, with trailer, which we had managed to borrow from Transport for our few days R&R.

After our short break in Maymyo we returned to Meiktila and I was thrilled to find a lovely newsy letter from Gilbert. He had caught up with Mrs T and Lois St John at Alfsea HQ and told them how wonderful we had all been and how we must now all have leave. He went on to say how sorry he was that the Wasbies were to be parted from the 36th but apparently there was no alternative, as the Division had completed its assignment. I felt very proud that he thought so highly of us all and was even more pleased to read the news that he was to fly home at once in order to stand for Parliament.

Gilbert, bless him, had also sent a couple of bottles of Murine eye drops which I asked him to try and find for me as we were all suffering from sore, irritated eyes.

We then flew on down to Rangoon, arriving there on 27 May 1945. We were so glad to see the back of Meiktila. It stank, mentally and physically. We were weary and after all this time were getting fed up with pigging it in tents in either excruciating and unrelenting heat, humidity and dust, or being constantly damp and sodden, surrounded by deep mud during the monsoon. I just hate to think what the poor soldiers must have felt like having to fight in such difficult conditions.

It was about this time that the news of Victory in Europe came through, and it is with a certain amount of shame that I admit, and so did the others, that to all of us out in Burma it didn't feel like the end of hostilities. It certainly made no difference to any of us, we just carried on as normal as the war had yet not ended in the East.

Now that the end of our attachment to the 36th Division had finally come about, I felt we had been the luckiest of all the Wasbie teams. We would not get such an interesting posting again. Our time with the 36th Division had been grand, if tiring. I would not have missed the experience for anything. I often wonder exactly what the men and the officers thought of us. I know most were in favour of us being with them but some definitely were not, feeling that it was not the place for women. We felt maybe our female presence was a reminder of the life they were missing and families they had had to leave behind at homes not just in England but in many parts of the world.

There were petty envies and jealousies, although I must say we did our best to keep off serious 'boyfriends', and indeed it was no trial, as we were too busy and far too tired to even think about any meaningful relationships, it just wasn't the place for this. Our role, after all, was to man the canteens and serve the troops equally and to the best of our ability. At the same time we endeavoured to boost morale and bring some form of normality to the often traumatic lives of those battle-weary men, and it was my sincere hope that we did in some way manage to do this. We certainly received a fair number of letters of thanks and appreciation from some of the men in the Division.

Rangoon – 27 May 1945

Although we were all overjoyed to leave Meiktila for Rangoon, once again the utter devastation and chaos which greeted us on our arrival there was completely shocking and took a while to forget. I suppose such extensive destruction was bound to have been inflicted on many a major city and Rangoon was in the most frightful state. The Japs really had done their utmost to annihilate it. It was totally wrecked and was one of the most forsaken places we had encountered.

A heavy emptiness prevailed and it was intensely eerie to venture down what once must have been a busy and bustling street to find simply nobody around. Weeds and long grass grew on open ground and fungi sprawled up the walls of most commercial buildings and shops, the majority of which had been bombed and/or ransacked, leaving windows broken and doors smashed. The Water Works and Lighting Company had been wrecked, people's homes had been abandoned with empty little gardens neglected and overgrown – a truly heartbreaking and tragic sight. One felt it would be an almost impossible job to rebuild or ever get things back to normal, and the situation certainly wasn't much better by the time I moved on in October.

Immediately after arrival in Rangoon we were allocated a static canteen but it was not until 3 June that we had any idea where we would be based. We were sent out to Mingaladon Airstrip to work. The same old crew, except for Fleurette and Vivian who now had their own team at last and went up to Tharrawaddy to open canteens for the troops up there.

The canteen we opened was in a large tent out at the airfield, and it was not long before the monsoon started here as well, and no amount of trench digging around the mess tent prevented water seeping in when the rain lashed down. There was no way of locking the place up which meant all equipment and provisions had to be removed and stored every night at Wasbie HQ, the most secure location away from the airstrip. Of course everything had to be returned to Mingaladon to be set up again each morning. Failure to do this was sure to lead to most of our stuff being pinched within a matter of hours of closing up the canteen at the end of each day.

Mobile canteens were also set up, taking goods and cakes to gun crews and other troops in the area, as they were often unable to get to the static canteens during the day. Stores were still in rather short supply and a certain amount of rationing was necessary to ensure that everyone received a fair share of what was available. The fresh egg supply threatened to fail, supplies for sandwiches, sausage rolls and cakes ran out, not that cakes or sausage rolls could be made on a regular basis anyway as the firewood was often pilfered.

In addition to canteen work, the girls tried to take part as much as they could in social events with the men at the mess in the evenings. The game of darts was very popular. There was usually a good singsong and now and again some of the lads would read poems which they had composed during brief moments of leisure. We found these very touching and again realised how much the men appreciated our female presence and morale-boosting efforts in the war zones. Some were set to music, such as this one, sung to the tune of 'The Isle of Capri':

> 'Twas on the Isle of Ramree that I met her
> In Kaukpyu by the sunlit sea,
> She was a girl with a chinthe on her shoulder
> One of THE glamour girls of WAS(B).

> Two razor blades, shaving soap she did give me
> With a smile such as I've never seen
> When I looked in the eyes of that WAS(B)
> I left my heart in that mobile canteen.

> Then I was transferred down to Rangoon
> A city, that for me, had no charms,
> For I went to an RAF party
> And found her in another man's arms.

> I'm in a place called Tharrawaddy
> She is there, that sweet WAS(B), I mean
> So my heart cannot move any further
> 'Cos she works in the static canteen.

One of the Wasbies offered the following response, sung to the tune of 'Lili Marlene':

Working in the mobiles, throughout the Jap Campaign
Through dust and heat and monsoons, and lots of heavy rain,
Our cause never faltered, because it's right
To lay on 'char' to boys who fight
THE WAS(B) WENT TO BURMA,
    TO HELP TO WIN THE WAR.

Working in the canteens, with tea and buns and things,
For Army and for Navy and for the boys with wings,
And now that our job is nearly done
'Twas lots of work, but bags of fun,
THE WAS(B) WENT TO BURMA
    TO HELP TO WIN THE WAR.

Time has come for demob. Time for us to part,
The memories of Burma will linger in our hearts,
Of friends that we gathered down the road
Who rallied round to share our load
THE WAS(B) WENT TO BURMA
    TO HELP TO WIN THE WAR.

*

In early June it was announced that a Victory Celebration of the Allied Forces in Burma would take place in Rangoon on the fifteenth. There was to be a Victory Parade, followed by a March Past and Naval Review of warships in Rangoon Harbour, with military, naval and Air Force personnel, along with many civilians, in attendance throughout the day's celebration.

At very short notice we were told that the WAS(B) would form part of the Parade, causing a great deal of consternation as we had never been on parade before and knew very little about the drill. Also our uniforms were pretty tatty from our travels so we felt we would not look as smart as we should like. During one of our practice sessions, horror of horrors, 'Supremo' [Lord Mountbatten] turned up along with the Commander in Chief, ALFSEA [Allied Land Forces South East Asia], and a number of other senior officers, to practise with the rest of us, throwing most of the Wasbies into an even bigger fluster.

On the day of the parade all went well, apart from the fact that just as Lord Mountbatten began his address, the heavens opened and monsoon rain poured down, leaving us standing to attention trying to look smart, only to have our rain-soaked uniforms rather embarrassingly plastered to our bodies, hair totally dishevelled and to add further insult our faces slowly became more and more streaked with green dye from our new berets. We heard that a few of the chaps thought we looked rather fetching when wet – was that a compliment or not?

Over the next few months our work at the airstrip continued, although with the canteens operating at a much slower pace than in the past which gave me time, in the evenings, to catch up with my diary notes and read the latest Wasbie newsletter. I was delighted to learn that some of our favourite beauty products made by Max Factor, Dorothy Grey, Arden, Rubenstein and Cyclax would soon be available to us using our ration cards. The bad news was that the stockist was located in Calcutta, but Mrs T was doing her best to obtain supplies for us.

On the whole day-to-day life was relatively routine, quiet and uneventful. This provided an opportunity for some much-needed leave and so I decided to follow a long-held desire to spend some time in Srinagar, which would offer a welcome respite from the sweaty heat of Burma. A couple of the girls had been to Kashmir and sang the praises of its beauty and refreshing climate. Consequently, a group of us decided to take a trip up there for a bit of R&R. The next step was how to get there. It was a long journey. Travel permits, planes, trains, and a rickety bus ride were all involved before we eventually arrived on the shores of Lake Dal. We spent the next couple of weeks relaxing on a houseboat, enjoying copious amounts of gin, exploring and swimming. I even managed to accomplish a very wobbly aquaplaning session on the lake without mishap. All too soon our leave was over and we embarked upon the marathon journey back to Rangoon.

We soon settled back into the daily regime at Mingladon airfield where we heard from one of the Spitfire pilots that there were a number of troops north of Rangoon in the Sittang region who were marooned in paddy swamps, having been cut off by the Japs. They were without any supplies so Anne Richmond, one of my Canteen No.16 team at Mingladon airfield, organised a small group of Wasbies to make up little parcels of free cigarettes, enclosing short notes with each packet. These were dropped by the Spitfire pilots who were operating in the area, much to the amazement and gratitude of those unfortunate beleaguered men. Not only did this result in a charming thank you note from Brigadier J. S. Vickers on behalf of the stranded men of the 33rd Infantry Brigade, but also a mention for Anne in a local newspaper column with the heading 'Miss Anne of the Sittang'.

It was during this period I heard the frightful news that Frank Hunter had died on 4 August. It shook me to the core. We had been such good chums and the fact that he had died so close to the end of this beastly conflict was just devastating. It left me feeling extremely upset as, once again, I had lost someone very dear to me. What a waste of a vibrant, brave young man's life.

15 August 1945

At last the Japanese had surrendered after the Americans dropped the first ever atomic bombs on Japan, initially on Hiroshima on 6 August and three days later, on the ninth, another was dropped on Nagasaki with horrific consequences, leaving the Japanese with little choice but to surrender, finally bringing an end to hostilities in South East Asia.

Although the War was officially now over and the world was at peace once more, the Wasbies' job was not yet done and we had been briefed that it would not be long before Prisoners of War from Siam [Thailand] and Indo China [Vietnam, Cambodia and Laos] would start to come through Rangoon prior to being airlifted to Singapore, from where they would be repatriated.

Before we became really busy again, I sought permission to make a quick trip to Calcutta. I had learnt that Frank Hunter had been buried there and I wanted to say my goodbyes to a lovely man who had worked closely with the Wasbies during our time with the 36th Division and who had become a great friend. Through our work in the canteens at Mingaladon airfield we got to know most of the RAF crews who operated daily between Burma and India and I was aware there was occasionally a spare seat available. As a consequence, it was not too difficult to hitch a ride with Flight Lieutenant Dennis Woolfe and his crew travelling on the Twelfth Army Commander's Dakota, which was named 'Chinthe' and which happened to be doing some back-to-back flights between Rangoon and Dumdum airfield in Calcutta.

During the course of the return trip, one of the flight deck crew brought a 'Message: Captain to Passengers' information slip from Flt. Lt. Woolfe. This indicated our position, height and ground speed. There was also a handwritten addition under the section 'Points of Interest' which stated that the 7.30 BBC London News had announced: 'British Airborne Forces will land on Tokyo airfields on Sunday [26 August] and heavy naval units will enter Tokyo harbour. On Tuesday [28th] the main air and seaborne occupation will commence.' The note went on to state: 'The Emperor's envoy has reached Singapore; the Russians have taken 250,000 prisoners; Japanese envoys are with Chiang Kai-Shek to arrange the surrender of the forces in China.'

I was only away a couple of days and shortly after my return we became frantically busy once again. We had been briefed by our Commandant, prior to the arrival of POWs, as to what we might encounter and were instructed to remain as calm and dignified as possible. We should not show our horror, and definitely should not stare at the appalling physical appearance of some of the men. We were to show compassion and try to be as normal as possible.

We endeavoured to make the canteens especially welcoming with tablecloths, flowers and English newspapers. It was harrowing to watch the ex-prisoners arriving. After the desperate years of subjugation many were completely speechless, overcome with exhaustion but joy at their release. They proudly wore ragged shorts and shirts, their 'best' attire, and some had stitched carefully preserved regimental badges on to these 'special' clothes. As it was monsoon season, the Army had provided waterproof capes for the men to wear for their transfer to hospital. This new item of clothing was received with great appreciation.

Before the POWs left the area, the Wasbies offered them Scotch broth, tea, buns and, of course, the essential cigarettes. Many were bemused by the world around them – the aircraft, Jeeps and modern military equipment – and they listened in awe to chat about DDT and Penicillin. The current state of the war was a topic of great interest and some of the men produced precious photos of their wives and girlfriends, questioning the Wasbies about the most up-to-date women's fashions and hairstyles.

I spent just over four months in Rangoon before being notified that I was to be posted, with a team of girls, to the Dutch East Indies to assist with repatriation of POWs from that region.

PART FIVE

Post War

South East Asia and Dutch East Indies
1945–46

Singapore – 5 October 1945

And so on to the plane one early, bleak and dark morning at 0530 hrs to go to Singapore en route to Java. The usual bustling scrum ensued, getting everybody up, packed and ready, finally managing to get down to Rangoon's Mingaladon airfield five minutes early, only then having to wait two hours, which was of course the norm. However, tea was served to us by none other than 'Pickles of the Dean and Chapter', a nickname given, for some unknown reason, to one of the BORs who had been helping us out in the canteen. Finally, we got away in a very full plane carrying POWs.

It was not long before we all ended up having to wrap ourselves in blankets as the plane flew so high and, not being pressurised or heated in those days, it was freezing cold in the cabin. The sight of tough ex-POWs, who were on the aircraft with us on their way home to Australia, together with some of our BORs, huddled up and wrapped in blankets playing cards, was a little bizarre.

We arrived in Penang at midday and stayed there until seven o'clock the following morning. Penang was a lovely city: small, compact and moderately clean compared to what we had been used to, and for me, being the first real undamaged 'Eastern' city I had visited, it was fascinating. There were lots of tiny shops on either side of narrow busy streets, selling the most intriguing things and to us, who had not seen much in the way of civilisation for a while, these little stores were an absolute Aladdin's Cave of goodies. The streets were crowded and hot, with busy Chinese rushing about their daily business, bargaining over their wares with anybody who stopped to look. The little shops smelled of incense and slow-burning joss sticks, added to which was the aroma of strange and interesting food and dried fish, plus a multitude of different spices on sale in open jute sacks – these were the real smells of South East Asia.

Cigarettes were at a premium here and one could get 60 Singapore dollars per packet, so I am ashamed to say I took advantage of this and purchased three yards of white chiffon material in exchange for five packets of ciggies! I also bought an enchanting little soapstone figurine and a pair of pretty silver filigree earrings, after which we had a wonderful Chinese chow supper and then 'did' the night life with two war correspondents we had just met.

It was a most entertaining evening, although I thought some of the older ladies in our party should perhaps not have accompanied us. Unwittingly we sat ourselves down on 'hostess' chairs in one of the nightclubs and were removed pretty quickly lest we got picked up for a ten-cent dance, or probably worse. It was very sordid really, but an eye-opener for me as I had not come face to face with this type of thing before, although of course I had heard all about the girls and the night life along the way and it was fascinating to now actually experience in person such a place of perhaps somewhat 'ill repute'.

We left Penang the next day, arriving in Singapore at 11.30 a.m., only to find a worse muddle than we could ever have envisaged. Probably due to communications problems, nobody was expecting us so there was no accommodation and, of course, no real plans for what we should do nor where our actual destination would be. We were told Java was now completely out of the question as the Indonesians were out of control and running wild so it was considered unsafe for us to go there.

9 October 1945

Disorganisation and indecision continued for a few days, leaving us feeling a little uncertain as to our future. We had arrived on the sixth and it was now 9 October, still with no information whatsoever as to what we were to do. Ordinarily three days was not a long period of time but we had been so used to things happening quickly, and always at short notice, that it was unsettling not to have received any information or instructions as to our next posting. Two of our team's plans had been cancelled, so we were rather left in limbo, with no news of amended orders from WAS(B) HQ.

With not much to do we decided to go out to the Dutch Club that night to meet people and have a bit of fun to while away the evening. Seven of us all squished into a small borrowed Fiat car and off we went. How we managed to fit I have no idea, but transport was almost impossible to come by at that time, so squish we had to as it was too far to walk. Some of the Chinese girls were having a whale of a time at the club, and I have to say it did make one feel a little sick at the promiscuous way in which they were behaving toward the men.

We seemed to be out most evenings after this, together with others who were in the same boat as ourselves, and as was often the case, one chap did try to get a bit too friendly and I am afraid had to be put in his place. The Dutch Club was frequented quite regularly whilst we were in Singapore as was the Tanglin Officers' Club, where we had some really terrific parties before leaving for Medan.

We ended up having to stay in Singapore for nearly a month whilst awaiting orders. It was a fascinating city, like Penang, with a multitude of small shops and booths in which to browse, each containing many fascinating commodities, fabrics and knick-knacks. Most of the little booths and shops were run by petite Chinese women wearing oriental-style clothing. The atmosphere, sounds and smells were much the same as Penang and there was an air of energetic hustle and bustle with constant activity late into the night.

Singapore was a definite meeting place of the worlds and it was somewhere I shall always remember. There was an energy about the place with so much to see and do. It was the most fascinating and interesting city, home to so many different nationalities, their varying cultures and religions all mingling harmoniously.

One evening whilst chatting with some Navy officers we were offered the opportunity to go on board the light cruiser HMS *Glasgow*. We were thrilled and jumped at the chance. None of us had ever been on a battleship before so this was very exciting. I did receive strict orders from above to 'look smart, neat and soldier-like' as we were about to visit one of His Majesty's warships. I did try to follow these instructions and initially looked the part but after scrambling from charthouse to galley to engine room, through numerous doors and hatches, I managed to lose several kirby grips and hair pins, ending up a trifle dishevelled and rather cross. Although seemingly inconsequential items, they were difficult to come by but essential to me if I was to keep my long flyaway hair in check. After a bit of persuasion one of the crew helped me to retrace our steps and after a thorough search the missing items were eventually located and I tidied myself up!

During the course of another evening we met up with a number of officers who were on their way through from Batavia and Sumatra, and heard some of their stories about the terrible internment camps where thousands of women and children had been imprisoned by the Japanese in extremely overcrowded and unsanitary conditions: in buildings exposed to the elements, with open sewers running through many of the camps.

The women and children were treated in the most horrific and cruel manner with many dying of hunger. Starvation had been commonplace and dysentery and malaria were rife, with little or no medication available. Savage beatings, kickings and often head-shaving took place for the slightest transgression, such as not bowing or showing sufficient respect and deference to their captors. We were told tales of women and girls being raped and in some cases removed from the camps into forced prostitution. Some of the stories related to us about the barbaric and inhuman treatment of women prisoners at the hands of the Japanese were disturbing beyond belief.

Apparently an enormous number of women and children internees were still out there and we were surprised to hear that there were depots of stores and equipment still being guarded by Japs if you please. There were very few of our own troops around to take over at this point.

With Java still not being an option, I more or less rubber-necked my way down to Medan from Singapore.

Medan, Sumatra – 6 November 1945

A more perfect small model city I had never seen, so clean, and compared to our Burma standards, so untouched by war and strife. I wish I could explain one half of what I felt when I arrived in Medan. The cleanliness and general tidiness of the town, together with the strong Dutch influence in the architecture, were an unexpected surprise. High red-tiled roofs on the houses combined with typically muted and mellow Rembrandt colouring in all the interior decoration. Multi-coloured flags fluttered in the courtyard of our hotel and so many other things almost made one feel one was in Holland and not the East.

The flight was pretty uneventful; seven girls, two of whom were Red Cross, plus five Dutch doctors who had recently arrived from Holland (very pink-kneed!). To me they were most peculiar men, or perhaps it is just typical of our British way of thinking that we consider anybody who is different from us to be strange. However, there it was, they were peculiar to me. They never sat still for a single second at a time and didn't seem to realise that there were windows on their side of the plane as well as ours. They brushed us aside as if we were flies, stretching across to look out of the windows on our side of the plane, without even so much as an 'excuse me', or a 'beg your pardon', to gaze excitedly down at the same view of the sea as that from their side.

During the flight we were all permitted to go up to the cockpit in turn. I have to say I never realised how far into the depths of the ocean one could actually see. It was the most beautiful crystal clear deep aquamarine colour. One could even spot the odd large dark shadowy shape, possibly a shark, more likely just coral and seaweed, in the depths below.

We could also see the local fisher folk out in their little boats. It appeared they built dwellings out into the sea – there were countless strange little what appeared to be 'V'-shaped groynes or some sort of jetty-type structures stretching far out into the water, terminating with a little hut which had been constructed at the apex, where they seemed to live.

A small convoy of ships also came into view when we were nearing the mainland of Sumatra, adding to the increasingly interesting scene over which we were flying. Sumatra itself was surrounded by many small islands and from up in the air it was a spectacular sight. The countryside itself looked to be just as one expected. We gazed out at high volcanic mountains, dense jungle and fertile plantations. Small villages were scattered here and there, mostly consisting of small *atap* dwellings with palm-thatched roofs, a number of which were situated not too far from white coconut-fringed beaches and mangrove swamps leading down to the clear blue ocean.

We had to circle out over the sea for about half an hour to lose height as there were many dark, heavy rain clouds building up over the island through which we could not fly. The monsoon rains in this area were every bit as bad as those we had experienced in Burma. Here strong south-west monsoon winds, called 'Sumatras', would form squalls of such savagery that should a plane get caught up in one during flight it could, very likely, get torn to pieces by the extreme turbulence.

I was later to experience this type of violent turbulence on another trip I did between Medan and Singapore when we hit the tail end of one such storm. It was pretty terrifying and very unpleasant. It felt as if we had flown straight into a brick wall. However, during most of our current flight we just had the serene feeling of flying through light fluffy clouds which wafted softly by, disappearing gently behind us. It was only when we neared the island that the storm clouds built up and this particular flight started to become a little bumpy.

After landing at Medan airstrip and disembarking we were faced with a very uncomfortable situation, as we were waved in by Japanese, our baggage was carried by Japanese, and we were driven to the hotel by Japanese, all without guards. It made us feel uneasy and a little unnerved.

We were taken to the Hotel de Boer where we were greeted with superb comfort which really surprised us. We were to stay in the hotel whilst working in RAPWI [Recovery of Allied Prisoners of War and Internees] HQ. Being used to entering towns which had only just been liberated, and finding little protection from the elements, it was a joy to be given lovely bedrooms, complete with fans, running water and even clean sheets on the beds. The beds themselves all had a large meat-safe net arrangement round them, a necessary protection against the mosquitoes which were also pretty prevalent in this part of the world. It was like sleeping in a cosy little hut; very different to the traditional little tepee-type nets we had been using in Burma.

We had an excellent meal soon after we arrived, mainly made up of fresh fish and rice. We had been warned about the food vis a vis tummy upsets, but I felt sure that by now our stomachs were pretty used to coping with almost anything, and it was unlikely we would react to any unusual tummy bugs which might be in the food in Medan.

As I sit writing this account of our arrival, my little cornelian-coloured soapstone figurine and my gilt cross, purchased that evening, lie facing me. Seldom in recent months have I felt such satisfaction from the purchase of any two inanimate objects, but for some reason these simple little trinkets do give me such pleasure.

Shortly after our arrival I made contact with a Major Jacobs who was in charge of RAPWI and was one of the very few British in Medan. He was an extremely live wire, though he was not able to be of much help as he was in the process of handing over to the Dutch. He estimated this should only take him a couple more days, after which he would be leaving. Little did he and we know that it would in fact take considerably longer, as it was a period of total disorganisation during which chaos reigned supreme.

Major Jacobs was a most interesting man. He was a member of Force 136, and had been dropped into the area by parachute, as had other members of this Special Force, who we later discovered were a British-led, very small underground resistance group operating in the South East Asian theatre of war. They undertook sabotage operations, blowing up roads and bridges, supported by an effective local espionage network which kept them abreast of Japanese movements in the area.

He had arrived some six weeks or so before the actual recovery of Sumatra, and he had been treated almost as 'King of the Island' until one of the Indian Divisions arrived to take over. The situation was most extraordinary; the Dutch were almost non-existent, and those who were still there were almost incapable of any organisational powers whatsoever. We were told they had had a very bad time of it, and the prison camps in which many of them had been interned had knocked them for six completely.

British troops had not arrived yet so the Japs still had complete control over the country, there being no Allied Forces to take over responsibility from them. They would most punctiliously salute one at every opportunity, and the guard at the foot of the staircase in our hotel would present arms religiously whenever one of us went either up or down the stairs. They drove the vehicles, guarded the stores and ammunition dumps, and in general seemed to run the place. A situation we found very difficult to come to terms with.

There was at that time very little unrest as far as I could make out, only a rather passive resistance towards the Dutch, but security was still very definitely an underlying issue. At that point the Indonesians had not connected our arrival with the thought that we might be helping the Dutch retrieve their colony. We sincerely hoped that trouble would not flare up as it had in Java, as it would jeopardise the movement of thousands of Dutch internees who were being brought down from the hinterland, and would make things difficult here in the town for those of us who were dealing with their repatriation.

When purchasing a complete set of Sumatra stamps from the Post Office before it closed the next day, I met a very pleasant American officer who offered to give us a guided tour round the town, as we were not permitted to move about without an escort. So, off we trotted on foot to reconnoitre, me in the front with him and the other girls following behind in a line looking much like a school crocodile. We must have been a rather strange sight.

Our new acquaintance had been a businessman in pre-war Medan, and it was interesting to see how all the Chinese immediately recognised him, coming out of their shops to welcome him back. The stories he had to tell us about the Dutch administration of the place and its people were legion.

We had another terrific Chinese chow with him that evening which was most enjoyable, although I found shark fin soup to be a little odd – it was a sort of cross between tomato soup and a sago pudding with bits of bacon rind thrown in for good measure – not really to my taste and something I have not tried again since.

Initially we were running the IOR canteen and a large, empty shop was allocated to us for use as a tearoom, library/recreation room and a theatre for films and concerts. We attempted to offer food which we knew the Indians would enjoy, such as the sweet pink and white iced cakes which were so popular. There was also brightly coloured ice cream and soft drinks. The theatre concentrated on Indian films and concerts and also shows provided by Indian regiments.

Over in Padang, Western Sumatra, Bubbles was also having fun and games in her canteen, with their staff being threatened by the Indonesians for working with the British. In a newsletter she described a recalcitrant cook, a malfunction of the field ovens and over-kneaded pastry which resulted in very grey sausage rolls, and a lack of supplies meaning that ration biscuits had to be smeared in chocolate icing in order to be edible. She herself was bitten by the cooking fever and often missed dinner in an effort to produce something which the men would find worth eating.

Whilst here we have met some of the women and children who have been brought down from the prison camps; the joy with which they greeted us as fellow women, and the questions they asked, were moving to an extreme. They were desperate to hear news of the outside world, having been in isolated captivity for so long. Many of the women had only one dress to wear and when that was being washed had been forced to stay in bed, such as that was, to protect their modesty. Most of the young girls only wore a brassiere, and shorts made from the remains of ragged clothing which had become beyond repair.

The majority of women were reasonably well, considering the dreadful time they had clearly been through. The Japs had made them work out in the fields every day under the blazing sun. We were told that the look of health could actually, and especially in their cases, be very deceptive as they had not been treated well nor properly nourished, being fed only minimal, non-nutritious food rations in the camps. Their lives had been hard to bear and their stories were harrowing. In spite of the tragedies and hardship they had experienced, the children were still grand, spirited little kids, although rather wild and undisciplined.

Our workload was very heavy, not helped by the fact that we were trying hard not to tread on the toes of the Dutch Red Cross girls, who were unsure why we had come to help with what they considered to be their work. They appeared to have a slight mistrust and almost dislike of us English, unlike their compatriots who had been so badly treated and were only too thrilled to see us. We never understood the reason for their negative attitude towards us and any help we were trying to offer them. Although they needed our assistance in the form of supplies and ships etc., our personnel were not made to feel at all welcome and in fact we felt most uncomfortable at times. Later on, and after the arrival of more Dutch from Holland, things did get a little easier, although they continued to grumble a lot about our policies amongst other things.

As it turned out, my time in Medan was short-lived. After the first couple of weeks I started to make enquiries about the UNRRA [United Nations Relief and Rehabilitation Administration] jobs in Singapore. WAS(B) pay was simply insufficient to cover our expenses as the cost of living was so terribly high in Medan. I was also wondering how things were going to work out with no Area Commander to report to.

Knowing I would be returning to Singapore, leaving my team in Medan, I did have somewhat mixed feelings and doubts. The day before I left I had a rather stormy interview with the Dutch replacement RAPWI Commandant during which I had to exercise considerable self-control. He started off by saying in slightly broken English, 'You wear no Red Crosses, why have none Red Cross personnel been sent to help? You are Army and we do not want your help.' It was obvious that it would be an uphill grind, but I hoped that the comfort in which the girls were going to live, and the pleasantness of this little city, would be some form of compensation for some of the difficulties they were encountering, not least the snipers who were pot-shotting on a daily basis, meaning that we had not been allowed out without an armed guard.

Shortly after I left, and following the murder in Padang of a British Red Cross girl, Anne Allingham, a good friend of the Wasbies, Bubbles and her team were instructed they also would be returning to Singapore to await orders as to the future of the Wasbies in Sumatra, which seemed a little uncertain. However, just as they were due to leave, Bubbles went down with what was thought to be diphtheria, which meant instant quarantine for the rest of the team until her swabs had been analysed. Luckily the tests showed that it wasn't the dreaded diphtheria bug and the Wasbies were given clearance to travel.

My own flight was one of the most frightening I had ever undertaken, as mentioned earlier. Imagine sleeping peacefully on the aeroplane only to be awakened to find oneself catapulted off one's perch of reasonably secure boxes, in a sudden and very forceful fashion. The 'seats' on which the others were sitting collapsed, and we all ended up in an undignified heap of arms and legs. The plane had flown into some heavy storm clouds, with subsequent severe turbulence, resulting in an immediate and very sudden loss of altitude. I might add here that on glancing out of one of the small windows, the sea was NOT FAR AWAY! All most alarming, not to mention terrifying.

Once back in Singapore, and with my fuse as always rather short these days, I was pretty cross about the initial lack of accommodation, and I am sorry to say I rather flew off the handle about it. The only redeeming fact was that the FANY's [First Aid Nursing Yeomanry] arrangements were equally chaotic. I did eventually end up with an apology, and was assigned to the Red Cross depot at Sea View where we handled the distribution of Red Cross stores to the Dutch women and children POWs. We were to clothe in the region of 700 in a ten-day period, and I have to say when we were confronted with this seething mass of large shiny-faced Dutch women and children it seemed a somewhat daunting task.

As ever, humour came to our aid and we were able to enjoy some lighter moments. One evening, when relaxing with some RAPWI colleagues, I was presented with a very entertaining and completely unofficial 'Driving Licence' in place of a bona fide document which, due to the uncertain length of my stay, I had not bothered to obtain from the appropriate authorities in Singapore.

The accommodation at Sea View left much to be desired so we were transferred to the Raffles Hotel and made very comfortable indeed, with all mod cons including the luxury of a proper bathroom and exceptionally comfortable beds. The hotel was also being used as transit quarters for POWs during this period, accommodation being at a premium with so many of them coming through.

When Singapore fell, this well known, splendid and genteel colonial-style hotel had been renamed *Syonan Ryokan* by the Japanese and used as quarters for senior Japanese officers during their time of occupation. However, after the Japanese surrender it had quickly been cleaned up, reverting to its proper purpose as an hotel in September 1945.

January to April 1946

Shortly after my return I learnt from Wasbie HQ, which was now in Singapore, that I was to be promoted to the rank of Captain and was to become Area Commander, Java, leaving just after Christmas. My assignment was to organise the Wasbies' takeover of catering at the Toc H Club in Surabaya, which involved some of my team from Medan. The girls followed me from Singapore but their mobile van and equipment, being shipped from Sumatra, were still en route so, once again, we needed to open up improvised canteen facilities.

Initially there was no cook but the girls managed to train up an old Chinese. He put together his own little team and was soon able to provide a regular supply of sandwiches and sausage rolls, slab cakes, jam tarts, sponge cakes, ice cream and fruit salad. All went well until there was a festival day when all the cooks got drunk and ended up falling asleep covered in ice cream and half naked. On another occasion one of the girls was accused of serving stale cake to which she replied, 'It is fresh, made this morning.' 'No, no,' came the retort from the IOR in question, 'not made this morning, made tomorrow!'

In Surubaya we were in the company of 5th Indian Division, nicknamed the 'Ball of Fire' Division because their emblem depicted a red circle on a black rectangular background. They were commanded by Major General E. C. Mansergh, CBE, MC, and we remained with them until April. As always it was hard work, but fun, and in the evenings after a long day in the canteens, we relaxed with film shows, dances and, on one occasion, a piano recital by one Joseph Bodmer.

By early April we all knew we did not have much time left with the Wasbies and would soon be discharged and go our various ways to very different lives in the civilian world. In mid-April, after our short stint in Surabaya, we returned to Wasbie HQ to await our official discharge.

May to July 1946

Although not yet discharged, but with leave due, I decided to take a trip across to Calcutta and Darjeeling, accompanied by some chums who were also awaiting further orders. In spite of being aware that the start of the monsoon season was imminent, we decided to go anyway, booking our boat passages to Calcutta in early June. Our plan was to take a trip up to Darjeeling, a hill station in the Lesser Himalayas, known for its cool climate, picturesque forested mountain scenery, tea plantations and spectacular distant Himalayan panorama. The highlight of this visit was to be a ride on the Himalayan Mountain Railway 'Toy Train' up to Darjeeling.

We arrived in Calcutta after a short sea voyage and sorted out some accommodation at a local hostelry where we were able to store our main luggage, such as it was – after all, we didn't have much, having mainly lived in uniform for the past three years. Because of the weather we decided to go straight up to Darjeeling before the monsoon took hold and, after an overnight stay in Calcutta, booked the train trip for the following day, keeping fingers crossed that the weather would hold. June was the end of the short summer season and the hill station climate was more than likely to be damp and misty, if not pouring with rain – great for tea growing but not for visitors.

An early start and a good hearty breakfast set us up for the day ahead. We made our way to Howrah Station armed with light luggage and a packed lunch – drinks, sandwiches and a few regional titbits – which we would no doubt supplement with local food and tea at the many stops up to the mountains. We settled into the journey out of Calcutta and across the plains to Siliguri. We disembarked and made our way to where the narrow gauge Darjeeling Himalayan Railway service took over for the final 48-mile climb to our destination seven thousand feet above us.

There, puffing away gently, was the much-talked-of 'Toy Train', known as such because the engine and rolling stock were smaller than normal and operated on a narrow two-foot gauge track. The little B Class coal-fired locomotive, built in the 1880s, was painted a pretty cobalt blue. It had a tall chimney above its tubby boiler which was belching out a noxious cloud of sulphurous smoke. Perched on the front of the engine was a prominent, large, moon-like headlight and to us, the engine and its two small carriages truly resembled a toy train. It was an enchanting sight and brought a smile to all our faces. We boarded and settled down as the little engine began to chug its way slowly out of the station upwards to our final destination.

In order to assist the steep ascent, the track had been designed with a series of loops and reverses. Upon reaching the zigzag tracks the train would move forward and then back, and then forward again, gaining a little height each time. The railway ran through the high street of the villages that straddled the track and alongside, or in the middle of, the narrow road, hugging the bank on one side with often an eye-watering sheer drop on the other. It was certainly going to be an 'interesting' ride. We were mindful that the return trip would probably be even more stomach-churning.

Off we set at a slow pace – nothing fast about this train ride. An ear-shattering whistle sounded non-stop throughout the entire journey to alert any person or animal in the vicinity to the train's impending arrival; it would more than likely take a lot of steam to get going again mid-climb if we had to brake. The loops all varied in size, some short and some up to five miles each, with the most hair-raising being 'Agony Point' which circled around a high promontory with a precipitous drop on the outside: 'Agony' was rather an understatement. I don't really have a head for heights and it was petrifying!

The last station before Darjeeling was Ghum, which we had considered visiting as a day jaunt, enabling us to take a hike up to Tiger Hill which was known for its stupendous views of the Himalayan Kangchenjunga massif. As it turned out the weather was not conducive to doing this and anyway there were wonderful, uninterrupted views of the mountain range from Darjeeling with Everest, although a hundred odd miles away, visible on bright mornings.

Darjeeling was a pretty hill station surrounded by lush pine forests and tea plantations, reminiscent of Shillong. The streets were busy with a multitude of colourfully clad Indian, Tibetan and Nepalese tribal people. The most eye-catching were the Nepali women who wore traditional apparel, with very dramatic adornment – thick ropes of glass beads from which hung a chunky spool, apparently indicating that the wearer was a married woman, along with a string of large, embossed beads interspersed with roundels of scarlet felt. To complement their necklaces they wore huge hooped earrings, nose rings and to top it off a large bejewelled disc was perched on their foreheads. Their costumes were predominantly red and the accessories mostly gold, making for a particularly striking appearance. A very obliging, though rather stern-looking woman proudly allowed us to take a photograph of her.

Darjeeling was a fascinating and buzzing place, popular with civil servants and their families, military personnel and people like us, who were simply there to relax and unwind away from the heat and humidity of the lowlands. There was a vast amount to do and enjoy. The town itself provided many opportunities to search the bazaars for unexpected treasures, or to eat, drink and socialise at the local Country Club, always on the lookout for anyone we knew from our Wasbie travels. Further afield we rode horses, hiked the surrounding countryside and took a trip to Kalimpong, previously the gateway for trade between Tibet and India and renowned for its stunning, sheer forested escarpments on which perched tiny exquisite monasteries.

On our final afternoon we watched a beating of the retreat by the Gurkhas, who had a base there. It was a terrific sight with them marching proudly in their smart tartan uniforms, playing the bagpipes. They are such a noble race and had been a huge asset to the Army in the recent battles against the Japanese. It was wonderful to see them putting on a grand display so close to their home country of Nepal. It provided a fine ending to our visit and was made even more poignant by the fact that I had received my discharge certificate on 26 May and realised I was unlikely to ever visit this part of the world again. Knowing I was in Darjeeling, Nin Taylor had arranged for the certificate to be sent to me there for signature and return, by Forces Mail, to Wasbie HQ in Singapore.

We left Darjeeling in early June, having to brave the downhill return journey which, as anticipated, was even more hair-raising than the ascent – shades of the Goteik Gorge descent in Burma. The metal to metal of the train brakes against the lines screeched deafeningly almost the entire way down – loud enough to drown out the persistent sound of the whistle – until unscathed, but with ears ringing and jelly-legs, we arrived back at Siliguri ready to catch our onward connection to Calcutta.

Just before leaving Singapore I had received a note from Mrs T to say that I had been Mentioned in Despatches for services to the Wasbies during the period 16 February to 15 May, 1945, when I was with 36th Division in northern Burma. I had to admit to being rather thrilled at this recognition. However, when I arrived in back in Calcutta following the trip to Darjeeling I was astonished to receive a wire from Nin Taylor congratulating me on being awarded an MBE. This telegram was initially sent to me care of the YWCA in Darjeeling where we had been staying but missed me by a few days and so had been forwarded to Calcutta.

The news of the MBE came as a total surprise as I was only just coming to terms with the MID. Thrilled as I was, I did wonder why these recognitions had been bestowed on me when so many of the other girls were probably entitled to such accolades as much as I was. Without their tireless work and wonderful support my teams could never have coped the way they did. In fact I learnt later that Fleurette had also received a well-deserved MID.

Word got round and I was met with effusive congratulation, which I found slightly embarrassing, but my friends all insisted that the news called for a celebration.

It appeared everyone was delighted at the opportunity for a party and a special evening was arranged for 20 June. As always, the booze was flowing and we pushed the boat out, celebrating in style at Firpo's, an historic and rather splendid restaurant owned and run by Angelo Firpo who had also recently been awarded an MBE in the King's Birthday Honours List for his entrepreneurial services, presumably to the catering industry – the *London Gazette* was not specific.

Firpo's catered for all echelons of society from royalty, maharajas and high-ranking government officials and officers to the likes of ourselves. The menu was a fixed price *table d'hôte* irrespective of who the guests were. In addition to dinner there was a nightly cabaret and dancing. Firpo's was said to be the only establishment in India to have a sprung dance floor. We booked dinner, rather than luncheon, dolled ourselves up in our best evening wear and sat down to a three course meal, inclusive of soup and coffee, at a cost of five rupees.

After the meal and far too much gin, I was ceremoniously presented with a makeshift MBE. Someone had cleverly unearthed a snippet of genuine MBE medal ribbon which was pinned, with all seriousness, onto my evening dress. I accepted with due decorum, although still a little embarrassed by the thought of receiving a 'gong'. The celebration lasted long into the night and was great fun, with the following morning's sore feet and sore head a small price to pay.

Having spent a marvellous few weeks in Calcutta it was time to say goodbye to the extraordinary life I had led for the past three years and make my way to Bombay to catch the boat to England with my Wasbie chum Phyllis Jeffries. I had discussed with her, before she was posted to Japan, my desire to start afresh with a life away from all the memories of Kenya. She had very kindly invited me to stay with her and her family until I was settled and had found my feet and hopefully a job. Nin Taylor knew of my plan and had sent a note with my discharge papers, saying she had booked passage for me, along with herself and Phyllis, on board the SS *Canton*, a troop ship leaving Bombay in the last week of July.

I made my way by train across India to Bombay where I spent a few more fun days catching up with people I had met when I was there after arriving from Kenya in '43, going to picture shows and hunting for dress material, zips, buttons and other bits and pieces I was unlikely to find easily in post-war England. After years in uniform I was looking forward to making some attractive clothes for myself and knew that the clothing coupons we had been issued with upon discharge were only likely to provide me with a demob coat, skirt and two blouses. I was even lucky enough to have the privilege of attending a piano recital at the magnificent Sir Cowasjee Jehangir Hall on 3 July, the week before we sailed.

Although there had been great challenges during the past three years, our time with the Wasbies was an experience none of us would have missed. There were so many good things to remember: the letters of appreciation, not only from high-ranking military personnel but also from the officers and men we had met and served, the terrific welcome we always received wherever we set up a canteen and the many friends we had made along the way.

The Wasbies were a wonderful group of women, more like a family really. Ninian Taylor was a very fine leader as was Lois St John, her second in command. Their support, encouragement and appreciation of our endeavours was endless and never ceased to amaze me.

We had shared so many incredible experiences, met some extraordinary and wonderful people from all walks of life and many different cultures. The whole episode gave us all a great sense of achievement, and also taught me personally so much about myself and how to cope with situations I would never have been confronted with in civilian life. Most of us kept in touch for many years after the war, a number becoming lifelong friends.

Nin had been indefatigable and constantly on the move from place to place keeping an eye on us girls, keeping in touch with the military hierarchy and her finger on the pulse of where we were most required and would be most useful to the armed forces in India and Burma, later Japan and the Dutch East Indies. She was a true inspiration. So many wonderful stories which we would treasure for the remainder of our lives. Particularly memorable were the many notices we found pinned on trees reading: 'Wasbies please call', and the joy on the men's faces when our canteens lurched out of the trees into a steamy jungle clearing. They were thrilled to bits, even if we had little to offer other than a smile and a cup of char. I had a chuckle or two again over some of the poems which had been written by us and to us and which had been circulated in the Wasbie newsletters.

At the end of our time with the Wasbies when Nin wrote to thank us all in the form of a special newsletter to say farewell, she included copies of letters written to her by Lord Louis, General Slim, Lieutenant General Stopford, Lieutenant General H. R. Briggs and many other senior commanders, all of whom expressed their admiration and appreciation of the magnificent work done by the Wasbies during the Burma campaign.

The voyage home gave us the chance to spend many happy days in each other's company, relaxing and reminiscing and sharing these memories, together with the more disturbing accounts of alarming situations and narrow scrapes which some of us, particularly Nin, had encountered, especially when the Wasbies had to move out of an area at short notice because it had become too dangerous to remain.

As the *SS Canton* neared the English coast heading towards Southampton Water, we sighted the distinct white pinnacles of the Needles which reminded me of the giant baobab trees which also stood sentry at a harbour entrance so far away in Mombasa. I was about to face another milestone in my life and once again had misgivings as to whether I had made the right decision in not returning home to Kenya.

PART SIX

Return to Civilian Life

1946–1988

Before leaving Singapore, Maria had finally written her parents a letter telling them of the breakdown of her marriage, her divorce having been finalised on 28 June 1946. A reply from her mother eventually caught up with her after her arrival in England, at Phyllis's parents' house in Hampshire, where Maria was staying before moving up to London to find a job.

Joan's letter was sympathetic. She said that Allen was not sorry, and that she herself was not surprised. She had felt for some time that something was not right. She was glad that Peter had given Maria some happiness, but had always feared that it would not last. She hoped that Maria would put it behind her and 'Be ready to start life fresh in your heart as well as your mind.'

She encouraged Maria regarding her future: 'My dear, when you married, you took the course of your life into your own hands and ever since … you have done it very well and bravely.' She said that Maria 'must do what you think and wish and feel' and that wherever life led her in England or in Europe, 'Don't forget, if you want us we are here, and if you feel you would like to come home there is a warm and loving welcome always waiting for you.'

Joan and Allen had returned to Killean in 1945 as soon as the war was over, and in the same long letter she wrote that food supplies were good in Kenya and that she was getting fat, 'after four lean years in London'. Allen, however, was 'struggling with the farm – no nails, screws, cement, tools, etc.' Ordering materials required dozens of permits and reams of paperwork and then an interminable wait before they could be delivered. Joan was unhappy to find that Nanyuki was still overrun by the army, who had bought up everything they could and seemed set to remain in the form of a Brigade Command. They had shot so much of the local game, leaving herds depleted and the plains bereft of their rich pre-war fauna. The thought of their continued presence horrified her.

Luxury goods were unobtainable, both in Kenya and in London, or only available at prices beyond the reach of many. Joan wrote that on Oxford Street in 1945 the cost of a 'little cotton frock', which pre-war would have been around thirty shillings (£1.50) had risen to between £6 and £8. Evening dresses could not be had for love nor money; people were not allowed to make them, or at least, she said, that had been the case when she and Allen had left.

The returning Wasbies found that the situation was not much better in 1946. They had all been issued with ration books containing coupons which were cancelled each time they were used, whether it be for food, clothing or other day-to-day consumables. They had been advised that a utility rayon suit could be purchased for approximately £2 11s (the equivalent of almost £100 today), plus eighteen ration coupons. This was in addition to the demob coat, skirt and two blouses which had been issued to them on their arrival and which were also subject to the coupon system.

Although not particularly attractive, these items were useful as the few clothes they had managed to have made up whilst they were abroad were not suitable for the forthcoming winter months. On smart occasions and in the absence of stockings, which were nigh on impossible to find, women still resorted to the wartime expedient of painting a line down the back of their legs to simulate a seam. The 'make do and mend' regime continued for some while until rationing on clothes was lifted in 1949.

Many Wasbies kept in touch after they were disbanded, helping each other to settle back into civilian life, and not long after she moved to London, Maria was asked to help organise the first WAS(B) reunion tea party on 25 October 1946. She was only too pleased to do so, as it gave her the opportunity to get her teeth into something not only worthwhile but also fun. What was more, it offered a chance to step away from post-war drabness for the day and into a world of almost-forgotten style. This reunion was written up in one of the Wasbie newsletters which had been popular reading amongst them throughout the war, and Maria contributed a section on the marvellous and fashionable outfits which were worn by those who attended. In spite of the strictures of rationing – or, more likely, because of them – it is clear that the Wasbies relished the challenge of dressing up for the occasion, even if the prevailing colour appeared to be black:

Mrs Taylor, always affectionately referred to as Ma'am, looked as though she had just stepped out of Worth's Band Box in a very smart black dress and coat, complemented with a mauve and blue buttonhole and sable stole. Another two girls were also in black, Pam Tayleur in a suit with a fascinating black halo hat decorated with an ostrich feather pompom, and Nan Bruce-Scott who wore a mid-length coat and dress with a fox fur. This outfit was completed with a long string of pearls.

Fleurette Pelly looked extremely smart and tailored in a black suit as did Prue Banks. Phyllis Jefferies had combined two unusual colours with great success and looked lovely in a cinnamon wool dress with a black coat and bonnet.

Jean White, who was with her mother Cath, was soon off to Germany. She wore two shades of grey with a heavenly pancake hat and snood. Constance 'Spratt' Tayleur was there looking very smooth in midnight blue with matching coloured hat. I really envied Gay Tucker's Persian lamb coat; she looked very smart when she arrived wearing a small pork pie hat set at a very jaunty angle.

Mary McLaren wore a white lamb coat over a grey suit with a brightly contrasting red silk blouse. Jean Chater was in a powder blue dress with matching coat, and Elaine Cheverton looked very fetching in a black frock which she had combined with pale blue, as had I. Dosan Penty also attended looking glorious and so feminine and elegant in a beautiful soft peach floral silk sari. Last but not least, I must say our much *loved Lois St John wore a most charming ensemble with black fur stole over her shoulder and looked simply splendid, as in fact did everyone.*

As the reunion was such a great success, it was decided that they would continue to have some sort of get-together at least once a year. It was also agreed, at an after-party meeting, that the WAS(B) Newsletter would continue at a cost of five shillings per person per year to cover the cost of printing and postage. They had been united by war and wanted to continue to share their experiences, jokes and ditties for the foreseeable future of peace. At the request of the editor, however, the jokes submitted for publication were not to be too low in tone.

25 October 1946, at the first Wasbie Reunion: Maria presenting Lt. Col. Ninian Taylor OBE, WAS(B) commander, with a tablecloth depicting the badges of all the divisions and corps served by the Wasbies in India and Burma during the South East Asia Campaign.

The following year, the Wasbies were invited to participate in the first *Dekho!* Burma Reunion for the men of the Fourteenth Army, organised by the Burma Star Association, which was held at the Royal Albert Hall on 2 June 1947. It gave them the opportunity to meet again many of the soldiers they had shared experiences with and also a chance to put on their finery and present a completely different picture from the dusty, sweat-streaked 'jungle green'-clad spectacles that the men were more familiar with. The day was hot and sultry, more like Burma than London, but this didn't stop the Wasbies wearing their best outfits including hats, gloves and the occasional diamond brooch.

A *Daily Express* headline the following day exclaimed 'Mayfair girls recall the jungle war'. The journalist, John Deane Potter, who himself had been in Burma and India as a war correspondent, described the evening as joyful and nostalgic. 'Many of the men never envisaged,' he wrote, 'as they struggled and sweated along the dusty jungle tracks, sniped at and shelled by the Japanese, that such an occasion as this would ever come about.'

The men had difficulty recognising each other and made jocular comments about ties and lack of beards, then proceeded to talk animatedly about far-off days and battles long ago. They also failed to recognise most of the former Wasbies, and vice versa. But the part that the Wasbies had played in the theatre of war was loudly acclaimed. The newspaper article described how the 'Mayfair glamour girls talked with knowledge about the times they were surrounded by the Japanese when they went right up forward with the men, running canteens and social services.'

During the evening Maria caught up with one of the

36th Division team's favourites – friend and Wasbie 'camp protector', Gilbert Longden. He had embarked on what was to be a successful career in politics, going on to become MP for South West Hertfordshire, which constituency he held until 1974. He was also at various times a UK representative at the Council of Europe and vice-chairman of the British Council, and was knighted for his services in 1972.

The Albert Hall event was attended by more than 5,000 men – and a handful of women – all of them proud to have been part of such a significant period of history. The highlight of the evening was when General Slim took to the stage to deliver his speech. His appearance was met with a huge cheer and thousands of men shouting as one, 'We want Bill'. An army of Britons who had conquered the unknown Burma jungle now sat informally and shirt-sleeved in the auditorium of the Royal Albert Hall whilst generals, admirals and their old commanders joined General Slim on the podium, and concert performers during the evening included Vera Lynn and a very young Julie Andrews.

Both the Wasbie reunion parties and the annual Burma Reunions at the Albert Hall continued for a number of years, enabling former Wasbies to continue to catch up with the many people they had originally met in the strangest of places and in none too agreeable surroundings.

Maria also remained in touch with her old Kenya friend 'Flags' Atkinson, who continued his military career with the Royal Corps of Signals until he retired as a Brigadier in 1964. In later years, after retiring from the Army, Flags returned to England and became one of the thirteen Military Knights of Windsor, a position which he held for the remainder of his life.

All this was in the future, however, and Maria's most immediate concern was the question of what she was going to do to earn a living. Work was not easy to find at first, so she hunted down a second-hand Singer sewing machine. She had made most of her own clothes for many years using Butterick, McCall, Simplicity and Vogue paper patterns, the latter necessitating brushing up on her tailoring skills when it came to making up complicated jackets with fancy collars and revers. Some of her less accomplished girlfriends would also ask her to run up suits, frocks and gowns for them, which kept her in pocket money until she could find more regular employment.

She undertook a number of temporary jobs until eventually she was offered a permanent post with British Nylon Spinners (later Courtaulds) in their fashion department. One of her duties was to compere at fashion shows, which she found rather daunting at first, but she soon learnt to control her nerves and became more confident after the initial couple of presentations. Couture had always inspired and excited her, so this particular job was a lucky find, and although the days could be long and stressful, she loved being part of the dazzling world of fashion, especially following the austerity of the war years.

As time passed she could not help becoming involved with the everyday trials and tribulations of the young women she worked with. Maria loved acting as a mother-hen figure to the occasionally naïve younger models as it brought out the nurturing and protective instincts she had developed with her Wasbie girls. Sadly she never had the children she longed for, so her role as mentor to her more junior colleagues provided an outlet for her caring and maternal nature.

Maria with two of her modelling team, prior to going out on the catwalk.

*

Through Maria's work with British Nylon Spinners, the unexpected happened and she met and fell in love again with a truly exceptional, kind and loving man who was great fun and had a terrific sense of humour – Ronald Holroyd. 'Happy', as he was fondly known by his close friends, lived in Yorkshire. He was a busy man – chairman and managing director of Sanderson and Co (Engineers) Ltd., managing director of Moore and Avery Ltd., textile machinery manufacturers in Todmorden, and he also ran his own small business in the woollen trade.

Happy travelled widely, often to Central and Eastern Europe, and Maria often wondered whether these trips involved more than simple wool trade business. He did have numerous contacts around the world. However, he never elaborated on the reasons for the many unusual stamps in his passport and Maria didn't feel the need to question him. He always made time for her and they thoroughly enjoyed getting to know each other during their lengthy courtship, eventually announcing their engagement before marrying in October 1957. To Maria's great sorrow their marriage was not to last long. Happy was not a well man and passed away prematurely in April 1958, aged only forty-six. They had been married a mere six months.

22 October 1957 – Maria and Happy's wedding day. L to R: best man Patrick Black, Maria, Happy, and Happy's sister Margaret.

On honeymoon – happiness at last!

As a former Territorial Army officer, at the outbreak of the Second World War Happy had become a captain in the 122nd (West Riding) Field Regiment, Royal Artillery (apparently known as the Halifax Mashers) and saw active service in Malaya. At the fall of Singapore on 15 February 1942 he was taken prisoner, along with many thousands of other British and Commonwealth soldiers. He, along with his fellow servicemen, was initially imprisoned in Singapore's infamous Changi prisoner of war camp, where he remained until 26 June 1942. Thereafter they all began their journey to hell, in the most inhumane and despicable conditions, to prison camps in Thailand to work on the construction of the notorious Death Railway from Bangkok to Rangoon, where for every sleeper laid, one man was to die.

The men were herded into metal-sided cattle trucks with little ventilation and no sanitation. The wagons were so crowded that the men could only stand; there was insufficient room to sit, let alone lie. The journey took five days and five nights to reach Bang Pong, the first prison camp. During the gruelling journey there was only a thirty-minute respite stop per day when they received a meagre ration of food – mainly boiled rice, which was to be their staple diet until their liberation.

Their initial task on reaching Bang Pong was to build the actual POW camp – open-sided bamboo barracks with *atap* roofs housing up to 200 men in extremely cramped conditions. These rustic structures would house arriving POWs at the starting point of the railway construction. It was whilst he was incarcerated by the Japanese that he became known as 'Happy' Holroyd, a nickname given to him in recognition of his constantly jovial and cheery disposition in the face of the atrocities with which they were all confronted and had to endure. The nickname remained with him for the rest of his life.

Happy stayed in Bang Pong for three months before being moved on to Chungkai, which became the HQ Main Base Camp and 'Hospital', where he was held for two years.

After Chungkai he moved on to Nakhon Pathom and

subsequently Tha Makham, where the steel bridge over the River Kwai was located. He was there when it was eventually bombed and partially destroyed towards the end of the war. He spent his last five months of captivity in Kanchanaburi Camp where he was to endure life under the sadistic and savage Japanese camp commandant Captain Nagouchi, who was hunted down after the war, prosecuted for war crimes and hanged. Happy was liberated to Rangoon in August 1945. Although Maria had been at Rangoon airstrip helping with incoming POWs at the time Happy would have arrived, neither of them remembered one another from that traumatic period.

Happy was a well-built man, and, according to the letter he wrote to his mother upon arriving in Rangoon, at the worst period his weight went down to just over 7st 4lb (102 pounds or 46kg). He was one of the majority who contracted dysentery and other diseases caused by the inhuman conditions in which they were kept. They had all been starved and over-worked, hacking through the jungle and rocky mountainsides with the bare minimum of hand tools, to level the ground to lay the 400-mile rail track across Thailand to Burma.

All the camps were squalid, rat-infested, and riddled with lice and became a sea of mud and raw sewage in the monsoon. Prisoners suffered from malnutrition, cholera, malaria, beri beri, tropical ulcers and a number of other ailments. As is well known, all prisoners were treated with extreme brutality, and Happy was very fortunate to survive. He did not like to talk about this horrific period in his life, but not surprisingly it led to poor health and ultimately to the kidney failure which caused his untimely death.

A few months after Happy's death Maria's great friend Tina Martin, who had been diagnosed with cancer, also passed away. Tina was an American who had made her home in London. Maria had met her not long after she first came to England after the war, sharing Tina's flat in Draycott Place for a number of years before she moved to a flat of her own in Pont Street, just round the corner from Sloane Square. Her friendship with Tina was probably the closest of her life; Maria had no immediate family in England, and Tina became for her like a surrogate sister. For more than a decade they were inseparable, and after Maria met and fell in love with Happy, their closeness continued unaltered, the three of them often socialising and holidaying together.

This was perhaps the most difficult time of Maria's life, more so even than the long drawn-out ending of her first marriage. The deaths of two people so very dear to her within such a short time of one another had a profound effect on her. She had thought herself pretty resilient, having come through both heartbreak and war, and having coped, using only her own resources, with everything that had been thrown at her. But this was different. She was settled now; she had believed that, finally, she had found the happiness she had always longed for, and to have it snatched away from her so completely and so cruelly was more than she could bear. For some time she was plunged into a state of near-despair, and struggled to regain her sense of joy and purpose.

Phyllis came to the rescue once more. She was now Phyllis Shingles, having married, and was living in Kent. She suggested that Maria move back down south to be near her and her husband, Raymond, and away from everything which reminded her of that brief but special period with Happy, or the lively and frenetic years in London with Tina. Maria duly packed up the home in Halifax where she had lived for a short while with Happy, and moved to the small but exceptionally pretty and historic town of Cranbrook on the edge of the High Weald, nowadays an officially designated Area of Outstanding Natural Beauty. Phyllis stood by her every inch of the way and helped her to deal with her shattered emotions whilst she pieced together, once again, a fresh life for herself in the new home which Phyllis had helped her to find. An added bonus was that another of her dearest Wasbie friends, Merle Hannay (née Landrey), also moved down to Kent, and in later years came to live in Cranbrook itself.

Once settled in Causton Cottage, Maria picked herself up, dusted herself off, and in true Wasbie fashion got on with her life, reverting to her sewing skills yet again to keep herself busy. She converted the attic of the cottage into a work room. She taught herself upholstery and, in addition to making beautifully tailored items of clothing for local ladies, she also stripped, repaired, re-polished and re-upholstered small pieces of period furniture. She was kept so busy that it was not long before she formed a little sewing circle of girlfriends, and they had great fun making beautiful curtains and other soft furnishings for many residents of Cranbrook and neighbouring villages.

The picturesque seventeenth-century cottage where Maria spent the rest of her life was turned into a beautiful snug home with the most exquisite little garden, which she tended and nurtured into something quite breathtaking every summer. Her garden was the envy of all her friends.

She developed a passion for roses, her favourites being Whisky Mac and the spectacular white floribunda, Iceberg, which flowered in abundance each summer in her tiny garden and behind the white-painted railings outside the front of her little house.

She continued to enjoy the theatre, attending musical recitals, plays and shows whenever she could, at the Theatre Royal in Brighton, Chichester Festival Theatre and of course many of the playhouses in London, going to a variety of productions from drama and comedy to classical ballet. She was very amused to hear from one of her friends that the television show *It Ain't Half Hot Mum* was based upon the exploits of BESA, the Bengal Entertainment Services, one of the concert parties which, as an offshoot of ENSA, had entertained the troops in the Far East at the time when she was in Burma.

She developed a love for the ballet, attending many of Frederick Ashton's wonderfully choreographed productions often danced by Margot Fonteyn or Moira Shearer, the two prima ballerinas of the time, and on a few occasions she was privileged enough to see Dame Margot partnered with Rudolph Nureyev, a memory which remained with her and about which she enthused when she introduced me to ballet after my emigration from Kenya to England in the late 1970s.

She never lost her desire to travel and explore the world. In 1950, with her brother Fionn and Tina Martin, she had embarked on a three-month Grand Tour of southern Europe and the Mediterranean taking in, amongst other places, Monte Carlo, San Remo, Porto Fino, Genoa and Rome. Visiting historical and scenic locations remained a lasting joy, and in her later years, when she finally became less physically active, she loved to read about them and to watch travel documentaries on the television.

*

Friday, 20 May 1988

Maria had been to the hairdresser. Mrs Boniface, her dedicated and delightful daily, had been. The cottage was pristine, brass and copper shone, furniture was polished and gleaming, and the clean fresh smell of beeswax permeated throughout. Supper dishes were washed up, tomorrow's list was on the kitchen counter, the evening news was over and the TV turned off – it was time to retire: two cigarettes and a read in bed before dropping off to sleep.

It would seem she sat down on the end of her pretty, lace-draped bed – a headache, perhaps? She knew nothing. The final curtain came down and she toppled gently to the floor. Even in death she did it befittingly: no fuss, no hospitals, fully clothed, hair immaculate, elegant to the last. My best friend and beloved 'Ria had gone. She was only seventy-one.

I was bereft and felt cheated by the unfairness of the grim reaper, even though I knew she was suffering from emphysema – those cigarettes having finally caught up with her – and was half expecting the call when it came that shattering Saturday morning. I miss her to this day.

Postscript

How many readers will be asking themselves the one question I cannot answer – which is: *'What became of that cat?'* – I have no idea. Maria does not say. It would be nice to think it might have ended up with a family in Maymyo, where Fleurette used to live and perhaps still had connections.

Maria had intended at one time to expand on her journal, with a view towards turning it into a book herself. In London, four years after the war, she wrote of making a start. Before long, however, her busy life and its daily concerns intervened, as they tend to do, and she put it away. In later years, she did not even like to talk about the Second World War, and shut down any attempt on my part to do so, which is why the discovery of her papers was such a surprise to me. It was as though, after Happy's death, having come through and found peace and contentment in Cranbrook, she had closed the door on her previous life, lest opening it should prove altogether too painful a reminder.

The only time Maria returned to Kenya was for my wedding in 1969. Allen had died in 1949 and Joan in 1956. Her sister Grizel, my mother, stayed on in Kenya, where she became a successful racehorse trainer. Her brother Fionn went back after the war, in which he served with the Westminster Dragoons, RAC (Royal Armoured Corps). He was offered the post of district officer in the Colonial Service (later Her Majesty's Overseas Civil Service), rising to be senior district commissioner, Provincial Administration, before eventually returning to England, where he became secretary of the Council for the Protection of Rural England and was awarded an OBE.

My brother took Maria up to Nanyuki to see Killean, by then owned by a Kenyan family. The house stood until the early 2000s. Sadly it subsequently began to fall into a state of disrepair, although strangely the interior fabric and oak panelling remained largely intact. The pepper tree still stands in the driveway.

Nanyuki continues as a thriving community with many of the farms and ranches still being run by the younger generations of those families who emigrated at the same time as ours a hundred years ago or more. It is now a very different country to the one Maria and I grew up in.

Appendix 1

Letters of Appreciation

After the war a number of senior generals and commanders wrote expressing their admiration for the Wasbies and recognising the vital part they played in supporting the forces in South East Asia. The following pages include the two forewords written by Viscount Mountbatten and General Slim for the official WAS(B) history, published in booklet form by War Facts Press (now sadly long out of print), together with letters from Generals Briggs, Stopford and Mansergh and Air Marshal Saunders of the RAF. The final concluding letter is Ninian Taylor's farewell to her Wasbies on their disbanding in 1946.

FOREWORD TO THE W.A.S.(B.) HISTORY

I am glad to take this opportunity of expressing my admiration for the splendid work done by the Women's Auxiliary Service (Burma) since its formation in January, 1942.

The "Wasbies," who have the distinction of being the only women's service in Burma, played an important part in the Burma campaign. They shared the hardships and difficulties of the troops all the way from Rangoon to Maymyo, and later to Shwebo; and were evacuated from Myitkyina on the last plane to leave Burma, on 5th May, 1942.

Teams of "Wasbies" worked in various parts of Assam and Arakan. They were evacuated from Imphal during the siege; but they returned four months later, and moved right down through Burma with the 14th Army—earning their place in the history of that famous Army. Although they were living and working in the most uncomfortable conditions, they always had the welfare of the troops at heart; and they were able to do much to alleviate the hardships of the campaign.

The "Wasbies" are continuing their good work, with teams in the Andaman Islands, Java, Sumatra, and Japan; and on behalf of the forces in South East Asia Command I wish to express our thanks and appreciation for what they have done for us in the past and to wish them every success in the future.

7th May, 1946.

Rear Admiral, The Viscount Mountbatten of Burma,
G.C.V.O., K.C.B., D.S.O., A.D.C.

FROM GENERAL SIR WILLIAM SLIM

I first met the Women's Auxiliary Service (Burma) during the testing time of the 1942 Retreat from Burma. Then they not only performed essential services for the Army, but played a great part in helping the many thousands of unfortunate refugees—British, Burmese and Indian—who were being driven from their homes in circumstances of terrible hardship. In this, and in the many air raids on defenceless Burmese towns they showed the highest standard of devotion and courage.

Later, reorganised in India, they joined the Fourteenth Army and devoted themselves with the same efficiency to the welfare of the troops. They carried their duties throughout the re-conquest of Burma, right up to forward formations. Their contribution, not only to the material welfare but to the morale of the Army, was a very real one. The men of the Fourteenth Army were proud to see them wearing their Army Sign, and they will long remember them for their unselfish cheerfulness, their tireless service, and for the breath of home they brought to them.

W. J. SLIM,

General Sir William J. Slim,
G.B.E., K.C.B., D.S.O., M.C.

2nd April, 1946.

H.Q., BURMA COMMAND.

RANGOON.

1946.

Dear Mrs Taylor

     I am informed that next month has been fixed for the official disbandment of the Women's Auxiliary Service (Burma).

     In view of this I would like to place on record the Army's deep appreciation of the services that have been rendered by WAS(B) from the time the Corps was formed in 1942 up to the time of its disbandment.

     The way in which the rough and smooth of the campaign in Burma has been shared by all ranks of the WAS(B) with the troops, has been no small contribution to morale, and the popularity of the WAS(B) canteens has always been high.

     Shortage of supplies and equipment provided many difficulties in running efficient canteen services, but the genius of improvisation was always present to provide something for bored troops or weary travellers.

     All ranks of the WAS(B) I am sure will regard their services as a great experience and a proud achievement.

     On behalf of all troops in Burma Command, I wish you all good fortune in the future, and give you assurance that the name of WAS(B) will rest in an honoured niche in our memories for many years.

               Yours sincerely,

               Lieut-General.
          G.O.C.-in-C, BURMA COMMAND.

Lt-Col. Mrs. NINIAN TAYLOR, M.B.E.
     Commandant WAS(B).

HQ. Burma Command,
No. 2208/2/A-4,
S.E.A.C.
28th January, 1946.

H.Q., A.L.F.S.E.A.

On vacating command in Burma, I should like to place on record my appreciation of the magnificent work done by the W.A.S.(B.) during the Burma Campaign and since it ended.

I have seen the teams of this organisation working throughout the battle from Jorhat through Kohima, the Kabaw Valley, Mandalay, and on to Rangoon. They have toiled with their Mobile Canteens through mud, dust, heat and rain, sharing the hardships of the troops, but they have always delivered the goods, and their services have been enormously appreciated by British, Indian and African soldiers alike.

When the war ended, W.A.S.(B.) was the first to open static canteens in Burma, which contributed very materially to the morale and welfare of all three services.

I understand that the organisation is shortly to be disbanded, and I should therefore be grateful if the contents of this letter could be communicated to its Commandant.

M. G. N. STOPFORD,

Lt. Gen. Sir Montague G. N. Stopford,
K.B.E., C.B., D.S.O., M.C.

General Officer Commanding-in-Chief,
Burma Command.

From:- Maj Gen EC MANSERGH, CBE, MC

DO No.1016 A

5 INDIAN DIVISION
SOUTH EAST ASIA COMMAND.

11   APR   46

Dear Mama

     I want to thank you and the WAS(B) detachment for the splendid work and co-operation with which you have served 5 Ind Div.

     Your services whether in Toc H, the Library or on Mobile duty have been of tremendous value to the men from both the amenity and morale raising view points. It is also appreciated how much hard work is necessary to ensure the high standard which you have maintained. For this all ranks are very grateful.

     Apart from your exacting duties the amiable social forbearance of the WAS(B) often after exhausting days has in no small measure decreased the cares and improved the tempers of harrassed officers and staff - For this I am grateful!

     Many thanks and good luck.

Yours

E. Mansergh

Mrs. M. PILBROW

FROM: AIR MARSHALL SIR HUGH SAUNDERS,
         K.B.E., CB., MC., D.F.6., MM.

Headquarters,
Royal Air F orce,
Burma, S. E.A. Air Force.

REF : AMC/183.   12th May 1946.

D ear Mrs. Taylor,

I understand that the W.A.S.(B).'s officially disband
next month, and I would therefore like to take this opportunity to thank you, and through you, all W.A.S.(B). ladies
who did so much for the Royal A ir Force throughout the War
in Burma.

All ranks of the Royal Air Force owe a great debt of
gratitude to the WAS(B).'s for their grand work at Royal
A ir Force Stations, and all ranks are very sorry that the
WAS(B).'s are disbanding.

Yours sincerely

H. SAUNDERS.

Lt. Colonel Mrs. Ninian Taylor, M.B.E.,
Commandant, WAS(B).
RANGOON.

Headquarters,
WAS(B)-
BURMA COMMAND.

30th. May, 1946.

ORDER OF THE DAY.

I greatly regret that I have been unable to say goodbye to all of you personally.

I would like to take this opportunity of thanking you, one and all, for your loyalty to me, your hard work, and your devotion to duty. The WAS(B) has always been renowned for its esprit de corps and stern sense of duty at all times. For the high record of service during the Campaign when at all times you were found prepared to meet any eventually I am justly proud of you.

Some of us have served together for many years, others for a short time, but I know we all feel proud to have served in an Army that fought so gallantly to bring peace to the world.

Now that you are all dispersing to various parts of the earth I trust that you will keep in your hearts the comradeship and loyalty to your fellow creatures for which you were beloved in the WAS(B).

To one and all I say farewell with great regret. I am proud to have been your Commandant. God Bless You All.

Chief Commander,
WAS(B).

Appendix II

The Organisation of the British Army

For non-military readers who may not be familiar with the composition of an army, the role of a company, battalion, or division and their relation to one another, the following is adapted from information provided by the National Army Museum on their website and is used here with their kind permission. Note that terms such as squadron, troop or battery, which apply to cavalry or armoured units only and which do not appear in Maria's diary, have been omitted.

Section

A section will normally consist of 7 to 12 men and is part of a platoon. Sections are usually commanded by a non-commissioned officer (NCO), often a corporal.

Platoon

A platoon is part of an infantry company and is further divided into three or four sections. A British platoon usually consists of 25 to 30 men and is commanded by a lieutenant.

Company

A company is part of a battalion and is commanded by a major. Companies will usually consist of between 150 and 200 men, be lettered A through to D and be made up of at least two platoons.

Battalion

A battalion is a regimental sub-unit of infantry or signals troops numbering between 500 to 1,000 soldiers. It normally consists of three or more companies and is commanded by a lieutenant colonel. Traditionally, most British regiments have had more than one battalion; but different battalions of the same regiment have seldom fought together. During the Second World War, for example, one battalion may have been fighting in Europe while another battalion belonging to the same regiment was fighting in South East Asia.

Brigade

This is a formation consisting of three battalions or three cavalry or armoured regiments and is commanded by a major general or a brigadier. During the World Wars a brigade numbered between 3,500 and 4,000 men.

Division

A division is made up of three infantry, cavalry or armoured brigades and is commanded by a lieutenant general or a major general. Divisions are usually equipped to operate independently in the field and have a full complement of supporting reconnaissance, artillery, engineers, medical, supply and transport troops. During the World Wars the average British division numbered around 16,000 men.

Corps

A corps is a tactical formation made up of two or three divisions and is commanded by a lieutenant general. Corps are normally identified by Roman numerals.

Army

An army is a formation consisting of two or more corps and is commanded by a general or a field marshal. An army during the Second World War numbered about 150,000 men.

Maps

Map 1. (overleaf)
Lines of Communication Northern Burma:
December 1944 – April 1945

Map 2. (page 306)
Lines of Communication China – Burma – India:
1943 – 1945

KEY TO MAPS

TROOP MOVEMENTS (except as marked otherwise)

➤ Allied　⇨ Japanese　⟐⟩ Chinese

━▸　▭⇨ coastal

⚭ ✚ Airfields　◉ All weather　◯ Fair weather

━━ Main roads　+++++ Railways　〜〜 Rivers

NATO SYMBOLS

⊠ Allied　⌐⋈⌐ Japanese　⋈ Chinese

⊠ Infantry　⊠ Lorried Infantry　⊠ Parachute　⊠ Headquarters

I Company　II Battalion armoured/artillery regiment　III Regiment

X Brigade　XX Division　XXX Corps　XXXX Army

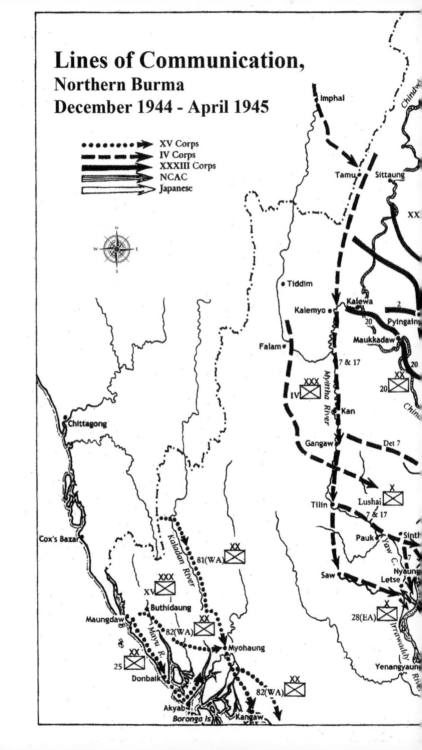

Lines of Communication,
Northern Burma
December 1944 - April 1945

XV Corps
IV Corps
XXXIII Corps
NCAC
Japanese

Imphal

Chindwin

Tamu

Sittaung

XX

Tiddim

Kalemyo

Kalewa

2

20

Pyingaing

Maukkadaw

20

Falam

7 & 17

XXX
IV

Myittha River

XX
20

Chin

Kan

Chittagong

Gangaw

Det 7

X
Lushai

Tilin

7 & 17

Cox's Bazar

Pauk

Yaw C.

Sinth

7

Saw

Nyaung

Letse

Kaladan River

81(WA)

XXX
XV

Buthidaung

82(WA)

XX

X
28(EA)

Irrawaddy River

Maungdaw

Myohaung

Moyu R.

XX
25

Donbaik

Yenangyaun

XX
82(WA)

Akyab

Boronga Is.

Kangaw

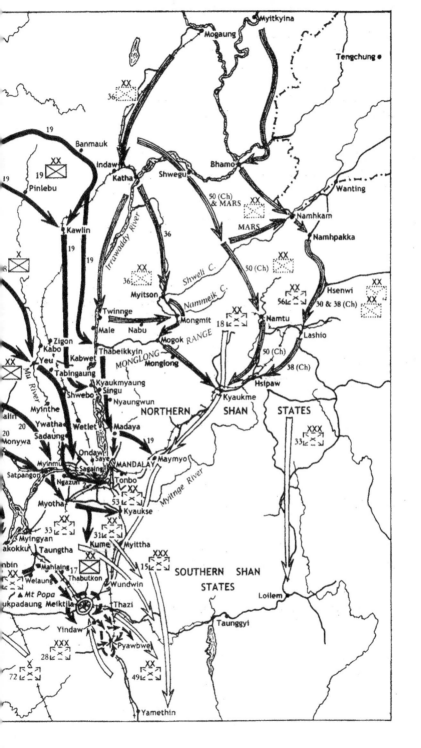

Lines of Communication
China - Burma - India 1943 - 45

Acknowledgements

Grateful thanks to my dear friend Madeleine Fowler, whose support and encouragement initially spurred me on to knuckle down and piece the story together and stop prevaricating. Madeleine ensured I kept going and we both joined a local creative writing group to further our writing endeavours. It was through Madeleine that I was introduced to Sandie Huntington, who spent endless hours with me over a number of years researching, editing and proofreading, until we were both satisfied that the manuscript was complete to the best of our ability and we could source no more.

My additional thanks go to the following people who were also of great assistance throughout my writing journey:

Kevin Patience, like me, grew up in Kenya, and his vast knowledge of trains and Kenyan history helped me with the accuracy of the manuscript in respect of both locomotives and of early Kenya, in the hope that no Kenyan '*fundis*' will pick up on any possible inaccuracies relating to the Kenya section.

Margaret Arnaud (née Sothers), ex-Wasbie, who served in Burma and was transferred with eleven other girls to the WVS working in Japan at the end of the War. Margaret was very generous in her support, providing me with endless photographs, publications, newsletters and other written material, together with hugely descriptive personal memories of her own time as a very young Wasbie.

Prue Brewis, ex-Wasbie, who remained in touch with Maria after the war. She was extremely helpful when I first started this project and was able to point me in the right direction on a number of queries and was always very supportive when I called. Prue has, sadly, now passed away, as have Bubbles Clayton and Fleurette Pelly, whom regrettably I was never able to contact.

Philip Crawley, of the Burma Star Association, who assisted me at the outset of this project. The Burma Star Association website offers a very comprehensive history of the Allied Forces attached to South East Asia Command, and their campaign against the Japanese during the Second World War. This site enabled me to ensure that the timelines and the details of incidents in Maria's notes and journal were correct, as did James Luto's magnificent book, *Fighting With the Fourteenth Army in Burma – original war summaries of the battle against Japan 1943–1945.*

Constance 'Spratt' Halford-Thompson (née Tayleur), ex-Wasbie. Constance joined Fleurette Pelly's team serving in Therrawaddy towards the end of the war, having been denied her request to join Maria's team. She said, 'Everybody thought so highly of Maria, and she was such fun to be with.' Constance, who became a prolific and extremely accomplished artist producing many wonderful horse racing and yachting pictures, was fascinating to meet – she gave me so much insight into the lives of these girls who lived amongst the troops out in the jungle. She was a mine of information, full of wonderful stories and amusing anecdotes of her own. Constance remained good friends with Fleurette until Fleurette died in 2006.

Sally Jaffe, author of *Chinthe Women – Char and Wads on the Front Line*. Sally very kindly provided me with some newsletters and contact details of Wasbies who remembered Maria. Her delightful little publication is full of anecdotes and photographs obtained from Wasbies and from the personal papers of her mother, Ninian Taylor, the Wasbies' commanding officer.

I owe grateful thanks too, to the following people who provided me with photographs and records of servicemen associated with Maria's time in South East Asia. Dorian Leveque of the British Library for providing me with access and copies of Indian Army service records, also Debbie Horner, who researched and obtained several images for me. David Read of the Soldiers of Gloucestershire Museum. Gordon Leith, curator of the Royal Air Force Museum. Martin Skipworth, head of research, Royal Signals Museums. Keith Andrews, researcher, COFEPOW (Children of Far East Prisoners of War), a charity devoted to perpetuating the memory of the prisoners held by the Japanese after the fall of Singapore. Keith was able to provide me with copies of Ronald 'Happy' Holroyd's Japanese POW record, which I was then able to pass on to his son's family. Happy's widowed daughter-in-law, Vivien, then very kindly gave me access to more of Happy's own personal papers and photographs.

Huge thanks go to my friend Jane Anderson-Wood, who spent many hours tweaking photographs in order to get the best possible resolutions out of some of the old images I wanted to include in the book.

I owe so many people!

The following websites also had some very helpful information and where needed, researchers who were only too willing to assist with queries: ww2talk.com, forces-war-records.co.uk, hut-six.co.uk and the Commonwealth War Graves Commission (cwgc.org).

Without the help of these interesting, dedicated people and organisations I would have struggled even more to obtain the detailed information required to make this story so fascinating to compile.

My admiration and thanks go also to Berni Stevens, my wonderful cover designer, who has finished off my long journey with a truly inspired image for the front cover and brought the story to life in a single encapsulating vision.

The team at Troubador have been unfailingly helpful and efficient, especially my Production Manager, Rosie Lowe, who could not do enough for me.

Finally, I am eternally grateful to my long-suffering editor, Sally Partington, whose endless patience and tireless work, combined with her expertise and knowledge of this particular genre, has turned my manuscript into a more publishable narrative. Hopefully Maria's memoir may take its place alongside similar publications Sally has worked on in the past in conjunction with the Imperial War Museum and the National Army Museum.

Bibliography

Books:

Burma: The Forgotten War, Jon Latimer, John Murray, 2005
Fighting With The Fourteenth Army in Burma, James Luto, Pen and Sword, 2013
The Campaign in Burma, His Majesty's Stationery Office, 1946

Booklets and magazines:

Chinthe Women: Char and Wads on the Front Line, Sally and Lucy Jaffee, Tenterbooks, 2002
Into Burma, published by the War Department, Government of India
The Wasbies, War Facts Press, London 1946
Wasbie Newsletters kindly supplied by Margaret Arnaud and Sally Jaffe

Websites:

ww2.talk.com
burmastar.org.uk
cwgc.org
forces-war-records.co.uk
hut-six.co.uk
iwm.org.uk
nam.ac.uk

Wasbie interviewees:

Mrs Margaret Arnaud
Mrs Prue Brewis
Miss Nancy 'Bubbles' Clayton
Mrs Elizabeth Ormerod
Mrs Constance Halford-Thompson
Mrs Merle Hannay

Additional Research:

British Library
Burma Star Association
Children of Far East Prisoners of War (COFEPOW)
Commonwealth War Graves Commission
Imperial War Museum
National Army Museum
Soldiers of Gloucestershire Museum
Royal Air Force Museum
Royal Signals Museum

Photographs:

Writer's private collection
British Library
Kevin Patience
Imperial War Museum
Soldiers of Gloucestershire Museum

The Burma Star Association Registered Charity No 1043040

Providing Support

Since undertaking benevolence work the charity has distributed over £5 million to people throughout the United Kingdom and wartime allied countries. Assistance takes many forms including: residential, care and nursing home fees; respite care; building repairs and maintenance; paying removal expenses; provision of powered wheelchairs, riser/recliner chairs and stair lifts; payment of debts and the provision of specialist medical and domestic equipment. These are just some of the ways in which the Association's benevolence operates.

Today the Association still has some 1,800 members worldwide, with 28 branches functioning in the UK and 4 overseas.

Kohima Epitaph

When you go home,
Tell them of us and say,
For your tomorrow
We gave our today.

Please donate to this worthy charity
via www.burmastar.org.uk
Thank you